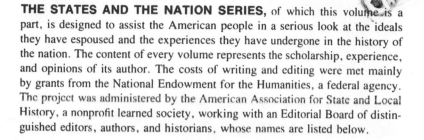

Minnesota

A History

William E. Lass

**With a Historical Guide prepared by the editors of the
American Association for State and Local History**

W. W. Norton & Company
New York • London
American Association for State and Local History
Nashville

W. W. Norton & Company, Inc., 500 Fifth Avenue, New York, N.Y. 10110

W. W. Norton & Company Ltd., 37 Great Russell Street, London WC1B 3NU

Library of Congress Cataloging in Publication Data

Lass, William E.
  Minnesota: a history.

  (States and the nation)
  Previous ed. published with subtitle: A bicentennial
history.
  Bibliography: p.
  Includes index.
  1. Minnesota—History. I. American Association for
State and Local History. II. Title. III. Series.
F606.L35   1983   977.6   83–11461

ISBN 0-393-30145-1 (pbk.)

Printed in the United States of America

3 4 5 6 7 8 9 0

*This volume is dedicated
to those students whose interest,
enthusiasm, and questions over the
years have helped deepen my own
appreciation of Minnesota*

Contents

Historical Guide

TO MINNESOTA

prepared by the editors of the
American Association for State and Local History

Introduction

The following pages offer the reader a guide to places in this state
through which its history still lives.

This section lists and describes museums with collections of valuable artifacts, historic houses where prominent people once lived, and
historic sites where events of importance took place. In addition, we
have singled out for detailed description a few places that illustrate
especially well major developments in this state's history or major
themes running through it, as identified in the text that follows. The
reader can visit these places to experience what life was like in earlier
times and learn more about the state's rich and exciting heritage.

James B. Gardner and Timothy C. Jacobson, professional historians
on the staff of the American Association for State and Local History,
prepared this supplementary material, and the association's editors take
sole responsibility for the selection of sites and their descriptions.
Nonetheless, thanks are owed to many individuals and historical organizations, including those listed, for graciously providing information and advice. Our thanks also go to the National Endowment for
the Humanities, which granted support for the writing and editing of
this supplement, as it did for the main text itself.   —*The Editors*

Grand Portage

Grand Portage

★ Northern Minnesota brings to mind images of iron mines and frigid snowbound winters. A remote and thinly peopled place, it is far off the well-traveled roads—on the way to nowhere else. The remotest part of it is probably the far northeast corner, where the Pigeon River (the

Great Hall at Grand Portage

international boundary) flows down off the Canadian Shield into Lake Superior. Indeed, that area is so remote that—as Minnesota historian Solon Buck once complained—cartographers have the unfortunate habit when drawing Minnesota maps of detaching the area from the rest of the state and isolating it in a little insert. Thus pictured as if an afterthought of geography, this part of northern Minnesota would seem largely left out of the state's history as well. But in fact, it figured in the history of the land that would become Minnesota well before white men ever broke the sod on the farming frontier far to the south.

Long before Minnesota became a state in 1858, this small area was the hub of an enormous commercial empire. It stretched 3000 miles, from Montreal on the St. Lawrence River to Fort Chipewyan in Canada's far northwestern wilderness. Its center was Grand Portage, "the great carrying place." White men first came to this region not to stay, but rather to harvest and market the wealth nature held out for the taking. The wealth came in the form of a homely gregarious animal— the beaver—whose fur, for hats and other garments, was the rage of European fashion in the eighteenth and early nineteenth centuries. An easy prey, the beaver was trapped relentlessly across the Great Lakes and beyond, so that even before the American Revolution trappers had penetrated north and west of Lake Superior to the countless lakes and streams that fed into Hudson Bay and the Arctic Ocean.

The route back to market was by water down through the Great Lakes. To reach it, men sought a connection between the northward-flowing lakes and streams to the northwest and Lake Superior. The Pigeon River was the best such connection, though before it reached the lake, falls and rapids made passage by canoe impossible. Trappers therefore sought a portage and found one on what would become the American side of the river. It started at a small natural harbor on the lake, about eight miles south of the river's mouth, and ran about nine miles north and west to a place on the river above the falls and rapids. Though steadily uphill, the trek was passable and in time became, every summer, a funnel for the wealth of a continent.

The first recorded visit by a European was in 1722, though French traders had likely known of it even earlier. Certainly the Indians had. But the French lost their Canadian empire at the end of the Seven Years War (the French and Indian War in America) in 1763, and it was under their British successors that Grand Portage enjoyed its heyday. As the new masters of North America, enterprising Britons (especially the Scots) quickly exploited the abandoned French trading routes throughout the Great Lakes. They soon found themselves at Grand Portage, where by 1768 independent traders had made a clearing for a meeting place at the Lake Superior end of the trail. The British government in Quebec had opened the fur trade to anyone who applied for a license, and by the 1770s the competition was fierce and sometimes violent. To ease hostilities and make the fur trade more efficient and secure from competition with the well-established Hudson's Bay Company, the Montreal traders experimented with several loose cooperative associations. Finally, in 1779, they established the famous North West Company. Grand Portage became its inland headquarters and the object of a yearly trek by traders up from Montreal and trappers down from the Canadian wilderness.

For several weeks each summer, the Company's stockade was alive with activity. From Montreal the firm's partners came to tally accounts, inspect the year's harvest of furs, pay the men who had trapped them, and make assignments for the season ahead. With them they brought the supplies needed both for the rendezvous itself and by the trappers in the woods in the winter to come. One such inventory, transported in twelve canoes with 102 canoemen, included 1000 gallons of spirits, 24 casks of wine, 90 bags of ball and shot, 150 guns, 150 bales of dry goods, 12 boxes of iron ware, 12 "nests" of brass kettles, 100 packages of tobacco, 50 kegs of tallow and lard, and 60 kegs of pork. At Grand Portage the small armada of birchbark canoes that plied back and forth across the lakes was maintained, and the beaver pelts were pressed and baled for the long voyage east. Along with the serious business went much revelry, feasting, and exchange of news and stories among men who worked for months and even years in wilderness solitude. The portage itself saw the voyageurs carrying tons of furs and trade goods over the rugged nine-mile path that rose from 600 feet above sea level at Lake Superior to 1360 feet at Fort Charlotte on the Pigeon River. Each man commonly carried two ninety-pound packs over the trail and two more back, making the eighteen-mile round trip in about six hours. Though later improved so oxcarts could use it, it remained primarily a footpath.

Though Minnesota is rarely thought of in connection with the Revolutionary War, remote Grand Portage saw military activity then. Despite the rebellion in the colonies far to the south and east, the British fur trade through the lakes continued, and in 1778 a small detachment of His Majesty's Eighth Regiment of Foot was dispatched to Grand Portage to show the flag and bolster the loyalty of doubtful traders and Indians. But American independence changed matters in time at Grand Portage. Under the terms of the Peace of Paris, which ended the war in 1783, Grand Portage became American territory, though it did not immediately pass into American hands. The boundary as initially defined was somewhat vague, and for a number of years the British traders of the North West Company conducted business as usual at Grand Portage. Indeed, the 1780s and 1790s saw the height of the fur trade there.

Only after the British at last surrendered their military posts on the Great Lakes to the Americans, and only when American customs inspectors threatened to tax the fur wealth that was being imported duty-free over Grand Portage, did the North West Company decide to look for another route to the interior. In 1803 they moved thirty miles up the shore of Lake Superior, safely inside Canada, to Fort William, whence over the Kaministikwia River and Dog Lake they reached the boundary waters to the northwest. Grand Portage—the stockade on Lake Superior, the trail, and Fort Charlotte on the Pigeon River—subsequently fell back into obscurity, even though John Jacob Astor's American Fur Company continued to use it for several more decades. In time the fur trade itself disappeared, and with it all vestige of what once had been the busiest crossroads in the Old Northwest.

Today a vestige has been recovered and reconstructed. Under the auspices of the National Park Service, archaeologists from the Minnesota Historical Society uncovered the location of the Lake Superior stockade and the sites of the major buildings. Several reconstructions now suggest what a great rendezvous post was like. The largest of the buildings is the "Great Hall," the place where the partners of the company came to do their business, feast, and celebrate at rendezvous time. Also at the site are a canoe warehouse that houses two authentic birchbark canoes, a fur press where the beaver pelts were packed tightly into hundred-pound bales, and a kitchen which prepared abundant meals for the partners, voyageurs, and trappers. The stockade, intended as much for privacy as for protection, surrounds the post, and the trail up to the site of Fort Charlotte is open for hiking.

This remote corner of Minnesota, once the center of a vast fur-trading empire, is today a quiet and lonely place, perched bravely between the rocky shore of Lake Superior and the still awesome northwest wilderness. It is an example of a natural pathway once thrust to great prominence by the accidents of geography and the whim of the market. That prominence was fleeting, and, as the little insert maps containing northeast Minnesota suggest, too easily forgotten.

Old Fort Snelling

Minneapolis

★ The expansion of the new American nation across a whole continent is one of the epic stories of the nineteenth century. Other nations too had undergone territorial expansion, the new lands commonly becoming colonies or provinces governed from afar by older, more settled areas. But in the United States, expansion entailed no such conventional empire-

Living history on the parade ground

building. Rather, as Thomas Jefferson described it, western America was destined to become an "empire for liberty." It became so through the process of state-making, whereby new territory, after meeting certain standard requirements, was admitted to the federal union on an equal basis with the oldest of the eastern commonwealths. Thus the citizens of North Dakota and Wyoming came to enjoy the same rights and bear the same duties as the citizens of Massachusetts and Virginia.

States were not made all at once, however; and in the preliminary stages whereby the Old Northwest and Minnesota in particular began to move toward statehood, Fort Snelling played a key role. Much of the land that would become Minnesota was part of Thomas Jefferson's famous Louisiana Purchase, by which for $15 million Napoleon sold to the United States some 800,000 square miles of land between the Mississippi River and the Rocky Mountains. Although the deal was struck in 1803, American authority over the vast region awaited a formal American presence. It took some time, but within two decades the Americans effectively took possession of what legally was theirs. In 1804 Jefferson sent explorers Lewis and Clark across his "Purchase," and beyond it to the Pacific Ocean; a year later Zebulon M. Pike (whose name now graces one of America's highest mountains) was dispatched to explore the upper Mississippi River and scout sites for permanent fortifications. One of them, at the confluence of the Mississippi and Minnesota (then called the St. Peters) rivers, became Fort Snelling.

Fort Snelling actually was part of a larger plan for an ambitious system of outposts and connecting trails that John C. Calhoun, Secretary of War under President James Monroe, hoped would secure this vast territory—and with it the rich fur trade—from British (Canadian) intrusion. But most of the plan remained just a plan, which gave Fort Snelling—alone for nearly thirty years in the Northwest—special significance. The army first arrived in August 1819, under the command of Lt. Colonel Henry Leavenworth. Making their plans known to the local Sioux Indian chiefs, the soldiers began trying to settle in. At first Leavenworth picked a bad spot not far from the southeast end of the modern Mendota Bridge; after a first difficult winter he moved to higher ground on a bluff above the Mississippi River. There he began a square log fort, which he never finished. Apparently unsatisfied with Leavenworth's slow start, the army abruptly replaced him in the summer of 1820 with Colonel Josiah Snelling. Southeast of the site of his predecessor's wooden fort, Snelling raised the imposing stone structure that to this day bears his name.

"To adapt it to the shape of the ground on which it stands," Snelling used an irregular diamond shape. As much as he could, he built with limestone quarried from the river bluffs. Necessary timber was cut on the Rum River and floated downstream to the fort. A water-powered sawmill at the Falls of St. Anthony converted it to lumber. The fort, which majestically commanded the junction of the two rivers, consisted of a stone wall connecting four corner bastions—one semi-circular, one pentagonal, one hexagonal, and one round—designed to provide the best lines of fire against possible attackers. Inside was accommodation for a garrison of several hundred men and some of their families. The two enlisted men's barracks, one of wood and one of stone, contained married soldiers' quarters, twelve-man squad rooms, the company storeroom, and, in the cellar, the kitchens. Twelve sets of officers' quarters, which housed officers and their families, a separate kitchen, and a large central room for plays and dances, were located across the parade ground. The first hospital and library on the upper Mississippi occupied an adjacent large building, while the fort's commanding officers from Snelling onward enjoyed a substantial house to themselves (with post headquarters on the lower level).

Smaller support structures completed the establishment. A heavy masonry magazine stored in the 1820s some 50,000 musket cartridges, ample artillery shells, and 1,000 pounds of gunpowder. A storehouse with a lift well to each of four storage floors sheltered the food, clothing, and tools that were shipped up the Mississippi every year by steamboat. What could not be imported (and that was much) had to be made and maintained at the fort. Workshops contained a bakery, blacksmith shop, and places for a carpenter, a wheelwright, harness makers, and an armorer. For things not part of army issue, soldiers and their families could go to the sutler's store, which filled the role of a post exchange. There was a school building, which also served as the Protestant church. A well at first supplied the post's water, which later had to be hauled up from the river. To protect it all, cannon in the pentagonal tower were trained down the north and east walls, while the hexagonal tower guarded the south and the west. The two rivers came under the sights of the semi-circular battery, while the round tower, with musket slits all around, was the fort's defensive strong point. A guardhouse, manned day and night, held the only jail in the territory.

Thus equipped and fortified, Fort Snelling loomed a powerful symbol of the American presence on this northwestern frontier. Though prepared to, it never had to defend itself, which is probably a good measure of how well it met the hopes of its planners. It helped keep the peace both between whites and Indians and among the Indians themselves. Its reassuring walls offered shelter in time of unrest and sociability in a remote and lonely region. It oversaw the largely peaceful process of white settlement that by 1849 won the Minnesota country status as a territory and full statehood just nine years later. It served so well, in fact, that by the late 1850s the army sold it to a private land developer who proposed to build a new city—to be called "Fort Snelling"—on the site. The Civil War intervened, however, and the post was soon reactivated as an induction and training center for the thousands of Minnesotans who served the Union cause. Barracks, storehouses, and stables mushroomed until Snelling's old fort grew to five times its original size.

After the war, though no longer a lonely frontier fortress, the fort remained an active post and served as a prime provisioning depot and administrative headquarters for forts farther west on the Great Plains. In 1898 it once again mustered off Minnesota soldiers, this time to the Spanish-American War, and again in the twentieth century to two world wars. By the time the army finally left in 1946, 126 years of hard military service had taken their toll. In 1956 a highway threatened to pass through the old fort grounds. Happily, a determined preservation campaign took hold, and through the combined efforts of local citizens and state government (notably the Minnesota Historical Society, which now administers the site), the site of Old Fort Snelling was set aside as a state historical park and the old fortress meticulously restored and reconstructed. Staffed by costumed guides and featuring a number of living-history demonstrations, it offers today's visitor a vivid glimpse back to the days when this was the far northwestern outpost of American civilization.

That civilization grew in time from thirteen to fifty states, in a unique step-by-step process that assured new territories equal status with old ones. The orderly extension of American power and authority into the western wilderness was the first part of that story. Old Fort Snelling, one of the most powerful symbols of that authority, therefore marks an important moment in the westward growth of the American nation.

Split Rock Lighthouse
Lake Superior

★ Nature endowed Minnesota more richly than she did many states: fertile farmland, thick pine forests, and enormous deposits of iron ore. Minnesota's history is in part the story of how, from nature's endowment, men made wealth. The wealth was not Minnesota's alone. Minneapolis flour was known around the world; Minnesota lumber built homes and fences far out on treeless prairies; iron from the Mesabi and Vermillion ranges went into the locomotives, skyscrapers, appliances, and automobiles that made the American standard of living a veritable wonder of the world.

Light tower

Unlike wheat and pine trees, which were transformed into flour and lumber close to home, iron left Minnesota in much the form that nature had given it. Ore boats carried the reddish dirt down the lakes and rivers to the huge mills at Gary, Detroit, Cleveland, Erie, and Pittsburgh, whence came steel. A crude extractive process, iron mining in northern Minnesota required reliable transportation out of the

state. To make it reliable on Lake Superior, some of the most dangerous water in the world, was no easy matter. Split Rock Lighthouse on
the treacherous north shore is a symbol of one era's solution.

In addition to containing all the excitement of storms at sea, of ships
and sailors dashed helplessly on the rocky shore, and of lighthouse
men gallantly keeping the light burning, the story of Split Rock is also
the story of economics in the ore business, which by the turn of the
nineteenth century was growing prodigiously. The first shipment of
2,000 tons of ore left the harbor of Duluth-Superior in 1892; by 1910
the figure had risen to 25 million tons, with another 5 million tons
going from Two Harbors on the north shore. Through the Soo Canal
at the eastern end of the Lake passed more tonnage than was handled
by the more famous canals at Suez and Panama, while even in its short
eight-month season Duluth-Superior was outstripping in crude tonnage
both New York and London. The number of vessels on the lake also
grew. United States Steel alone operated 112 freighters in 1901, and
the companies represented by the Lake Carriers' Association owned
over 500 bulk carriers. Although Lake Superior is an enormous body
of water and was hardly crowded, it does narrow considerably at its
western end between the Chaquamegon Peninsula and Duluth-Superior. Here passed all the ore boats.

Profitable operations in the steel and iron-ore business, as in any
other, depended in part on reducing expenses of operation, which entailed some risks. It was known, for instance, that in accord with company policy ore boats commonly ran at high speed even in thick
weather: delay meant money and perhaps jobs lost. The boats themselves were designed to carry maximum burden in the most economi-
cal fashion and thus were frequently underpowered: larger engines
meant less payload. Few ships were insured: exorbitant premiums for
such high-risk business meant deeply diminished rewards. The gamble
paid off most of the time, though there were times when it threatened
not to. One of the most memorable of them was the great gale of
November 1905, which drove half a dozen freighters aground on Lake
Superior's rocky north shore. Though some were salvaged, the dam-
age cost their owners dearly, and over the next two years the ore
carriers mounted a campaign for the cheapest form of protection they
knew: a lighthouse and a fog signal to be built and maintained by the
federal government in the vicinity of Split Rock.

The result was an appropriation of $75,000 and construction of the imposing lighthouse that still stands at Split Rock. Construction began at the isolated promontory, then accessible only by water, in the spring of 1909 under the direction of Ralph Russell Tinkham, a civil engineer who eventually became chief engineer of the entire federal lighthouse service. Supplies arrived by boat and were either landed in a small cove or hoisted directly up the face of the cliff with a large steam-powered derrick. Trees and brush first were cleared from the site and temporary living quarters then erected, and then work on the station began. The light tower itself rose on a skeleton of steel girders rooted in the rock outcropping and, in the second season of construction, took on its final octagonal brick shape.

Its beacon represented, for the era before radio navigational aids, the latest in technological refinement. Even though electricity was in wide use by 1910, lighthouses, because of their often remote locations, commonly relied on older forms of illumination. No exception, the new beacon at Split Rock employed a powerful incandescent oil vapor lamp whose wickless kerosene vapor flame produced a brilliant white light that was reported visible more than sixty miles away. The twin lens panels consisted of both reflecting and refracting prisms that concentrated the light source into two powerful beams. When rotated, it produced the characteristic lighthouse flash that swept the horizon every ten seconds. Imported from Paris, France, the Split Rock lantern and lens assembly weighed over six tons and, when mounted atop the tower, loomed 168 feet above the surface of the lake. The fog signal equipment likewise relied on non-electric power. Twin gasoline-driven air compressors (one to guard against mechanical breakdown) powered a siren that emitted a thunderous two-second blast three times a minute.

Adjacent to all the magnificent hardware rose the buildings needed to maintain it. The keeper and his two assistants occupied a trio of solid two-story houses, each with three bedrooms, bath, kitchen, pantry, and living and dining rooms. Nearby barns were later converted to garages. In the cove to the west, a dock and boathouse were built to help land supplies, and in 1915 they were joined to the top of the cliffs by an elevated tramway that vastly improved the station's access to the water. Sharing the rock headland with the light tower, the original construction derrick hoisted the bulkiest supplies until the completion of the tramway. Nearby the pillbox-like oil house stored the kerosene burned by the great beacon.

It was all self-contained, solid, and built to last. Physically, much of it did, though as the years passed some things changed. Most notably, the completion of the North Shore highway in 1924 opened the station to access by automobile and quickly ended its isolation. Tourists flocked there and ended the keepers' once quiet life. The Civilian Conservation Corps built a new access road in 1935, and when four years later the Lighthouse Bureau was absorbed by the United States Coast Guard, the Split Rock Station was spoken of as the most visited lighthouse in America. Meanwhile it continued to do the job it was built for, with a few concessions to changing technology. The old flywheel gasoline engines that powered the fog horn were replaced by diesels in 1932. With access by highway well established, the tramway up from the lake was dismantled in 1934. Electricity arrived in 1940 and the oil vapor lamp was replaced by a 1000-watt bulb. Electric motors rotated the beacon and drove the fog horn. Yet even with such improvements, modern navigational aids were making the station obsolete. The fog signal was discontinued in 1961, and the beacon flashed for the last time in 1969. The site remained a popular attraction, however, and in 1971 was opened to the public as a part of Split Rock State Park. Five years later the Minnesota Historical Society assumed its administration.

Today, the ore boats still pass close by on their way through Lake Superior's narrow western reaches. They still carry Minnesota's red iron-bearing earth down the chain of lakes to the mills and factories where it is transformed into wealth. Radar and other technological marvels guide them. The light at Split Rock has become a relic, though one well worth a visit as a reminder of how dangerous navigation on Lake Superior once was—and sometimes still is.

Other Places of Interest

*The following suggest other places of
historical interest to visit. We recommend
that you check hours of operation in advance.*

ALEXANDER RAMSEY HOUSE, *265 S. Exchange Street, St. Paul.* French
Second Empire mansion built in 1872 by first territorial governor of Minnesota; with period furnishings.

ANDREW VOLSTEAD HOUSE, *163 Ninth Avenue, Granite Falls.* Victorian
house of congressman whose name went on national prohibition legislation.
Privately owned.

CHARLES A. LINDBERGH HOUSE AND INTERPRETIVE CENTER,
Lindbergh State Park, Lindbergh Drive, Little Falls. Boyhood home of the
famous aviator, built in 1906; with historical materials on the Lindbergh
family.

THE DEPOT, *506 W. Michigan Street, Duluth.* An 1892 French Norman train
station housing the Lake Superior Museum of Transportation, with excellent
collection of railroad equipment used in Minnesota; St. Louis County Historical Society, with nationally important collection of paintings by Eastman
Johnson; and the Chisholm Children's Museum.

FOREST HISTORY CENTER, *state 76, Grand Rapids.* Reconstruction of a
turn-of-the-century logging camp; with tours and trail walks.

FORT RIDGELY, *off state 4, south of Fairfax.* Partial reconstruction of an
1855 fort built to defend white settlers against the Sioux; site of an 1862
battle.

GRAND MOUND, *state 11 west of International Falls.* Site of the largest
prehistoric burial mound in Minnesota, where the Laurel culture held sway
from 200 B.C. to A.D. 800; with exhibits.

HARKIN STORE, *county 21 northwest of New Ulm.* Restoration of a general
store from the 1870s.

HULL-RUST-MAHONING OPEN PIT, *Third Avenue East, Hibbing.* An open
pit mine on the Mesabi Range of Northern Minnesota's iron mining country.

IRON RANGE INTERPRETIVE CENTER, *off U.S. 169, Chisholm.* Geology, ethnic culture, crafts, and industry of the Iron Range.

ITASCA STATE PARK, *21 miles north of Park Rapids off U.S. 71.* First Minnesota state park (1891); includes prehistoric mounds, log structures, pioneer cemetery, and other buildings.

JAMES J. HILL HOUSE, *240 Summit Avenue, St. Paul.* The 1889 Richardsonian Romanesque home of the railroad magnate.

JEFFERS PETROGLYPHS, *county 2 east of Jeffers.* More than 2,000 carvings from two periods of Woodland life—beginning 3000 B.C. and ending A.D. 1750.

LAC QUI PARLE MISSION CHURCH, *R.R. 5, Montevideo.* Restored early-nineteenth-century mission established for the Dakota Indians near Joseph Renville's American Fur Company post.

LANDMARK CENTER, *75 West Fifth Street, St. Paul.* A preserved turn-of-the-century Romanesque federal court building housing the Ramsey County Historical Society, with major exhibits on topics relating to the history of the state's capital city and surrounding area; also includes galleries of the Minnesota Museum of Art, with exhibits primarily on American art and architecture.

LOWER SIOUX AGENCY, *county 2 east of Redwood Falls.* Site of first Dakota attack in war of 1862; with interpretive center on the struggle of the Dakota Indians.

MILLE LACS INDIAN MUSEUM, *U.S. 169 on shore of Mille Lacs Lake, Onamia.* Artifacts and dioramas on the Dakota and Ojibway Indians.

MINNESOTA HISTORICAL SOCIETY, *690 Cedar Street, St. Paul.* Headquarters of the state's historical program; houses the state's largest history museum and library and provides information about historic sites and resources throughout the state.

MINNEAPOLIS INSTITUTE OF ARTS, *2400 Third Avenue, S., Minneapolis.* Extensive collections and exhibits on a wide variety of paintings and other art, including American.

MINNESOTA MUSEUM OF MINING, *Chisholm.* Steam shovels, locomotives, and other equipment used in open-pit and underground mining in the Mesabi Range.

MINNESOTA STATE CAPITOL, *Aurora between Cedar and Park streets, St. Paul.* Designed by famous architect Cass Gilbert, built 1896–1905. Beaux-Arts Classical building still in use.

NORTH WEST COMPANY FUR POST, *county 7 off I-35 at Pine City exit, Pine City.* A reconstructed post of the early 1800s, with utensils and other items showing how the voyageurs worked and lived.

OLIVER H. KELLEY FARM, *U.S. 10 east of Elk River.* First headquarters of the organization that spawned the National Grange; in an 1860s farmhouse furnished with late-nineteenth-century items.

PIPESTONE NATIONAL MONUMENT, *U.S. 75 north of Pipestone*. Quarries where Plains Indians and others obtained the stone for their ceremonial pipes.

ST. ANTHONY FALLS, *Minneapolis*. Site of nineteenth-century milling operations that made Minneapolis the nation's largest flour-producing center.

SCIENCE MUSEUM OF MINNESOTA, *30 E. Tenth Street, St. Paul*. Extensive collections in archeology, anthropology, ethnology, and paleontology, as well as other sciences.

SIBLEY HOUSE, *Mendota*. Home of the first governor of Minnesota, built 1835–1863; includes a museum containing furnishings of mid-1800s.

SINCLAIR LEWIS MUSEUM AND INTERPRETIVE CENTER, *I-94 and U.S. 71, Sauk Centre*. Late-nineteenth-century boyhood home of the author, with his books and family furnishings; visitor center.

SOLOMON G. COMSTOCK HOUSE, *Fifth Avenue S. and 8th Street, Moorhead*. The 1883 Queen Anne home of the banker and politician and of his daughter Ada, president of Radcliffe; includes a museum containing family memorabilia.

TOWER SOUDAN MINE AND STATE PARK, *U.S. 169 north of Tower and Soudan*. Open-pit and underground mine, the first iron mine in the state.

UPPER SIOUX AGENCY STATE PARK, *state 67 south of Granite Falls*. Partially restored buildings at site of agency established 1854 by the United States government to instruct Sioux in farming methods.

W. W. MAYO HOUSE, *118 N. Main Street, Le Sueur*. Gothic house built in 1859, where Mayo practiced medicine before moving to Rochester and establishing the famous clinic with his sons.

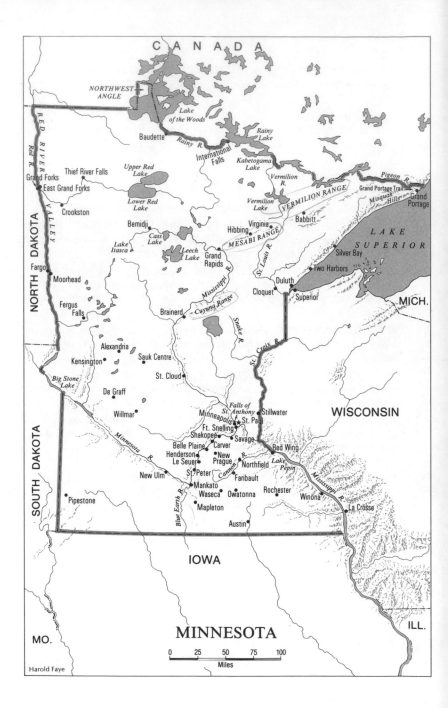

CANADA

NORTHWEST-
ANGLE

Lake
of the Woods

Baudette

Rainy R.

Rainy
Lake

International
Falls

Kabetogama
Lake

Pigeon R.

RED RIVER R.

Thief River Falls

Upper Red
Lake

Vermilion
R.

Grand Portage Trail

Grand Forks

Vermilion
Lake

VERMILION RANGE

Misquah
Hills

Grand
Portage

East Grand Forks

Babbitt

Crookston

Lower Red
Lake

Bemidji

Hibbing

Virginia

MESABI RANGE

LAKE
SUPERIOR

RED RIVER VALLEY

NORTH DAKOTA

Cass
Lake

Lake
Itasca

Leech
Lake

Grand
Rapids

St. Louis R.

Silver Bay

Fargo

Two Harbors

Moorhead

Mississippi R.

Duluth

Fergus
Falls

Brainerd

Cuyuna Range

Cloquet

Superior

MICH.

Snake R.

Alexandria

St. Croix R.

Kensington

Big Stone
Lake

Sauk Centre

St. Cloud

WISCONSIN

SOUTH DAKOTA

De Graff

Willmar

Minnesota R.

Falls of
St. Anthony

Stillwater

Minneapolis

St. Paul

Ft. Snelling

Shakopee

Savage

Belle Plaine

Carver

Red Wing

Henderson

New
Prague

Le Seuer

Northfield

Lake
Pepin

St. Peter

Cannon R.

Faribault

New Ulm

Blue Earth R.

Mankato

Owatonna

Rochester

Mississippi R.

Waseca

Winona

Pipestone

Mapleton

La Crosse

Austin

IOWA

MINNESOTA

0   25   50   75   100
Miles

MO.

ILL.

Harold Faye

Invitation to the Reader

IN 1807, former President John Adams argued that a complete history of the American Revolution could not be written until the history of change in each state was known, because the principles of the Revolution were as various as the states that went through it. Two hundred years after the Declaration of Independence, the American nation has spread over a continent and beyond. The states have grown in number from thirteen to fifty. And democratic principles have been interpreted differently in every one of them.

We therefore invite you to consider that the history of your state may have more to do with the bicentennial review of the American Revolution than does the story of Bunker Hill or Valley Forge. The Revolution has continued as Americans extended liberty and democracy over a vast territory. John Adams was right: the states are part of that story, and the story is incomplete without an account of their diversity.

The Declaration of Independence stressed life, liberty, and the pursuit of happiness; accordingly, it shattered the notion of holding new territories in the subordinate status of colonies. The Northwest Ordinance of 1787 set forth a procedure for new states to enter the Union on an equal footing with the old. The Federal Constitution shortly confirmed this novel means of building a nation out of equal states. The step-by-step process through which territories have achieved self-government and national representation is among the most important of the Founding Fathers' legacies.

The method of state-making reconciled the ancient conflict between liberty and empire, resulting in what Thomas Jefferson called an empire for liberty. The system has worked and remains unaltered, despite enormous changes that have taken place in the nation. The country's extent and variety now surpass anything the patriots of '76 could likely have imagined. The United States has changed from an agrarian republic into a highly industrial and urban democracy, from a fledgling nation into a major world power. As Oliver Wendell Holmes remarked in 1920, the creators of the nation could not have seen completely how it and its constitution and its states would develop. Any meaningful review in the bicentennial era must consider what the country has become, as well as what it was.

The new nation of equal states took as its motto *E Pluribus Unum*—"out of many, one." But just as many peoples have become Americans without complete loss of ethnic and cultural identities, so have the states retained differences of character. Some have been superficial, expressed in stereotyped images— big, boastful Texas, "sophisticated" New York, "hillbilly" Arkansas. Other differences have been more real, sometimes instructively, sometimes amusingly; democracy has embraced Huey Long's Louisiana, bilingual New Mexico, unicameral Nebraska, and a Texas that once taxed fortunetellers and spawned politicians called "Woodpecker Republicans" and "Skunk Democrats." Some differences have been profound, as when South Carolina secessionists led other states out of the Union in opposition to abolitionists in Massachusetts and Ohio. The result was a bitter Civil War.

The Revolution's first shots may have sounded in Lexington and Concord; but fights over what democracy should mean and who should have independence have erupted from Pennsylvania's Gettysburg to the "Bleeding Kansas" of John Brown, from the Alamo in Texas to the Indian battles at Montana's Little Bighorn. Utah Mormons have known the strain of isolation; Hawaiians at Pearl Harbor, the terror of attack; Georgians during Sherman's march, the sadness of defeat and devastation. Each state's experience differs instructively; each adds understanding to the whole.

The purpose of this series of books is to make that kind of understanding accessible, in a way that will last in value far beyond the bicentennial fireworks. The series offers a volume on every state, plus the District of Columbia—fifty-one, in all.

Each book contains, besides the text, a view of the state through eyes other than the author's—a "photographer's essay," in which a skilled photographer presents his own personal perceptions of the state's contemporary flavor.

We have asked authors not for comprehensive chronicles, nor for research monographs or new data for scholars. Bibliographies and footnotes are minimal. We have asked each author for a summing up—interpretive, sensitive, thoughtful, individual, even personal—of what seems significant about his or her state's history. What distinguishes it? What has mattered about it, to its own people and to the rest of the nation? What has it come to now?

To interpret the states in all their variety, we have sought a variety of backgrounds in authors themselves and have encouraged variety in the approaches they take. They have in common only these things: historical knowledge, writing skill, and strong personal feelings about a particular state. Each has wide latitude for the use of the short space. And if each succeeds, it will be by offering you, in your capacity as a *citizen* of a state *and* of a nation, stimulating insights to test against your own

James Morton Smith
General Editor

Preface

I have lived a third of my life in Minnesota, and I think I have come to know it well. I have read its literature, researched its history, explored its land. I live in the Minnesota River Valley not far from the spot where Pierre Charles Le Sueur spent a winter gathering furs and blue clay. When I drive west, I am soon out on the open, windswept prairie that early settlers found so inhospitable; but if I drive east, I reach a place where I can walk through a remnant of the now nearly vanished Big Woods. I have gone north where I have camped in the fragrant forests, walked in the red dust of the open-pit mines, picked up agates along the thundering shores of Lake Superior, and watched the ocean-going vessels riding at anchor in the harbor at Duluth.

Throughout my Minnesota years I have taught its history, sharing my interest and my knowledge with young people who are the descendants of pioneer Germans and Swedes, Norwegians and Finns, Irish and Poles and native Americans. Now, through this Bicentennial State History series, I am able to share my interest with a broader audience.

To try to tell the story of Minnesota within the limits of this book was a difficult challenge. It seemed first of all necessary to characterize both the state and its people. Chapter 1, "Minnesotans and the Land," does that and more: it also looks outward, providing glimpses of how the rest of the nation perceives Minnesota and the contributions Minnesota has made to the national image.

The chapters that follow are basically chronological. Because there are some who believe that the Vikings were the first white men on Minnesota soil, the Viking myth is the beginning. The exploits of those early explorers who ventured into what is now Minnesota without benefit of maps or geographical knowledge are recounted if for no other reason than to let the reader admire (or perhaps envy) their accomplishments. The traders who first encountered the native tribes and brought the dubious benefits of European civilization to them play a necessary part in this narrative, and much attention is also given to the pioneers who participated in frontier expansion—perhaps the single most significant force in shaping American character. It is necessary, too, to consider political development because Minnesota has a long tradition of government responsiveness to the people.

There is also, within this chronological framework, a common element: the land as a focal point. The quest for land and water passages drew explorers; the furs that traders sought were a natural product of the land and the climate. Settlers sought land and its produce. The Industrial Revolution in Minnesota exploited natural resources, and much of the state's twentieth-century experience has been one of soaring productivity and prosperity based on faster and more efficient utilization of resources.

The final chapter in this work places Minnesota in national perspective; it portrays Minnesotans who have had national impact, it describes the state's contributions to the national economy, and finally it considers the role of the land and environment in Minnesota's future.

This history would not have been possible had it not been for the contributions of others. I have, first of all, benefited from the research and writings of earlier historians, and recognition of their efforts is indicated in the footnotes and in the Suggestions for Further Reading. For their assistance during the preparation of this book, I am indebted to certain individuals. My wife, Marilyn, not only shared the joys and the vexations of the task but helped locate materials and was involved in all phases of the work. Velma Joneson, typist par excellence, was continually gracious and punctual. And for their aid in easing my day-to-day obligations at Mankato State University, I sincerely thank my colleague Phyllis R. Abbott and Elwood B. Ehrle, former dean of the School of Arts and Science at Mankato State.

WILLIAM E. LASS
Mankato, Minnesota
December, 1976

Minnesota

A History

1

Minnesotans and the Land

URING the spring of 1965, Minnesota reeled under a succession of blizzards, floods, and tornadoes. Through it all the state legislature debated daylight saving time with great fervor. Residents took it all in stride, quipping that a Minnesotan was someone with snow in his yard and water in the basement of his roofless house, who did not know what time it was. The experience reminded Minnesotans of two of the elemental forces that run through the fabric of the state's history—nature and government.

Minnesotans have always been close to nature. The geographic forces which influenced the past are still very much a part of their lives, for geography is active and evolving. Minnesotans have been shaped by the land, and they in turn have shaped it. Through this interaction the people and the institutions of today's Minnesota have emerged.

Minnesota's bountiful waters have molded the state's character just as surely as the search for scarce water has influenced much of the Great Plains and the American Southwest. Minnesotans refer to their state as the "Mother of Three Seas," because her waters contribute to three distinct and separate drainage basins. Most of the state's land is drained by the Mississippi and its tributaries, which flow to the Gulf of Mexico; but the land that lies to the north and west is drained northward to Hudson Bay, while the area about Lake Superior lies in the

Gulf of St. Lawrence drainage. If Minnesota had been land-locked, her history would be far different: the water connections were the paths to the interior for French and British explorers and for the American frontiersmen, and they are plied yet today by modern vessels.

The Mississippi River flows from its small beginnings in Lake Itasca past Bemidji, Grand Rapids, St. Cloud, over the Falls of St. Anthony in Minneapolis, on past Hastings, Red Wing, Winona, and out of Minnesota on to the gulf. It was important to the Indians who plied it for hundreds of years before white men set eyes upon it, but they did not comprehend its grandeur. Tribes living along its banks called it by various names and used that portion of it which served their purposes; but white men popularized the name Mississippi, an Algonquin word which, when applied to rivers, meant "great water."

Those who traveled on the Mississippi River in Minnesota found that when they reached the Falls of St. Anthony, they had to portage before they could resume navigation. Thus the falls were the practical head of Mississippi River navigation. Indians congregated at the falls; fur traders built their posts there. This in turn led the United States Army to build its first installation in Minnesota—Fort Snelling—near the falls. Two of Minnesota's greatest industries, sawmilling and flour milling, developed about the Falls of St. Anthony because of the water power available there. When manmade aqueducts, dams, and canals threatened to destroy the falls, they were dressed with a concrete apron which makes them look today very much like a large spillway. Although the natural beauty has been lost, the falls are still important as a source of hydroelectric power. More than any other geographic feature, the Falls of St. Anthony contributed to the development of the state's only truly metropolitan area.

The Mississippi below the Falls of St. Anthony has always been more or less navigable, but it has not always had a deep channel. Steamboats, which were the heart of Minnesota's economy for almost half a century, often had to stop running by August or early September because the river was so low. The river, like the falls, has been altered: the Army Corps of Engineers must provide a nine-foot navigation channel. The project, now nearly half a century old, has stimulated commercial barge traffic moving coal upstream and grain downstream, but it has also created problems which distress ecologically minded Minnesotans and Wisconsinites. The sand and silt dredged from the channel are piled along shore, creating unnatural dunes and sand bars and destroying vegetation and habitat. Through such agencies as the Mississippi River Parkway Commission of Minnesota and the recent Esthetic Environment Task Force, Minnesotans have struggled to bring about an awareness of the need to achieve a balance between economic use of the river and preservation of its natural features.

The Mississippi River above the falls was a major canoe route for the fur traders, and it had its steamboat era in the 1860s and 1870s in the St. Cloud–Little Falls area, but it is best known for the years of mystery surrounding its source. In their struggle for empire in North America the great powers of Europe—France, Great Britain, and Spain—used the Mississippi as a natural boundary to demark their claims even though its source was unknown. At the close of the Revolutionary War, Great Britain and the United States made the unknown source of the river an important factor in determining the northwestern boundary of American claims. After years of wrangling, the boundary was settled diplomatically, resulting in that odd configuration of the northern boundary of Minnesota known as the Northwest Angle. Not until 1832 did Henry Rowe Schoolcraft trace the Mississippi to its origin in Lake Itasca, about thirty miles southwest of Bemidji. Schoolcraft put together knowledge about the nature of the Mississippi which whites had collected piecemeal—often from Indians—since the Spaniard Hernando de Soto first saw the river in 1541.

Despite the ravages of steamboatmen who cut untold quantities of wood for fuel along its banks, and lumbermen who leveled the white pine along the Mississippi above the falls, the river has retained much of its natural beauty. The broad valley, the swiftly moving water and verdant islands and banks, are not so greatly changed from the time of early explorers, and there remain places along the river where there is no sound other than that of flowing water or leaves moving in a summer breeze. The Mississippi, like many of Minnesota's other waters, offers the opportunity to be with nature—something that means a great deal to Minnesotans.

The longest tributary to the Mississippi in Minnesota is the Minnesota River, which drains much of southern Minnesota and runs in a rough "V" from Big Stone Lake on the South Dakota border to its juncture with the Mississippi several miles below St. Anthony Falls. The French called it the St. Pierre's River; British and early Americans, the St. Peter's. The Sioux Indians, however, had a more descriptive name, "Minnesota," which meant cloudy waters—like the turbid river at flood stage. Such waters looked like a roiled, cloudy sky, and so the name was translated into English as "sky-tinted waters." Today the "land of sky-blue waters" is mentioned so often that the true meaning of the name has been obscured. The Sioux name was given to Minnesota Territory, and three years later Congress, responding to a petition from the territorial legislature, officially changed the river's name from the St. Peter's to the Minnesota.

The Minnesota, like the Mississippi, was an important route for fur traders and explorers and was thought by both French and British to be a possible link in the fabled Northwest Passage—the mythical all-water route through the continent. The beauty and fertility of the land in the Minnesota River Valley was extolled from the beginning of its exploration, in accounts of men such as Jonathan Carver, Joseph Nicollet, and William Hypolitus Keating. When the valley was wrested from the Sioux by the United States government in the famous treaties of 1851 and subsequently opened for settlement, throngs of pioneers rushed to establish claims in "Suland."

The Minnesota River provided pioneers with access to southern Minnesota and was plied by steamboats in the years before railroads, but it has never really been profitable for commercial navigation purposes. Steamboats could usually ascend no further than New Ulm or Mankato in early spring when the water was high, and by late June the head of navigation would be yet further downstream—at St. Peter, Henderson, Chaska, or Shakopec. Despite numerous suggestions and proposals for river improvement over the years, only the very lower portions have been improved enough to permit barge traffic. In recent times Savage has become headquarters for huge grain terminals which are fed by caravans of trucks from throughout southern Minnesota, and the barges haul the grain downstream from there.

The St. Croix River, yet another major tributary to the Mississippi and part of the Minnesota–Wisconsin boundary, was followed by fur traders and explorers as they moved from the north–south highway of the Mississippi to the east–west thoroughfare of the Great Lakes. Because of the immense stands of white pine on its upper reaches, the St. Croix Valley was one of the first areas to be claimed when the land was legally opened to settlement. And at Stillwater, lumbering's "Queen of the St. Croix," a loose assemblage of Yankee lumbermen, fur traders, and other frontier boosters met in 1848 at the Stillwater Convention which led to the formation of Minnesota Territory. Inhabitants of the St. Croix Valley proudly call it the "Birthplace of Minnesota."

The Upper St. Croix, one of eight original components of the National Rivers System under the federal Wild and Scenic Rivers Act of 1968, is one of the most scenic rivers on the continent. Its cascading waters, sometimes clifflike banks, and numerous parks and natural areas have become focal points for outdoor activities—fishing, camping, canoeing, hiking, climbing, cross-country skiing, snow shoeing—all activities important to Minnesotans not only recreationally, but economically.

Minnesota shares the St. Croix Valley with Wisconsin because Congress believed that the river was a natural boundary, a sentiment not shared by the original settlers of the St. Croix. They believed that there should be unity in the valley, and they fought vigorously to have the entire valley left outside Wisconsin (and thus potentially in Minnesota) when Wisconsin became a state. The movement failed but the sense of regional identity remains. For once, hindsight and foresight agree, for political unity as envisioned by the pioneer politicians of the St. Croix Valley would be an obvious advantage to the many thousands of Wisconsinites who work in the Twin Cities.

Every river has a valley, but the dictates of custom have

reserved a special place for the Red River Valley. It is "The Valley" to Minnesotans. Only the uninitiated call it by more formal names. A student of geography feels compelled to refer to the Red River as the Red River of the North to distinguish it from the Red River which separates Oklahoma and Texas. And he also must explain that the name comes from the spectacular sunset-lit Red Lakes whence the main tributary to the Red River flows.

The Great Plains are flat, but even a Kansan or a Nebraskan will concede that he has not seen flat until he has seen "The Valley." The rich black soil is the bed of the gigantic Glacial Lake Agassiz, whose remnants are still evident in Red Lake, Lake of the Woods, Lake Winnipeg in Manitoba, and hundreds of smaller lakes. Furs and land were the magnets that drew settlers to the Red River Valley. Usually there was a certain order in the frontier process, with the fur trader passing on before the pioneer farmers arrived. But because of the visionary Scottish Lord Selkirk, this pattern was violated in the Red River area. Selkirk brought English, Scottish, and Swiss settlers to his New-World colony near Winnipeg as early as 1811, at a time when fur traders believed that part of the world to be theirs. The Selkirkers found the soil fertile enough, but they also found hostile half-breeds, droughts, floods, grasshoppers, and great suffering and tragedy. Many of these disillusioned colonists fled up the Red River into the United States, and thus the valley became one of the paths into Minnesota. Later it was the route of the famed Red River carts used by American traders who linked St. Paul and Fort Garry (Winnipeg) in commercial alliance long before the age of roads or railroads. But the valley is best known for the advent of bonanza farming in the 1870s when, in the golden age of wheat, it became one of the greatest breadbaskets in the United States. Today the valley is recognized as the producer and processor of a diversity of agricultural products—wheat, sugar beets, sunflowers, potatoes, and a variety of vegetables.

The longest continuous waterway in the Hudson Bay drainage area is the system of lakes and streams connecting North Lake west of Lake Superior to Lake of the Woods—the border watershed which is the legal boundary separating Minnesota and Canada. French and British explorers in their persistent search for the Northwest Passage traveled over the boundary waters and, as they did so, claimed vast hinterlands for their countries. For a long time these waterways were the world's greatest fur-trade route, and the lore of the area speaks of the voyageurs who paddled hundreds of miles through unmapped wilderness in search of beaver. Much later these waters were important to lumbermen for the movement of logs and the processing of lumber and paper pulp products. Today, the meaning of the boundary water region lies beyond the diplomatic and the economic. Much of that heavily forested zone is in such areas as the Superior National Forest and the recently created Voyageurs National Park near International Falls. Parts of the Boundary Waters Canoe Area within Superior National Forest are a designated wilderness that provides a glimpse of this land the way it was before the advance of European civilization. The tug of war between those who want the boundary waters area to remain untouched and those who advocate controlled timber cutting and extraction of mineral resources has not yet been resolved.

The St. Louis River is the dominant stream in that part of Minnesota which lies in the Great Lakes watershed. Fur traders used the river to move from Lake Superior to the Mississippi by way of the Savannah Portage, and they also traveled up it and then down the Vermilion River to reach the boundary waters. Like most of the rivers that drain into Lake Superior, however, its natural head of navigation is only several miles inland, and those coming off Lake Superior into the St. Louis were soon challenged by a series of cataracts that rushed through the dells which are now part of Jay Cooke State Park southwest of Duluth. Voyageurs could portage their canoes around the falls, but no one ventured onto the St. Louis with larger boats. Millions of logs were moved down it, but even they could not be passed through the dells without sluices. As a result, important sawmilling centers such as Cloquet developed upstream to challenge Duluth, the Lake Superior port situated not far from the outlet of the St. Louis.

Minnesotans who travel to less watery places will often find

strangers staring at their automobile license plates and asking:
"Are there really 10,000 lakes in Minnesota?" A precise answer would be "No, there are actually 15,291." Minnesotans
have always made an effort to count the lakes, but they have not
been consistent in defining one. The 10,000-lakes tradition is
rooted in the promotional literature of Minnesota Territory—a
tradition reinforced by mapmakers and geologists. The motto
was put on the license plates about a quarter-century ago as an
inexpensive and effective way of publicizing one of Minnesota's
outstanding features. But since that time the definers have been
at work. Today in Minnesota, any basin of at least ten acres
which is partially or completely filled with water is a lake.
When the Motor Vehicle Division of the State Highway Department announced in 1975 that it intended to discontinue the
motto on license plates, protest was immediate and loud. Minnesotans were moved by their affection for their lakes, but the
announcement touched another nerve: citizens had not been con-
sulted. For nonelected government officials to make such a decision was contrary to the deep conviction of Minnesotans that
issues must be publicly aired and debated. The decision was
reversed.

A visitor to the state might sometimes get the impression
from overhearing Minnesotans that there is only one lake in the
state: "The Lake." On summer weekends and holidays many
communities seem deserted as Minnesotans throng to "the
lake"—whichever one is most convenient—pulling motor boats
behind them. Long before recreational boating became popular,
most of the lake shores fell into private hands, so public access
has been a lively issue in Minnesota. Major lakes now have
public access, but often not much more than a spot from which
to launch or land a boat. The motorboat has for many become
almost a necessity. Motorboating and its accompanying water-
skiing boomed during the last three decades, but recently there
has been a sharp revival in canoeing. The birch-bark canoes of
the Chippewa Indians and the voyageurs have been replaced by
aluminum craft, and that which once was a necessary mode of
transportation has become a form of recreation and relaxation.
Minnesotans find that canoeing toughens the body while it

soothes the mind—that it has a naturalness in harmony with the elements.

If there is a single distinctive lake in Minnesota, it is Lake Superior, which Minnesota shares with Wisconsin, Michigan, and Canada. Lake Superior, one of the world's largest fresh-water lakes, has a certain awesomeness. To the Chippewa it was "Kitchi Gamma"—great water—and to Henry Wadsworth Longfellow in the *Song of Hiawatha* it was "shining Big-Sea-Water." The surface of the lake can be mirror smooth one day, and on the next roll in waves violent enough to break up the largest ships. The beaches of Lake Superior are strewn with curious, flat oval rocks that fit into the palm of the hand—rocks fashioned by thousands of years of water action. Even the shores suggest its enormity. In places such as Palisade Head the lake laps and pounds away at the foot of vertical cliffs rising hundreds of feet to the rocky terrain above. Tradition has it that Chippewa warriors as a test of manliness tried to shoot arrows up the escarpment.

French adventurers first crossed Lake Superior in the mis-taken belief that it led to yet greater seas, and for nearly two centuries it was navigated by French, British, and American traders who were the cutting edge of the white man's inexorable push into the wilderness. Later the lake was important in the movement of Minnesota wheat, lumber, and iron ore to eastern markets; and in recent times with the completion of the St. Lawrence Seaway the world has been brought to Minnesota's door at Duluth, the western terminus of the seaway. Minnesota seems a midland state, a notion dispelled when one stands at the waterfront in Duluth and watches freighters bearing the flags of Japan, Norway, the Netherlands, Great Britain, and a host of other nations.

Lake Superior is used for boating and fishing, but most visi-tors see it from the unbelievably beautiful North Shore Drive running from Duluth to the Canadian boundary. Every summer the highway, from which one can almost continuously see the lake, is filled with thousands of vehicles and sightseers. There is, however, a less attractive side to the Lake Superior story. The lake, because of its great breadth and depth and the absence of major industrial centers on its shores, was unspoiled by man-made pollutants for many years. But in recent times it has been threatened by the vast deposits of taconite waste that have been shoved into its waters at Silver Bay, Minnesota. Thus the future of Lake Superior has become a highly emotional issue—a classic case of conflict between economic interests and environmental concerns.

Minnesotans' appreciation of the value of their environment is not a recent thing. The first state park, at Lake Itasca, was started in 1889 before the lumbering frontier had run its rampant course; public funds purchased thousands of acres of land to protect the area about the headwaters of the Mississippi. Visitors to Lake Itasca State Park today can see virgin stands of white and red pine and view the source of the Mississippi much as it presented itself to Henry Rowe Schoolcraft more than a hundred years ago. The same principle that guided the selection of Itasca as a park site before its desecration has been applied to other sites in Minnesota. Throughout the state, one may visit parks that preserve virgin stands of timber, waterfalls and unimproved streams, natural vegetation and wilderness areas.

Minnesota has an economic diversity based on its three greatest natural resources—fertile soil, forests, and iron ore. There is a tendency, though it is not accurate, to associate the first one with southern Minnesota and the other two with the northern part of the state. Minnesota in a broad sense has only two parts—north and south, in much the same way as South Dakota has an east-of-the-Missouri area and a west-of-the-Missouri, or Nebraska has a south-of-the-Platte area and a north-of-the-Platte. In Minnesota, however, there is no physical demarcation separating north and south. There are, instead, rough categorizations suggested by the shape of the state—which is nearly twice as long north-south as it is wide east-west—and solidified through custom and activities. Minnesotans think of the Twin Cities as being the borderland between north and south, when in fact Minneapolis and St. Paul are well south of the state's midpoint near Brainerd. But Brainerd to southern Minnesotans is north, because there is no well-developed concept of central Minnesota. Northern Minnesotans, who admittedly are closer to the North Pole than are southern Minnesotans, delight in promoting their regional identity. Thus the radio station of Pine City, which is actually south of the latitude of the state's geographical center, advertises itself as "The Voice of the North."

North means an area not so rich in terms of dollars nor so heavily settled as the south; but it also means more lakes, more forests and wilderness areas. The south in many ways is more like neighboring Iowa than it is like northern Minnesota. It is predominantly intensively cultivated farmland that is very much a part of the Corn Belt.

North and south in Minnesota are not all-inclusive. The Red River Valley, which is really in the northwest, is within the geographical north but not the colloquial north. It is "The Valley," agriculturally oriented and therefore unlike most of the forest and mining sections of the north. Likewise there tends to be a north-of-north area in much the same way that the United States has a west of the west: If Wyoming is west, California is somehow beyond the west. In the same way Minnesota has a boundary area which is usually described in those terms. A person traveling from southern Minnesota who says he is going north really means someplace like Bemidji or Grand Rapids, but if he goes further north to Baudette or International Falls he is "up on the boundary."

Other parts of the north also have a regional identity. Shape and promotional literature clearly identify as "The Arrowhead" that northeastern triangle bounded by Lake Superior, the St. Louis River, and the international boundary. And Minnesotans talk of "The Range" and "The Range Towns." "The Range" is not a cattle range, nor a mountain range like the Big Horns or the Grand Tetons; rather it is the Mesabi Iron Range. There are, of course, three iron ranges in Minnesota, the Mesabi, the Vermilion, and the Cuyuna, but only the largest and the richest is "The Range." The others, except in the very immediate locale, are always called by their proper names. As the notion of range is deeply imbedded, so also is the idea of the range towns. It is not necessary to enumerate Chisholm, Hibbing, and Virginia. They are distinct enough, to be sure, but to Minnesotans the meaning of "the Range Towns" is clear.

With the exception of the northeast, where the Misquah Hills formation provides a rugged landscape, and the hilly portions of the southeastern part of the state, the land is gently rolling. These contours are the result of glaciation, for over a period of nearly a million years practically all of Minnesota was gouged, shaped, and leveled by four distinct glaciers which not only graded the land but deposited a rich topsoil as well. In the post-glacial period, forests developed over about seventy per cent of the state and the remainder was open prairie. The forest was an extension of the eastern forest belt that stretched from the Atlantic beyond the Mississippi. In Minnesota all of the area east of the Mississippi was forested with the exception of the excessively swampy areas, and the forest extended west of the river irregularly for about 30 to 125 miles. Within the timbered area there were both coniferous and deciduous forest zones. The zone in which the large conifers, such as white and red pine, spruce, and tamarack, were the dominant trees encompassed most of the area east of the Mississippi and roughly north of Pine City. There were some coniferous stands west of the Mississippi, but generally the western fringe of the forest belt from Canada south was composed of deciduous trees. At about the latitude of St. Cloud, south of the coniferous forest, the deciduous belt widened considerably. Within the deciduous zone there was one particularly distinctive area—the Big Woods, so named because of its extent and the massiveness of its trees. The Big Woods lay in an irregular triangle, its corners at St. Cloud, Mankato, and Northfield.

Minnesota's pioneer farmers first looked to the Big Woods. They had come from the forested areas of the eastern United States and western Europe, and the Big Woods in which elm, oak, maple, and other hardwoods commonly grew over 100 feet tall proved to them that the land was fertile. But these pioneers were interested in farming, not lumbering; so they cleared the land rapidly by burning, and most of the hardwood forest was soon devastated. If one wants today to know what the Big

Woods were like, he may visit Nerstrand State Park, an area set aside because of its stand of virgin timber.

Because of the coniferous forest, much of Minnesota was a lumberman's frontier—a frontier which started before agriculture and then developed apace with the farming frontier. The lumberman's assault on the vast stands of white pine undid thousands of years of nature's bounty in less than a century. As the coniferous forests were cleared, the agricultural belt pushed northward into the cutover area so that today the relative proportions of forested and open land have been nearly reversed from that of the zones before white man.

Iron mining, Minnesota's third frontier activity, developed within the coniferous forests. All three of the iron ranges were in heavily timbered regions; when iron ore was found on the Mesabi, its discoverers scraped away layers of pine needles to reveal the iron-laden red soil beneath. Pine trees were stripped away as the great open-pit mines of the Mesabi were developed, and all of the pioneer mining companies operated lumber camps for a time.

Pioneer farmers were not attracted to Minnesota's prairie area. Perhaps they believed that it, like the rest of the Great Plains, was the Great American Desert. Because there were other places with wood and water, they saw no need to challenge a treeless land that lacked navigable streams. Not until the advent of railroads, liberal land laws, and an enticing wheat market in the 1870s and 1880s were farmers led out of the wooded areas onto the prairie.

Little of the prairie described so aptly by Ole Rölvaag in his *Giants in the Earth* remains. There are a few small tracts in Minnesota that man did not violate because they were too rocky, and there are some others—such as the small preserve about the Jeffers Petroglyphs and another maintained by the Minnesota chapter of the Nature Conservancy near Brownton— that were deliberately left as man found them. Although the prairie is now mostly cropped and trees have been planted where none grew naturally, there is yet a recognizable openness and contour to the land. Looking across the corn and soybean fields, one still sees the land roll and slope gently to distant horizons, and the trees in shelter belts or around the farmsteads seem artificial. Man-planted prairie trees are like so many large cornstalks, symmetrically arranged in neat rows, reaching for a sky that seems much too high for them.

North Dakotans and Canadians understand Minnesota's climate, but Iowans are glad that Minnesota stands between them and northern winters. And people in yet warmer climes enjoy the anecdote about the Minnesota farmer who was informed that, as a result of a land resurvey, he was now living in Wisconsin instead of Minnesota. "Thank God, no more cold winters," he wrote in his diary. In like vein, Mark Twain wrote that the coldest winter he ever spent was a summer in Duluth, and Duluthians themselves tell about the cab driver who, when asked by a visitor "How is summer in Duluth?" responded "I don't know yet. I've only lived here fourteen months."

Territorial newspapers, promotional literature, and letters sent back east by new Minnesotans exuberantly proclaimed the invigorating healthfulness of the climate and the purity of the dry winter air. During the 1860s and 1870s healthseekers by the thousands sought restoration at Minnesota's resorts and spas. Even after medical opinion shattered the notion that climate spawned or discouraged disease, Minnesota resorts and spas continued to exist, but with a changing emphasis. Resorts originally began in the southern part of the state and along the Mississippi River, but they gradually spread northward into the cutover area left by the lumbermen, springing up alongside the deep, cold glacial lakes so ideally suited to game fish.

Modern Minnesotans are more subtle than the pioneer boosters; when they boast, they speak of the theater of seasons—the verdant growth of spring, the water sports of summer, the brilliantly colored autumn leaves, and the diverse winter sports. Minnesotans have adapted to their climate. They ski, and they send skiers to the Winter Olympics. They invented the snowmobile and have used it until it has become an ecological issue. They fish through the ice, entering into the spirit of it so wholeheartedly that entire villages of fish houses ranging from shacks to carpeted, heated cabins spring up almost before the lakes are completely frozen over. Hockey is a favorite winter sport, and Minnesota has provided more Olympic and professional hockey players than any other state. Thousands enjoy ice skating and the nationally famous Shipstad and Johnson's Ice Follies which originated in the Twin Cities. St. Paul has since 1886 sponsored a Winter Carnival complete with King Boreas and a spectacular ice palace.

Minnesotans nevertheless are still defensive about their climate, and they were offended during World War II when a newscaster, in attempting to put the awfulness of winter on the Russian front into meaningful terms, said that Minnesotans at least would understand it. More recently, in response to the metric trend, weather forecasters began citing temperatures in both Fahrenheit and Celsius scales, and many Minnesotans protested. On the Celsius scale, Minnesota could easily record temperatures below zero most of the winter.

There was more truth in the likening of Minnesota to Russia than Minnesotans care to admit, for the temperatures of St. Paul, Duluth, and Moscow are roughly comparable. Like all the interior land masses of the northern hemisphere, Minnesota is a land of temperature extremes. Winter's cold has reached a low of −59°F, but summer's heat has soared as high as 114 degrees. Minnesota is dry compared to Seattle, but wet by the standards of Miles City, Montana; and during all seasons the winds blow across Minnesota's flat terrain. Windiness, like the other elements, is relative. Most of Minnesota is windier than the "Windy City" of Chicago, but not so windy as North Platte, Nebraska; Clinton, Oklahoma; or hundreds of other places on the Great Plains.

Climate, however, is not simply something that people live in. Climate is formative. Cold winters made possible the furs that attracted Minnesota's first businessmen. Lumbermen used the snow and ice to move logs economically. Hard winters and short growing seasons showed immigrant farmers from milder climates that the customary plants, animals, and methods were not suited to Minnesota. Through trial and error, and with professional assistance from the University of Minnesota and the United States Department of Agriculture, Minnesotans shifted from winter to spring wheat, developed regional varieties of alfalfa, corn, and soybeans, and adapted dairying to the rigors of the land. As agriculture has adapted to climate, so too have industry and all other aspects of life. Cold winters and hot summers necessitate large heating and cooling plants, more insulation, and the construction of basements. Because of the demands of both heat and air conditioning, there are heavy drains on energy. Minnesota has, in fact, not produced its own supply of energy since the days when wood was the common fuel.

Even in their politics and government, Minnesotans have been influenced by geography, for geographic factors were determinants in the drawing of political boundaries and in the development of diverse economic sections with all the attendant political interplay. Sectionalism is as old as Minnesota politics, stemming from the time when a little group of fur traders and lumbermen, loyal to the small area between the Mississippi and the St. Croix, channeled their sectional cohesiveness into a political activism that divorced them from Wisconsin and led to the formation of Minnesota Territory.

Since Minnesota became a state in 1858, north–south division has been the most evident. It originated because of the great length of the state and was nurtured as the interests of a predominantly agricultural people collided with those of people whose livelihood depended on shipping, iron mining, and tourism. Lawmakers from the north and from the south have always been conscious of their own sectional interests; thus the legislature has a long history of political compromises which have affected numerous acts and plans of state agencies. Through the years roads, schools, and state institutions have been built or located in open recognition of the natural interests of both north and south.

Urbanization has created yet another kind of sectionalism. With industrialization in the generation following the Civil War, Minneapolis and St. Paul became the core of an urban area that far surpassed any other in the state. Because of this single large metropolitan area Minnesotans have developed concepts of "The Cities" and "outstate." To go to the Cities means to go anywhere in the metropolitan area, be it Minneapolis, St. Paul,

or one of the numerous suburbs, but the boundaries of the outstate are not quite so clear—except that anything removed from
the immediate environs of the metropolitan area is in it. If out-
staters take the term too literally they are offended, but outstate
does not really mean that there is an "instate" in Minnesota; it
only suggests that modern Minnesota has both a rural and an
urban identity. And it further suggests that the rural–urban character has caused some strain. Throughout much of the state's
history, metropolitan residents resented the political clout of the
outstate legislators—often thought of as farmers even if they
happened to be lawyers, doctors, or businessmen. But rapid
population growth in the urban area and one man–one vote representation have reversed the roles. Today there is concern in
outstate Minnesota about what sometimes appears to be the
oppressive will of the majority which has resulted in the use of
state funds for improvements or programs in the Twin Cities,
something justified by metropolitan legislators on the grounds
that "What's good for the Cities is good for the state."

Minnesotans have unbounded faith in government to solve
those problems which seem too big to handle save by collective
action, a tradition of reliance on state government that dates to
the first year of statehood. Minnesota Territory was peopled
amidst the boosterism and inflationary spiral of the mid-1850s;
when the Panic of 1857 came, it was not only an economic ca-
lamity but a betrayal of the promise of instant prosperity. Pioneer Minnesotans were too impatient to wait out a depression.
Instead they committed their infant state to underwrite
$5,000,000 worth of railroad bonds to stimulate business—an
example of pump-priming nearly three quarters of a century
before the New Deal.

When railroads emerged as the villains of the 1870s Minnesotans again turned to the state. Government regulation seemed
the answer to rate fixing, rebates, and discrimination against
small shippers, and so the Minnesota legislature created a
railroad commission in 1871 as a first step toward bringing corporate giants under control. Minnesota's Senator William Windom suggested federal regulation of railroads fifteen years before the Interstate Commerce Commission was finally

established in 1887. The same faith in government caused a Populist-dominated legislature to pass a law in 1893 providing for state-owned terminal grain elevators, a measure that was, however, struck down by the conservative state supreme court.

Minnesotans have been concerned with public morality, also. A sense of Yankee propriety and orderliness, or perhaps (as critics have suggested) an overdeveloped morality, caused the pioneers of Minnesota Territory to pass a prohibition measure. Modeled after a similar law in Maine, the Minnesota version did little to rid the frontier of liquor, but it did provide a certain tradition that led to the formation of a very active Prohibition Party in the late nineteenth century. When the movement finally succeeded nationally it was a Minnesotan, Representative Andrew Volstead, who introduced the congressional measure putting the Prohibition Amendment to the federal constitution into effect. Volstead was a legalist, not a moralist, but even he had no qualms about government acting in the interests of public morality. Today, there is much interest in many states in challenging the Supreme Court ruling against capital punishment. In Minnesota capital punishment was abolished in 1908, and the suggestion of reinstating it has not been publicly advanced.

Minnesota has always been fertile ground for protest movements. During the last century Minnesotans have actively participated in three great reform movements—Populism, Progressivism, and New Dealism—all of which have aimed at more government regulation. Minnesotans insist on openness in government and on being involved. They expect forthrightness in their politicians and demand public exposure of issues. Minnesota has been relatively free of major political scandals and this tradition of openness and public involvement in decision making helps account for that record. So does the independence of its voters and politicians.

Throughout Minnesota politics there has been a marked distrust of big business. Minnesota's first experience with rampant capitalism was during the Panic of 1857. Thousands of Minnesotans were ruined by the panic, which particularly affected moneyless frontier areas. Frontier people who liked to think that

they controlled their own destinies believed they had been ma-
nipulated by eastern speculators. The distrust of many of these
pioneers toward big business was revealed during the debate
over the controversial Five Million Dollar loan. A clever car-
toonist portrayed the railroad schemers as striped gophers in top
hats. The symbolism was well conceived; the railroad promoters
were as despicable as the accursed gophers that devastated
crops. Because of the wide circulation of the cartoon, Minnesota came to be known as the "Gopher State."

Railroad villainy was one of the principal concerns of the National Grange started by Oliver Kelley of Elk River. Later Ignatius Donnelly led an emotional campaign against monopolies
and became the chief spokesman of the shortlived Anti-
Monopolist or Independent Party. Distrust of business and the
Minnesota belief that big-money men, particularly railroad fi-
nanciers and millers, suppressed the common man account for
much of the vigor with which Minnesotans participated in the
Alliance and Populist movements. Hostility toward railroads
was so intense that John Lind, a Populist who served as governor from 1899 to 1901, promoted his early political career by
representing farmers in a number of successful lawsuits against
railroads whose crime was that sparks from their steam engines
caused fires in wheat fields. Lind's successor, the basically conservative Samuel Van Sant, also moved to check the power of
railroads by instituting a suit against the Northern Securities
Company, the massive railroad combination whose later dissolution was the first step in the making of Theodore Roosevelt's
reputation as a trust buster. The anti-business sentiment first
directed against railroads has persisted in Minnesota. Big business took little comfort in the changes wrought by Progressive
and Farmer-Laborite legislatures. The overriding reform philosophy demanded that big business be regulated and taxed relatively hard, an attitude still discernible in present-day Minnesota.

A persistent theme in Minnesota politics has been the belief
that much of life is a struggle between competing economic
classes. Ever since the Panic of 1857 the notion of a have-and-
have-not society has prevailed, and the search for solutions for

the economic ills of society led Minnesotans into reform and third-party movements. The Grange, the Anti-Monopoly Party, the Greenback Party, and the Farmers' Alliance movement, all strongly supported in Minnesota, were too singular of purpose to accomplish broad reforms. But they all contributed to Populism—a movement that met the same fate as other third-party movements but nonetheless conditioned political development in the state.

In a national perspective there is a tendency to think of the Progressive Period as being interrupted by World War I and the 1920s and then re-emerging during the New Deal. In Minnesota there was much less of a hiatus because of the Farmer-Labor movement, which led to the formation of a successful third party. Agricultural discontent especially enabled the Farmer-Labor Party to surpass the Democratic Party by 1918 and to outdistance both Democrats and Republicans by 1930. The eight-year reign of the Farmer-Laborites accounts for much of Minnesota's tradition as a liberal state, a tradition reinforced by the merger of the Democrats and Farmer-Laborites in 1944 as the Democratic-Farmer-Labor Party. Out-of-state newscasters, puzzling over the DFL, find it convenient to say that that is what they call Democrats in Minnesota; but Minnesotans know it is far more than a different nomenclature. It is an amalgam of culture, philosophy, and tradition that is unique to Minnesota.

Minnesota is said to have a liberal tradition, but it can be said that the state has a conservative tradition, also. Political philosophies have ranged from the unabashed state socialism of Arthur C. Townley, the founder of the Farmer-Labor movement, to the ultra-right-wing Commission of Public Safety that worked to suppress seditious activity and other dissent during World War I. This range of political faiths has insured a legitimate two-party system in Minnesota. One party may dominate for a long period, as the Republicans did following the Civil War, but both parties have always been well enough represented to assure debate on key issues. And the major parties have been far enough apart in their views to cause issues to be identified and debated. Republican-dominated legislatures traditionally relied on property taxes to raise revenue; but reformists starting with the Populists urged a graduated income tax, which was finally enacted in 1933 during Floyd Olson's administration after the Farmer-Laborites had captured the governorship and the legislature. The income tax was not augmented by a state sales tax until 1967, and then only with reluctance and after prolonged debate in which liberals railed against a regressive tax. As the tax was finally approved, it did not apply to necessities such as food and clothing—a small victory at least for the liberals.

Senator Hubert Humphrey quipped recently that, contrary to what one might think, there was no provision in the state constitution requiring that a Minnesotan run for the presidency. But the state's record of producing national leaders is long and impressive. Senators William Windom and Cushman K. Davis were considered presidential timber by some; the immensely popular John A. Johnson was nominated for the presidency in 1908 and then, with his premature death the next year, became one of the great ifs in state history. There is a lingering belief that if he had lived, he rather than Woodrow Wilson would have been the Democratic candidate in 1912. Floyd B. Olson, the three-term New Deal governor, gained national recognition and was commonly considered to be a possible running mate of Franklin Roosevelt in 1936, but like Johnson he died at the height of his political career. Minnesota captured national attention with the election of the "boy governor" Harold Stassen, who vied seriously for the presidency in both 1948 and 1952 and who, like William Jennings Bryan of an earlier age, pursued the impossible dream well past his time. Over the past quarter-century one of the nation's best known political leaders has been Humphrey, who was a serious contender for the Democratic presidential nomination in 1960 and then served a term as vice president before becoming his party's presidential candidate in 1968. Divisiveness within the Democratic ranks over the Vietnam issue cost him the election—a divisiveness that was stimulated by the activities of another Minnesotan, Eugene McCarthy, who like Humphrey rose in party ranks after the formation of the Democratic-Farmer-Labor Party. Although Humphrey and McCarthy were the state's most serious presidential aspirants, Minnesota Senator Walter A. Mondale also campaigned for his party's nomination for a time in 1974. Mondale withdrew his candidacy but became a national political figure again in the course of being elected to the vice presidency in 1976.

Perhaps the most enduring trait of Minnesota's politics has been a certain maverick tradition. Minnesotans have been willing to experiment and to pioneer new political movements and philosophies. They have been influenced by the past but they are not bound by it. Concern for solving problems and shaping tomorrows has provided a hospitable environment for such men as the brilliant but eccentric Ignatius Donnelly, who was not able to convert his fame as a protester into victory at the polls, and Henrik Shipstead, who maintained the support of Minnesotans as he switched from Farmer-Laborism to Republicanism.

This, then, is Minnesota, a land of rivers and lakes, of ocean-going vessels and canoes, of forests and prairies and iron mines and cultivated fields. It is both urban and rural, liberal and conservative. Its people are diverse—Germans, Irish, Swedes, Norwegians, Finns, Bohemians, English, Icelanders, blacks, Indians, and a host of others. Minnesota's diversity is rooted in the past; and Minnesota is what it is today because of the men who searched her waterways for the Northwest Passage, because of the fur traders and the frontier speculators, and because of those who followed to cut timber or mine or farm, and who stayed to form a territory and a state.

Interlude

The Viking Myth

AGNUS ERICKSON, ruler of all Norway and Sweden and a militant Catholic, received word in 1354 that the Scandinavian colonists in far-off Greenland were falling away from the faith. He dispatched Baron Paul Knutson on an expedition to bring the errant ones back into the fold. When Knutson finally reached western Greenland, he found the settlements abandoned, so he went on to Vinland on the North American continent to find the colonists. He and his men searched three or four years about the Gulf of the St. Lawrence, but to no avail. Then Knutson reasoned that the colonists might have sought a place that more nearly resembled Greenland, so he moved north along the Atlantic coast for a thousand miles until he turned the tip of Labrador and entered Hudson Strait. Passing through the five-hundred-mile strait, Knutson skirted the shores of Hudson Bay for another fifteen hundred miles, finally reaching the mouth of the Nelson River. Knutson spent the long winter ice-bound in that vicinity. When summer at last arrived the Vikings decided on a yet bolder course. Some were left with the ship, but most went up the Nelson River, determined now not only to continue the search for the lost colonists but to claim new lands for the crown. The men moved into the interior by way of the Nelson, Lake Winnipeg, and the Red River. Traveling eastward from the Red River, they reached what is now Douglas County, Minnesota, in 1362.

One day some of the party returned from fishing and found ten of their companions killed by Indians. The frightened survivors fled but then halted to leave a record of their presence. They selected a slab of grey rock some two and a half feet long, sixteen inches wide, and about six inches thick and the rune master was asked to inscribe it appropriately. Working on the

25

two-hundred-pound rock for about two days, he chiseled out this message: "8 Swedes and 22 Norwegians on an exploration journey from Vinland westward. We had our camp by 2 rocky islets one day's journey north of this stone. We were out fishing one day. When we came home we found 10 men red with blood and dead. AVM save us from evil. We have 10 men by the sea to look after our ships, 14 days' journey from this island. Year 1362." [1]

After placing their handiwork on a little knoll about three miles northeast of the site of the future Kensington, Minnesota, the Vikings moved on. Despairing of ever seeing their homeland again, or even reaching their ship, they decided to spend the rest of their days in the wilderness. They moved west of the Red River, met the Mandan Indians in central North Dakota, and became the progenitors of blue-eyed, fair-skinned Indians.

This intriguing tale of Minnesota's discovery was the outgrowth of the unearthing of the Kensington Rune Stone in November, 1898, by Olaf Ohman, a Swedish immigrant farmer. While clearing land Ohman and his ten-year-old son found the stone among the roots of an aspen tree. The reticent Ohman, never at ease except when speaking his native tongue, showed the strange stone to some neighbors and permitted some Kensington merchants to see it, but he did not invite the attention of outsiders. Then, several months after the discovery, a Kensington lumber dealer solicited opinions about the nature of the stone. The initial responses were both voluminous and critical. Norse language experts immediately recognized the runic symbols but pronounced them to be a modern forgery done very shortly before the stone was found.

After the first flurry, interest in the stone lapsed. Ohman kept it on his farm, using it as a granary stepping stone, and there it languished until 1907 when it was rediscovered by Hjalmar Holand—the greatest champion of its authenticity. Holand, who had a long-standing interest in pre-Columbian Viking explorations, probably first learned of the stone in 1899 when he was a

---

1. Erik Wahlgren, *The Kensington Stone: A Mystery Solved* (Madison: University of Wisconsin Press, 1958), p. 3.

student at the University of Wisconsin. Eight years later, while researching a history of Norwegian immigrants, Holand visited Ohman and acquired the stone. Until his death in 1963, Holand publicized and defended the stone through numerous books and articles, letters and speeches.

Soon after acquiring the rune stone Holand tried to buttress its validity with the opinions of European runologists, but Scandinavian-language experts questioned the stone because a number of the symbols that appeared on it were unknown in 1362. Holand, undaunted, complained that "there is in Europe, a number of educators who tied down to their narrow little round of duties have been led to believe, through an unfortunate superstition, that all things American are tinged with humbug." [2]

Over the years Holand perfected his defense of the stone. Reacting to criticism that there was no Viking activity in North America in the mid-fourteenth century, he seized on the historical fact that Magnus Erickson had dispatched Paul Knutson to Greenland to reassert control over apostates and on this fact alone wove the Viking saga. Other than the king's order there is no record of Knutson, but Holand, working almost entirely from assumption and supposition, carried the Viking odyssey into the heart of North America where the stone was placed and where the Norsemen, by his reasoning, intermarried with the Mandans. In espousing the Mandan theory Holand chose to ignore preponderant scientific opinion that the seemingly white features of the Mandans resulted from inbreeding rather than from mixing with itinerant Europeans. Holand's ingenious case for the stone was given a wide audience with the publication of his book, *The Kensington Stone: A Study in Pre-Columbian American History,* in 1932.

The book gave those who believed that the stone was an authentic record of Viking discovery a satisfactory explanation of the Kensington mystery, and it also won many converts to

2. Hjalmar Holand, "The Kensington Rune Stone Abroad," *Records of the Past* 10 (September–October 1911) as quoted in Milo M. Quaife, "The Myth of the Kensington Rune Stone: The Norse Discovery of Minnesota," *New England Quarterly* 7 (December 1934):619.

Holand's cause. For those unfamiliar with the nature of historical proof and hoaxes, Holand had built a persuasive case.
Within a few years after the book's appearance one critic pre-
dicted in alarm that if the enthusiasm for the stone "be not
stayed by an exposition of the facts concerning it, it may
reasonably be anticipated that the zealots responsible for the
myth will ere long procure the enactment of a law requiring it to
be taught as true history in the public schools of Minnesota and
other neighboring states." [3]

Although Holand had sold the stone to a group of Alexandria
businessmen before his book was published, he continued as its
chief advocate. When critics attacked his theories, Holand responded with an emphatic retelling of his old arguments. Holand saw himself, like Knutson's men, a crusader, and he took a
particular delight in quarreling with academically trained critics
who were unimpressed with his logic and his selective use of
evidence.

Holand and other believers had some moments of elation
when the stone's validity was given boosts from other sources.
Some enthusiasts, reasoning that it dealt with the discovery of
America and not merely with a small part of Minnesota, arranged to have it exhibited at the Smithsonian Institution in
1948. Although officials of the national museum stopped short
of declaring it to be an authentic record, they certainly left a
favorable impression when one of them described it as "probably the most important archaeological object yet found in North
America." [4] The exhibit in the minds of many was an implied
endorsement, and because of it the stone was nationally
publicized—including coverage in the *National Geographic,*
which pictured the Smithsonian's curator of archaeology studying the stone and included the statement that "later studies indicate that it was carved by white men who had traveled far into
North America long before Columbus's first voyage." [5] With
this backing the stone was returned triumphantly to Minnesota

3. Quaife, "Myth of Kensington Rune Stone," pp. 619–620.
4. Wahlgren, *Kensington Stone,* p. 5.
5. Thomas R. Henry, "The Smithsonian Institution," *The National Geographic Magazine* 94 (September 1948):343.

and ceremoniously unveiled by Governor Luther Youngdahl on March 3, 1949, as part of the commemoration of Minnesota's Territorial Centennial.

By this time even those who thought the stone was a hoax had to recognize its significance in the public mind. Residents of Alexandria, the county seat of Douglas County and the possessor of the stone, began advertising their city as the "Birth Place of America," and under the leadership of the Alexandria Kiwanis Club a granite replica about five times the size of the Kensington stone was placed at the east entrance of the city in August 1951. The stone itself, however, was still not appropriately displayed. Then during 1958, the centennial year of Minnesota's statehood, the Alexandria Chamber of Commerce solicited donations from its businesses and civic groups for the erection of an area historical museum where the stone has been enshrined ever since. The stone's boosters displayed it as part of Minnesota's exhibit at the World's Fair in New York in 1964-1965, a move that contributed nothing to resolving the question of its authenticity but made the stone and Alexandria yet more famous.

Although the Kensington Rune Stone has enlivened discussions about Minnesota's beginnings and though there will always be those who believe in its authenticity, there is overwhelming evidence that the stone was a hoax. Authorities in runic languages have universally pronounced the inscription to be modern and are agreed that those who chiseled it were amateurs who probably had nothing more than some rather elementary runic sources at their command. Historians too, particularly Erik Wahlgren and the late Theodore C. Blegen, the most eminent Minnesota historian of the last generation, challenged the stone's authenticity, primarily because of the circumstances under which it was found. They thought it rather a strange coincidence that the stone was found by a Scandinavian in one of the most Scandinavian parts of a state heavily peopled by Scandinavian immigrants at a time when there was great popular interest in Viking explorations of North America. Then, too, Olaf Ohman and his minister friend, Sven Fogelblad, had a strong interest in Viking history and runes and had books that would have enabled them to make the inscription. Furthermore, Ohman and Fogelblad were fun-loving and quite capable of perpetrating a hoax to confound the academicians. There was a local rumor too, immediately after the discovery, that the whole matter was a prank.[6]

The very existence of the stone is sufficient proof of its authenticity to some, and the believers will always be challenged by the critics. Nevertheless, the myth is deeply engrained in Minnesota's tradition and will be of interest even to the disbelievers who may, as Erik Wahlgren suggested, come from afar to Alexandria where they will "witness, not an ancient runic monument, but a memorial to the pioneer settlers of Douglas County—and to the good sportsmanship of their presentday descendants." [7]

6. Blegen, in his book *The Kensington Rune Stone: New Light on an Old Riddle* (St. Paul: Minnesota Historical Society, 1968), p. 124, refers to tapes which he had never heard but which he believed would clarify the origins of the stone. A transcript of part of those tapes, strongly supporting the hoax rumor, has recently been published: "The Case of the Gran Tapes: Further Evidence on the Rune Stone Riddle," *Minnesota History* 45 (Winter 1976): 152–156.

7. Wahlgren, *Kensington Stone,* p. 181.

2

Europeans in the Wilderness

IKE much of North America, Minnesota was first claimed by the French who pushed westward into the heart of the continent by way of the Great Lakes. Their movement in the seventeenth century was part of an intense French rivalry with Great Britain and Spain for control of the vastness of North America. Goaded by this rivalry, and led yet further by the elusive dream of finding a northwestern all-water route to the Far East, France first claimed the St. Lawrence River area in 1536. Costly European wars prevented the French from pursuing this waterway, so they turned their interests to fishing. Commercial fishermen hauled in enormous catches from the Grand Banks of Newfoundland, established numerous stations on shore to salt and dry their fish, and began trading steel knives and other items to Indians for furs—becoming the first fur traders in North America. When European buyers recognized that beaver pelts from the wilds of Canada compared favorably to furs imported from boreal Russia, the French monarchy decided that the fur trade was a feasible commercial venture in its own right and chartered the Company of New France to colonize the lower St. Lawrence.

Under the vigorous leadership of Samuel de Champlain, who dominated New France for years, the Company founded Quebec in 1608. Though menaced by the English, the Dutch, and the powerful Iroquois confederation to the south, Champlain pushed his agents into the interior to stimulate the fur trade and to seek the ever beckoning water route through the continent. The goals complemented each other, for in seeking furs new tribes were discovered, peoples who might have information about western waters; and as the waterways became known, they benefited the extractive and transitory fur trade. The agents of Champlain's policy were his "Young Men"—men such as Étienne Brule and Jean Nicolet whom he sent to live among the Indians to learn their languages, to cement alliances, to carry on the fur trade, and to gather information about other bodies of water to the west.

The discovery of the Great Lakes excited Champlain; this must be the beginning of the route to the East. Outfitted with native guides, Champlain had traveled up the Ottawa River and discovered Lakes Huron and Ontario. Then, when Quebec was about a decade or so old, he learned of Lake Superior—the largest and westernmost of the great inland seas. Late in his career Champlain heard of yet another great sea southwest of Lake Huron upon whose shores lived people who might be Asiatic or, if not Asiatic, Indians who had met Asian traders. Aged and infirm, Champlain could not undertake this trip himself, but he sent out an expedition led by Nicolet. Though Nicolet's primary instructions were to extend the French alliance to western tribes and to lay the foundations for trade, Champlain also had the passage to Cathay in mind. Therefore, Nicolet was outfitted with "a grand robe of China damask, all strewn with flowers and birds of many colors." [1] The robe was sure to impress any Indians he met and would make him doubly welcome if the distant people proved to be Orientals.

Champlain's remote waters proved to be Lake Michigan and the "people of the sea" were Winnebago Indians whom Nicolet met at the site of Green Bay, Wisconsin, in 1634 when he debarked from his canoe garbed in the brilliant Chinese robe. Although he enriched the storehouse of knowledge about the interior and added the fourth of the Great Lakes to French maps,

1. Louise Phelps Kellogg, *The French Régime in Wisconsin and the Northwest* (Madison: State Historical Society of Wisconsin, 1925), p. 78.

Nicolet brought back questions as well as answers. For at Green Bay, on the mouth of the Fox River, the Winnebago told him that three days distant there was another stream issuing from a lake which led to a great water. That stream was probably the Wisconsin River or the Illinois River, and the second great water was apparently the Mississippi; but Nicolet could only report to Champlain that he had learned of yet more water to the west—water that flowed south.

Champlain died a few months after Nicolet's return; and with his death, French dreams of quickly penetrating the mystery of the unknown area west of Lake Michigan faded. Without Champlain, the Company of New France drifted into a long time of troubles—warring with the Iroquois, unsuccessfully fending off creditors, and striving to control the rebellious *coureurs de bois*, those unlicensed traders who often dealt with the Dutch and English. Of the dozens of men who defied the company, two, Pierre Esprit Radisson and Médart Chouart, the Sieur de Groseilliers, won enduring fame.

Groseilliers began his trading career in 1654. In 1656–1657 he and young Radisson went on an unlicensed but lucrative expedition into the Superior country. Two years later, emboldened by their first successful foray, they set out again. The second trip, undertaken in secrecy, carried them along the south shore of Lake Superior to Chequamegon Bay, where they built a rough log hut to cache some of their provisions. Moving inland, they wintered among the Ottawa on Lac Court Oreilles near present Hayward, Wisconsin, and there they learned of the Sioux to the west. Enticed by the fact that no Frenchmen had ever visited this powerful tribe, Radisson and Groseilliers traveled southwestward to meet the "nation of the beefe" or the buffalo-hunting Indians. The site of this famous meeting is unknown; since the discovery of Radisson's journal in the 1880s there has been speculation that the rendezvous was held at Knife Lake near Mora, Minnesota, but there is no real proof that the two adventurers ever left Wisconsin.

Radisson and Groseilliers retraced their path to Montreal in 1660, confident that because they carried back quantities of furs and brought reports of new country and new Indians, their unlicensed adventures would be forgiven. Instead of the heroes' welcome they expected, they were detained and stripped of their furs. Embittered, the two worked their way to England where they helped organize the Hudson's Bay Company and thus contributed to the downfall of the French empire in North America.

Although outside the law in the eyes of French officials, Radisson and Groseilliers contributed significantly to later exploration. They added much to the knowledge about Lake Superior and revealed the importance of the fur trade in that region. Further, they learned from the natives of Lake Superior about the interior route from Hudson Bay to Lake Winnipeg and correctly presumed that it was the easiest passage to the interior of the continent; and they learned that rivers from Lake Winnipeg flowed westward, perhaps even to the Western Sea. As the first white men to visit the Sioux, they observed these Indians before they had been influenced by the ways and tools of Europeans. Radisson, the diarist of the expedition, captured the exhilaration of young men in the wilderness—men in control of their own destiny—with his classical observation that "We weare Cesars being nobody to contradict us." [2] He found a certain comfort in the pristine wilderness, describing Lake Superior as the "delightfullest lake in the world" and wondering if the surrounding area might be a future "laborinth of pleasure" for the crowded masses of Europe who warred over "a rock in the sea." [3]

Men like Radisson and Groseilliers hastened the demise of the Company of New France, whose holdings were taken over by the royal government in 1663. Capable executives of Royal New France soon revived Champlain's dreams. Jean Talon commissioned the youthful explorers Louis Jolliet and Father Jacques Marquette to push inland from Green Bay in search of the Mississippi. On their famous trip of 1673 this pair, after crossing Wisconsin by way of the Fox and Wisconsin rivers, reached the Mississippi a few miles downstream from present Prairie du Chien and followed it southward for a month to the

2. Quoted in Kellogg, *French Régime,* p. 113.
3. Pierre Esprit Radisson, "The Western Lakes Region in Summer," in *With Various Voices: Recordings of North Star Life,* comp. Theodore C. Blegen and Philip D. Jordan (St. Paul: Itasca Press, 1949), p. 4.

mouth of the Arkansas. In disappointment they concluded that it led to the Gulf of Mexico, not to a South Sea that connected with the Pacific Ocean. But still, they had discovered the mouth of the Missouri River, which was a larger stream than the Mississippi at the point where the two rivers joined. Was the Missouri then the way to a western sea? Leaving that question unanswered, the two men led by native guides returned to Lake Michigan by way of the Illinois and Chicago rivers, thus pioneering two routes from that lake to the Mississippi for later explorers to follow.

The royal governor, Count Frontenac, was aggressive and soon French traders moved westward along the Chicago–Illinois, Fox–Wisconsin, and Lake Superior paths. While La Salle was establishing posts in the Illinois country the trade of Lake Superior, dormant since the time of Radisson and Groseilliers, was revived by Daniel Greysolon, Sieur Duluth. Duluth, sponsored by Quebec and Montreal merchants, set out from Montreal in 1678. After wintering among the Chippewa near Sault Ste. Marie, Duluth moved on to a rendezvous with the Sioux near where the city of Duluth now stands. The tribesmen escorted him inland to their principal village on the south shore of Lake Mille Lacs and there on July 2, 1679, he formally claimed the country for Louis XIV.

Satisfied that he had extended French suzerainty over the Sioux, Duluth returned to Lake Superior, leaving behind three engagés who were to visit other Sioux villages seeking information about the western sea. These men met Sioux warriors who told of having been on a campaign twenty days travel westward to a great lake that had salty waters. Ignorant of the breadth of the continent and equally ignorant of Great Salt Lake, Duluth assumed that his men had been told about the Pacific. At any rate, Duluth wintered at the mouth of the Kaministiquia (present day Thunder Bay, Ontario), convinced that a water route to the Pacific lay through the Sioux country.

The Sioux, confined to the forests of northern Wisconsin and northern and central Minnesota where they had emerged as a modern culture from earlier woodland stock, called themselves Dacotah, meaning roughly "ally," because they did not war against each other. The French at first used the Chippewa name "Nadouessioux," or "little viper," but soon abridged it to the meaningless and thus milder "Sioux." The Sioux welcomed the French alliance because it promised them the guns and ammunition that their arch-enemies, the Chippewa or Ojibwes, already had. The Chippewa had been pushed westward by the powerful Iroquois and equipped with firearms; they in turn pushed west from Sault Ste. Marie after the mid-seventeenth century, threatening to drive the Dacotah from their native forests. Ultimately the Chippewa did just that, forcing the Sioux into southern Minnesota and the prairies. The western tribes occupied much of the Great Plains across the Dakotas and into Nebraska and Wyoming, but for nearly a century after Duluth the eastern Sioux tribes held their ground.

Duluth's plans to find the salt water reported by his men were thwarted. While journeying down the St. Croix River in 1680, Duluth learned that a band of Sioux warriors was holding three white captives. Believing they were French and realizing that no French lives were any safer than those of the captives, Duluth overtook the Sioux hunting party and effected the release of the prisoners. The men proved to be emissaries of La Salle, led by Michel Accault and sent from the Illinois River to explore the upper Mississippi. Near the mouth of the Illinois they had been seized by the Sioux party which had carried them northward into Minnesota. Realizing the gravity of the situation, Duluth returned to the Sioux villages on Mille Lacs and upbraided the assembled Sioux chiefs for their effrontery to the Sun King's subjects, insisting that they abide by their alliance. Then he returned to Montreal. Although Duluth failed to find a way to the Pacific, he did reopen the Lake Superior fur trade and he added the Sioux to the French alliance. His explorations also fed the French expansionist mania with yet another story about a salt-water lake to the west.

Father Louis Hennepin, a Belgian who was diarist and cartographer for the Accault expedition, became an instant celebrity. He had carefully noted the actions and customs of his captors, who carried him past the picturesque falls of the Mississippi which he named in honor of his patron saint, Anthony of Padua. In 1683, only a year after he returned to France, he published his *Description of Louisiana*. With a keen sense of the reading appetite of Europeans, who were fascinated by the natives of North America, Hennepin emphasized those things which would seem bizarre to his readers. Though he was not overly concerned with geography, he did introduce the Upper Mississippi and its falls to thousands because his book was a best-seller in its time. Unfortunately, Hennepin fell victim to an inclination to exaggerate; by 1699, in a later work, he was describing the sixteen-foot falls of St. Anthony as having a drop of fifty or sixty feet.

In a sense, Hennepin exploited the wilderness, but most Frenchmen who ventured among distant tribes were interested in economic exploitation—the furs. During the 1680s Nicholas Perrot, who had long traded in the Lake Michigan area, extended his operations to the Upper Mississippi. He established Fort St. Antoine on the Wisconsin side of Lake Pepin, the widening of the Mississippi above the mouth of the tributary Chippewa River, and began trading with the Sioux. When the English announced a claim to the area and Sioux loyalty appeared to be wavering, French officials ordered Perrot to claim the Upper Mississippi for France again, even though Duluth had already done so and La Salle, upon reaching the mouth of the Mississippi in 1682, had claimed its entire drainage basin for Louis XIV. Intent upon overawing the Sioux, Perrot arranged an elaborate ceremony at Fort St. Antoine on May 8, 1689. There, to the sound of muskets, Latin chants, and shouts of "long live the king," Perrot claimed the lands adjoining the Fox, Wisconsin, and upper Mississippi as well as the country of the Sioux and the rivers St. Croix and St. Pierre; and lest some undiscovered area of value should escape the French grasp, Perrot also laid claim to "other places more remote." [4]

Throughout much of his career on the Upper Mississippi, Perrot was accompanied by his young lieutenant, Pierre Charles Le Sueur. Le Sueur stayed with Perrot from 1683 until at least the mid-1690s, trading not only with the Sioux but with the Chip-

4. Kellogg, *French Régime*, p. 242.

pewa on Lake Superior as well. During this time he met Sioux Indians who smeared their faces and bodies with a greenish blue clay they extracted from the banks of a stream that entered the St. Pierre's River from the south. Intrigued by the possibility that copper ore might be found along with the clay, Le Sueur visited the "mine" site along the stream that he called the Green River (the modern Blue Earth).

Le Sueur brought out specimens of the clay and purportedly had them assayed in France, where they were proclaimed to be copper-bearing. Le Sueur's desire to return to the Blue Earth River was frustrated for several years by difficulties in obtaining a royal permit: he also wanted to trade in furs, and the French market was glutted with beaver pelts. Ultimately, however, he received a patent to search for mineral wealth in the Upper Mississippi and to trade with the Indians for peltries and hides other than beaver. He was delayed yet another year when his ship was seized by belligerent English; then Canadian colonial officials, mistrustful of his purpose, also blocked his expedition.

In an extraordinary move, Le Sueur decided to reach the Upper Mississippi by way of the Gulf of Mexico. His path was at last made smooth through the fortune of being related by marriage to the Sieur de Iberville, the founder of Biloxi, Mississippi, and it was from there that Le Sueur undertook his voyage early in 1700. He and his party of about two dozen men reached the mouth of the Blue Earth early in October and constructed a small stockade named Fort L'Huillier after a French official who had befriended Le Sueur.

Working out of the fort, Le Sueur's men almost immediately began taking out the blue earth from the mine site a few miles upstream, scraping it out with knives and loading it onto canoes. Le Sueur seems to have come well equipped with trade goods, for he also struck up a lucrative business with the Sioux in which he gathered nearly four thousand beaver pelts. He and his men lived well, killing and butchering hundreds of buffalo which were numerous on the prairies west of the Blue Earth. He left Fort L'Huillier after less than a year, taking with him a reported two tons of blue earth—as well as the furs. Leaving behind a portion of his party who abandoned the post the following year because of the threatening Fox Indians, he was back in France within a few months; but he did not return to his homeland bearing untold mineral wealth. The blue earth apparently never reached France. Whether it was cast into the Father of Waters or simply abandoned someplace, no one knows. But Le Sueur successfully perpetuated the myth that he had worked a copper mine. Later chroniclers, particularly Benard de la Harpe, one of the first historians of Louisiana, reported Le Sueur's intention as accomplishment, and as a result tales of Le Sueur's copper mine on the Blue Earth River persisted for years. The mine was not finally declared bogus until it was visited by the English geologist George Featherstonhaugh in 1835.

Surely Le Sueur should have been able to identify copper, for when trading among the Chippewa and Sioux he had seen float copper, those pieces scattered by glacial action; and he had seen objects the Indians shaped from this copper, including musketballs fashioned when lead was unavailable. Given this knowledge Le Sueur should have had no difficulty in making a distinction between copper and the blue earth because of the difference in color, heft, and consistency.

Le Sueur was not without critics in his day. The intendant of New France suspected deceit in Le Sueur's expedition, speculating that "the only mines that he seeks in those regions are mines of beaver skins." [5] In light of Le Sueur's subsequent trade with the Sioux even though his license excluded beaver, this may have been the most accurate statement ever written about the first explorer of the Minnesota and Blue Earth rivers. But Le Sueur still must be credited with contributing to the geographical knowledge of the area in which he traveled. He sketched the region between Lake Superior and the Blue Earth River, and he obtained information from Indians who had been on the plains to the west. He calculated as best he could the latitude and longitude of significant stream junctures. Most important, he reported his findings to the famous royal geographer Claude Delisle, who issued a 1703 map showing much of the Upper Mississippi area.

5. Kellogg, *French Régime*, p. 350.

Le Sueur's expedition marked the end of an era in the fitful history of New France in the northwest. The exigencies of the War of the Spanish Succession, which found France again pitted against her age-old foe Great Britain, caused the royal government to abandon all posts and activities in the western Great Lakes region. The area lay dormant while armies in Europe struggled for control of North America. Peace was finally restored in 1713 with the Treaty of Utrecht by which France surrendered the Hudson Bay region to Great Britain.

This reversal proved to be a stimulant, and the French launched a broad campaign to strengthen their remaining hold in North America. The settlement of New Orleans was begun in 1718, and at the same time the French reoccupied the Lake Superior posts, hoping to draw the Indian fur gatherers away from the British at Hudson Bay. With the revival of trade, the French awakened anew to the task of finding an all-water route through the continent to the "Western Sea." It was a long way to the Pacific, and the French pinned their hopes on that Western Sea which would provide easy passage from the Great Lakes and the Mississippi River to the ocean.

Thus it was that the government of New France authorized a reconnaissance by the Jesuit priest Pierre François Charlevoix. So that the British would not divine his real purpose, Charlevoix conducted his business under the guise of a tour of missions. He questioned Indians at Green Bay about routes west of Lake Superior and the Upper Mississippi and then canoed across Wisconsin and down the Mississippi to the gulf. In his report of this 1721 trip he recommended two possible ways of reaching the Western Sea, which he believed lay southwest of Lake of the Woods. One suggested avenue was by way of the Missouri River, the other overland from a location on the Upper Mississippi. In the interest of economy the government chose the Upper Mississippi route without knowing that an expedition up the Missouri would have borne more fruit.

The Upper Mississippi expedition was launched in 1727 by the government of New France headed by Charles de la Boische, Sieur de Beauharnois, whose rule, like Frontenac's, was marked by westward expansion. Merchants underwrote the costs of constructing a post in return for a three-year monopoly of the fur trade, and Beauharnois provided a military escort. The fleet of canoes carried not only Beauharnois's men but also Jesuit missionaries, sent because the Sioux had told Charlevoix that they would welcome the Black Robes.

After a three-month trip which carried them through the lands of the hostile Fox Indians in Wisconsin, the group selected a site on the Minnesota side of Lake Pepin, about two miles from present-day Frontenac. There, on low ground along the Mississippi, they erected an enclosure "a hundred feet square surrounded by stakes twelve feet high with two good bastions." [6] The fort was named Beauharnois, and in November the men celebrated Beauharnois's birthday with a fireworks display which wrought terror among the Indians. But Fort Beauharnois was a failure. The Fox Indians made war, trade with the Sioux was not realized, and no expeditions set forth for the Western Sea. The fort was occupied intermittently for a decade and then abandoned.

When Beauharnois realized that the Fox Indians would prevent any expeditions from Lake Pepin, he looked for another way of reaching the west. His interests soon melded with those of Pierre Gautier de Varennes, Sieur de La Vérendrye, whom history remembers as the last of the important French explorers in North America—and the only one who was a native of Canada. He had served with distinction in the French army in the War of the Spanish Succession and after the war was rewarded with various commands, including that of a post on Lake Nipigon, north of Lake Superior. Here, on the border of an expanse dotted by thousands of lakes and laced with streams, he listened eagerly to Indian tales of water routes and the great sea that could be reached from Lake Superior.

Vérendrye was aware of the route inland by way of the Kaministiquia from Thunder Bay to Lac la Croix—it had first been used by Jacques de Noyon in 1688—and he learned of the route along the present Minnesota–Ontario boundary from the As-

6. Theodore C. Blegen, *The Land Lies Open* (Minneapolis: University of Minnesota Press, 1949), p. 57.

siniboine Indians, one of whom sketched the border lakes for
him on birch bark. Indian guides showed Vérendrye a trail, later
known as the Grand Portage, leading from Lake Superior to the
Pigeon River above the series of falls that blocked its lower
reaches, and led him on an arduous canoe route that had some
three dozen other portages and carried him across the Lake
Superior–Hudson Bay divide on Height of Land Portage and
through numerous lakes and the Rainy River. At last before him
lay Lake of the Woods.

Lake of the Woods could easily have been described as an
inland sea, but Vérendrye knew the Western Sea he sought lay
yet ahead, so he thought of Lake of the Woods as a likely
halfway point between Montreal and his unknown destination.
Therefore, to provide himself with a base of operations and a
way station, Vérendrye built Fort St. Charles during the summer of 1732. The small stockade was erected on the Minnesota
side of Northwest Angle Inlet about halfway between Rainy
River's entry into the lake and the lake's outlet into the Winnipeg River.

Vérendrye could have profited immensely from the fur trade
in that unexploited wilderness had he been content to limit himself to that activity, but his belief in the Western Sea drove him
on. The outflow from Lake of the Woods led him to Lake Winnipeg, a massive remnant of glacial Lake Agassiz, and canoe
routes from that lake drew him westward by way of the Sas-
katchewan and Assiniboine rivers. Vérendrye's quest took him
all the way from present-day Winnipeg, Manitoba, across the
prairies to the Mandan villages on the Missouri River. Always,
the Western Sea lay beyond. Later, two of his sons explored
through North Dakota and into Montana, Wyoming, and South
Dakota in the futile search for salt water. Debts and personal
tragedy at last defeated Vérendrye, and he abandoned his search
in 1744. Fort St. Charles lives to the present day, for in reconstructed form it stands on the ground where Vérendrye stood
and saw the Western Sea beyond Minnesota's horizon.

There is a certain sadness in Vérendrye's story; New France
had little time to use the western lands added by the Véren-

dryes. The defeat of Braddock's redcoats by the French and their Indian allies in the forests of western Pennsylvania touched off the last of four Anglo-French wars that ultimately brought the end of New France and the French phase of Minnesota's history. The fate of the vast lands placed under the *fleur de lys* by the Champlains, the Duluths, and the La Salles was decided on the Plains of Abraham before Quebec, and four years later, in 1763, France formally relinquished her North American holdings to Great Britain.

French flags were taken down with the end of the struggle for the continent; but through activities spanning a century, the French introduced Minnesota to the world. They did not find the seas they sought, but they found major waterways, and they left at least some legacy of maps. The traders made a beginning in the fur trade and, whether for good or for bad, they began the process of making the Indians dependent on white man's goods and tools.

Minnesota's French tradition has been perpetuated by names left upon the land—some of them given by the French themselves, others in memory of them. Thus there are counties named Mille Lacs, Roseau, and Lac Qui Parle and another called St. Louis, after the river named by Vérendrye in honor of King Louis IX. Hennepin became the name of a county and a major avenue in Minneapolis, and Le Sueur had a county, a river, and a town named in his honor. Although many French names have been lost through translation—Lac la Pluie to Rainy Lake and Lac du Bois to Lake of the Woods—and some changed beyond recognition, such as the transformation of the River des Embarrass to the Zumbro—others are still evident in Lake Pepin, Lac la Croix, Grand Marais, Frontenac, Pomme de Terre, Belle Plaine, Le Center, and Faribault.

Though French influence in the fur trade technically ended with the British conquest, it lingered nonetheless. French remained the essential language of the trade, and the British and later American fur companies were filled with the French Canadian voyageurs who carried their names and their culture among the tribes. These French Canadians soon found that Great Britain, like France, encouraged but two activities in its new kingdom—the fur trade, and exploration for a route to the Pacific.

The annals of British exploration in Minnesota are not nearly so long as the French, but they are colorful, and the highlight of them has to be the adventures of Jonathan Carver. Carver was yet another pawn in the game of seeking the Northwest Passage. His career as a traveler was inextricably bound with that of his sponsor, Robert Rogers, a rugged New Englander whose heroic deeds as a frontier ranger during the French and Indian War made him known from the colonies to Great Britain. While serving at Detroit, Rogers heard tale after tale from French voyageurs and Indians about the unknown interior and the myriad water routes. His interest was further piqued through conversations with Arthur Dobbs, the aged governor of North Carolina. Dobbs, a testy Irishman, had devoted much of his life to the search for a Northwest Passage; years before meeting Rogers, he had concluded absolutely that there was a connecting strait from Hudson Bay to the Pacific. Dobbs not only was convinced that the strait existed, but he believed that the Hudson's Bay Company knew of it. Dobbs was dedicated to the point of sending a party of explorers to Hudson Bay and fanatical enough to denounce the leader of the expedition as part of a conspiracy of silence when he reported that he could find no strait to the Pacific. It did not take long for Dobbs's zeal to conjure up for Robert Rogers visions of marching from the Upper Mississippi overland to the Pacific, skirting the ocean's shores, and finding at last the elusive strait to Hudson Bay. But for such an enterprise Rogers wanted royal backing. Though he had powerful friends in England, he was not able to win support for his expedition from British ministers who were struggling with the staggering debt of the recent European war. Instead, he received the command of the military post at Michilimackinac. Once back in Boston, the undaunted Rogers schemed to use this command to launch a small private expedition.

For leader of the expedition, Rogers chose a former ranger associate, James Tute, known for his courage and resourcefulness. Second in command was James Stanley Goddard, a veteran fur trader, well known among the Indians of the western Great Lakes. As map maker and draftsman, Rogers engaged the unemployed Jonathan Carver, then fifty-six, whom he had first met during the recent war when Carver was an officer in a colonial unit. Some of Dobbs's suspicious nature must have communicated itself to Rogers, for he never revealed the expedition's real purpose to Carver but merely instructed him to winter near the Falls of St. Anthony and map the area west of the Mississippi in that sector. Carver made his way from his Massachusetts home to Michilimackinac at the western end of Lake Huron, and in September 1766 he left with some traders on a journey that carried him across Wisconsin from Green Bay to Prairie du Chien. From Prairie du Chien he paddled upstream, accompanied by only two companions—a French Canadian and a Mohawk Indian. He arrived among the Sioux Indians near St. Anthony Falls in November and wintered with them on the Minnesota River.

Tute and Goddard, who had left Mackinac some two weeks after Carver, wintered among Indians near Prairie du Chien. Rogers had instructed Tute that his goal was to move from Lake Huron to the Pacific, which he would finally reach by following the great river "Ourigan" after wintering twice enroute. But Rogers also had more immediate aims, which account for the separation of Tute and Goddard from Carver. Penniless and hounded by creditors, Rogers hoped to recoup himself through the Indian trade, so Tute and Goddard at Prairie du Chien were to persuade the tribesmen to meet with Rogers in a grand conclave at Mackinac.

Whatever hope these men had of reaching the Pacific was lost after the first winter. Carver was completely out of touch with the other two for months and Tute and Goddard, away from the infectious enthusiasm of Rogers, grew increasingly skeptical of the scheme of crossing the Sioux lands to a second winter's destination far out on the Canadian prairies. Tute was also well aware of Rogers's slim purse and wisely decided not to gamble on his getting provisions to the second wintering ground. After Carver joined him and Goddard at Prairie du Chien in the spring, Tute decided to move far northward to the fur trade rendezvous of Grand Portage in the hope of receiving further word and supplies from Rogers.

The trio found Grand Portage bustling with dozens of traders, none of whom bore goods from Rogers. At last, after a three-week wait, word arrived. Rogers could not send supplies, but still he urged his men to carry out their grand mission. Under these circumstances, the thought of starting for the Pacific held no appeal for the demoralized explorers, and Carver noted that they "universally agreed to return to Michillimackinac and give over our intended expedition." [7]

For Carver, however, the end had not yet come. He made his way to England, where his life changed drastically. Separated from his homeland and his family, he married an English-woman, fathered a second family without divorcing his American wife, and spent the rest of his days hoping to persuade the Crown to reward him for services as an explorer.

In 1778, Carver's *Travels Through the Interior Parts of North America, in the Years 1766, 1767, and 1768* was published and became instantly popular. It soon appeared in other editions and ultimately was translated into many foreign languages. As the first book in English about the Upper Mississippi, it has become one of the classic accounts of the region. The book was really two books in one. The first section was authentic, although it suffered for want of accuracy since Carver evidently wrote it without having at hand the diaries he had written en route. Even in this section his account sometimes surpassed belief, as when he described the hissing snakes of Lake Erie or the forty-pound trout caught two at a time through the ice. But the second part, a lengthy exposition of Indian manners and customs followed by descriptions of wilderness plants, animals, and birds, was another matter. In writing this section, Carver liberally copied verbatim passages from the accounts of Charlevoix, Hennepin, Lahontan, and others. Perhaps Carver can be forgiven his plagiarism, since in his day it was common and aroused no particular ire among readers, and perhaps his enthusiastic exaggera-

7. *The Journal of Jonathan Carver and Related Documents, 1766–1770*, ed. John Parker (St. Paul: Minnesota Historical Society Press, 1976), p. 132.

tions of the natural wonders of the wilderness can also be excused; but Carver was less than honest about his part in the expedition, and that is more difficult to forgive. Rogers was not mentioned except as "governor" of Michilimackinac, Tute was not mentioned at all, and, said Carver, Goddard was "a gentleman that desired to accompany me." [8] It may have been that Carver hoped through such deception to dupe government officials into rewarding him for his enterprise.

It is no wonder Europeans read Carver's account avidly. His descriptions were often vivid—the terrain in the Lake Pepin vicinity he saw as "the most beautiful and extensive prospect that imagination can form. . . . Verdant plains, fruitful meadows, numerous islands, and all these abounding with a variety of trees that yield amazing quantities of fruit, without care or cultivation. . . ." [9] And the River St. Pierre, he said,

> flows through a most delightful country, abounding with all the necessaries of life . . . wild rice grows here in great abundance; and every part is filled with trees bending under their loads of fruits, such as plums, grapes, and apples; the meadows are covered with hops, and many sorts of vegetables; whilst the ground is stored with useful roots, with angelica, spikenard, and ground-nuts as large as hens eggs. At a little distance from the sides of the river are eminences, from which you have views that cannot be exceeded even by the most beautiful of those I have already described; amidst these are delightful groves, and such amazing quantities of maples, that they would produce sugar sufficient for any number of inhabitants. [10]

Not content to limit himself to the country he had actually seen, from Indian reports and his own speculations Carver made intriguing though not always accurate comments on western geography. He had information that the sources of the Minnesota and Missouri rivers lay within a mile of each other, and he had learned from the Sioux and Assiniboine that the four great rivers

8. J[onathan] Carver, *Travels through the Interior Parts of North America, in the Years 1766, 1767, and 1768,* 3rd ed. (London, 1781; reprint ed., Minneapolis: Ross & Haines, 1956), p. 105.
9. Carver, *Travels,* p. 55.
10. Carver, *Travels,* p. 100.

of North America all started from the same highlands, with the
Mississippi flowing south, the St. Lawrence east, the Bourbon
(Nelson) north to Hudson Bay, and the Ourigan west. Like
Rogers, Carver believed in the great river of the west. He may
have been writing about the stream that was later named the
Columbia, but neither it nor any other river of the far west was
ever known to the natives as the Ourigan. Many years later Car-
ver's Ourigan became Oregon.

Carver also popularized the belief that there was a great
mountain range in the west. It was three thousand miles long in
its extent north from Mexico, he said, and it divided the waters
of the Gulf of Mexico and the Gulf of California. Could this
have been anything other than the Rocky Mountains? Carver
called them the Shining Mountains, "from an infinite number of
crystal stones, of an amazing size, with which they are covered,
and which, when the sun shines full upon them sparkle so as to
be seen at a very great distance." [11]

Carver's obsession with his great adventure lived beyond him
not only because of his book. Shortly after his death, Carver's
first biographer revealed a deed under which Carver purportedly
had been granted a huge triangle of land in western Wisconsin
by the Sioux. But the deed was obviously fraudulent, and efforts by the heirs and others to have the grant honored were ultimately rejected by Congress. Still, in the Minnesota River
Valley where Carver lived with the Sioux a town and a county
bear his name; and not far distant is the model community of
Jonathan.

Great Britain was not monopolistic as France had been, and
the fur trade was opened to all comers to increase competition
and encourage productivity. Soon Scots and New Englanders
became the lords of the wilderness, and they dominated it until
the close of the War of 1812. Most of the British trade centered
on Lake Superior, but some traders canoed from Lake Michigan
to the Mississippi by the Fox-Wisconsin passage and worked
from Prairie du Chien along the Upper Mississippi and its tributaries, especially the St. Croix and the Minnesota.

11. Carver, *Travels*, p. 121.

One of the earliest British traders in this Mississippi trade was Connecticut-born Peter Pond, who was in his early thirties when he led a trading party to the Minnesota River in 1773–1774. Pond was a ruffian, but he had a sense of history and he kept a diary of this trip. Virtually uneducated, Pond spelled instinctively, phonetically, his writing unencumbered by punctuation. "On acount of the fase of the Cuntrey & Soile the Entervales of the River St. Peter," he observed in describing the Minnesota River Valley, "is Exsaland & Sum Good timber the Banks Bend the Intervals are high and the Soile thin & lite the River is Destatute of fish But the Woods & Meaddoues afords abundans of annamels Sum turkeas Buffeloes are Verey Plentey the Common Dear are Plentey and Larg. . . ." [12] Pond later joined the North West Company and traded in the distant Athabascan country. He had, and deserved, a bad reputation because he was a known murderer, but he also had an uncommonly strong interest in geography.

Of the dozens of British trading posts built in Minnesota, none compare in magnitude to Grand Portage, at the start of the nine-mile "great carrying place" connecting Lake Superior and the Pigeon River. For nearly four decades this post, situated in a sweeping bay on Lake Superior with the rugged pine-clad hills of northeastern Minnesota rising above it, was probably the single most important fur trade location in the world. From here large canoes and other vessels that hauled the rum, guns, powder, ammunition, blankets, cloth, tobacco, kettles, axes, and beads out from Montreal could go no further, and it led to the start of a two-thousand-mile-long canoe route into the Canadian interior.

Jonathan Carver observed that it was the place where Indians customarily awaited traders, though it was but a bare meeting ground, and the British first used it as a rendezvous site without benefit of stockades. During the next decade independent traders built houses with stockades around them, until by 1778 Grand

12. "The Narrative of Peter Pond," in *Five Fur Traders of the Northwest,* ed. Charles M. Gates (Minneapolis: University of Minnesota Press, 1933; reprint ed., St. Paul: Minnesota Historical Society, 1965), p. 56.

Portage was a virtual village in the wilderness, with as many as five hundred people coming and going through the season.

Grand Portage took on a new importance during the 1780s and 1790s under the influence of the North West Company. The company erected a huge stockade enclosing sixteen buildings, including a great hall. The post was occupied year round, but every July and August it burgeoned with the arrival of canoes from Montreal laden with goods that had been sent out many months before from London. The boatmen for the Montreal–Grand Portage trip were usually young French Canadians who returned to Montreal the same year. These men were called *mangeurs du lard,* or pork-eaters, because they cooked their dried corn and peas in grease, and the name came also to signify their status as greenhorns. Each year some of the pork-eaters stayed in the fur trade country and thus became *hiverants,* or winterers; in common fur-trade parlance, "Northmen." The social distinction between the pork-eaters and the Northmen was so strong that they did not even occupy the same campgrounds. Most of the voyageurs, whether *mangeurs du lard* or *hiverants,* were legally engagés: apprenticed servants, bound to the company by the advancement of an outfit and trade goods. Some of the more enterprising engagés worked their way out of debt and became independent traders, but many others stayed bound for long years as their debts to the company accrued with each passing season. It was difficult to succeed in a situation where prices paid for pelts were meager and trade goods cost ten to twelve times the original London prices.

The bourgeois, or director of the fur trading post, and his clerks packed the goods for the overland trip to Fort Charlotte on the Pigeon River where the North canoes were assembled for the western trade, but the voyageur carried them. With two or even more ninety-pound packs held high on his back by a portage strap around his head, the voyageur would toil through the hilly terrain, ascending nearly 800 feet as he traversed the nine-mile path. Mud, rocks, and swarms of mosquitoes must have caused these men to give voice to more than the *chansons* for which they are so well remembered. Those who toiled over the great carrying place surely must have wished for a better way, but there was none: carts and wagons required roads and animals, impractical in a business that was both seasonal and transitional.

At Fort Charlotte the birch-bark canoes that had come in from distant posts deposited their beaver, weasel, mink, fisher, and marten pelts along with bear skins and buffalo hides and took on a cargo of trade goods. Each of the large North canoes could carry almost a ton and a half of cargo and was manned by four or five men. When the canoes were loaded for trade, the Northmen departed for the interior once more. Many times the voyageurs who had carried trade packs uphill to Fort Charlotte would make the return trip bearing packs of furs downhill, back to Grand Portage. These furs were taken by canoe to Montreal and then to the great market in London, which attracted buyers from all across Europe. Some of the Grand Portage furs were caravaned across Russia and sold eventually in China.

Grand Portage's glory was brief, for it was abandoned by the North West Company in 1803. The boundary drawn between the United States and Canada at the end of the Revolutionary War was vague in the region west of Lake Superior, and the partners of the North West Company became increasingly uneasy about the possibility that the post was really on American soil and thus subject to American customs officials. When the British removed themselves from Detroit and Mackinac in 1796, Grand Portage seemed alone and unprotected, and the North West Company sought an alternate depot. The Kaministiquia waterway from Thunder Bay to Lac la Croix had been known for many years, but it was longer and more rigorous than the Grand Portage way. Nevertheless, the North West Company built Fort William at the mouth of the Kaministiquia and moved its base of operations.

For the British and for the North West Company, Grand Portage had been something more than a fur trading post. It was an outpost to adventure. Alexander Mackenzie, partner in the North West Company who followed the river named after him to the Arctic, and who was the first man to cross North America, used the post as the starting point for both his expeditions. David Thompson, astronomer and surveyor employed by the North West Company who was responsible for mapping much of northern Minnesota and western Canada (and the Pacific Northwest), worked out of Grand Portage during his search for the northern source of the Mississippi, as did Dr. John McLoughlin, another North West Company partner who gained fame in the Oregon country.

The shift to Fort William signified increasing recognition by the British of America's intent to assert herself in that enormous country which was hers by diplomatic right. The French and the British who explored and exploited Minnesota had as goals the development of commercial routes and trade with the Indians. These men were removed from their native governments by thousands of miles of ocean; their posts were outposts of civilization. But American aims were vastly different. America was a young nation, a growing nation, concerned with placing her stamp on that which was hers; concerned with the fur trade, yes, but also with determining and enforcing permanent boundaries and exploring for the sake of ascertaining potential economic wealth. The Indians had to be dealt with—not just as trade contacts or as allies, but in such a way that they would not impede the settlement which was inevitable.

Although the British abandoned Grand Portage, they did not desert their posts in the interior of the Old Northwest. They stayed on at Fond du Lac near the mouth of the St. Louis River; at Sandy Lake, near the western end of the Lake Superior–Mississippi canoe route through Savannah Portage; at Leech Lake; at Pembina in the Red River Valley; and wherever else they had a foothold. But those footholds were challenged time and again by an American government determined to control the Northwest country.

3

America Asserts Herself

ITH the exception of George Rogers Clark's expedition through southern Illinois and Indiana there was little American military activity in the Old Northwest during the Revolutionary War; and even Clark's venture only temporarily interrupted British control of the Illinois country. British traders in the western Great Lakes country paid scant attention to the war. It was inconceivable to them that Great Britain would ever surrender the west, and they were bitter when they learned of the provisions of the Treaty of Paris. Under it, American claims were extended to the very heart of the continent and Great Britain agreed to a northern boundary that gave most of the Great Lakes trade area to the Americans.

Late in the war American diplomats Benjamin Franklin, John Jay, and John Adams met with Richard Oswald, the British envoy to the peace talks, to consider perplexing northern boundary settlements. Franklin had a simple solution—Great Britain could just relinquish the whole of Canada to the United States. The British countered with a suggestion that perhaps the Ohio River was a suitable demarcation. Serious discussion then dealt with the possibility of using the forty-fifth parallel westward from the Connecticut River to the Mississippi. There was legal precedent for such a line, since it was the southern boundary of the old province of Quebec, but it presented problems: if drawn to the Mississippi, which it would have reached where Minneapolis now stands, it would have crossed the St. Lawrence River and the Great Lakes, leaving southern Ontario to the United States and much of Michigan, Wisconsin, and central and northern Minnesota to Great Britain. The idea was finally abandoned because it did not respect the natural flow of waters and because of its inconvenience to British fur traders. Finally the diplomats agreed to the American suggestion that the boundary follow natural water routes leading from the St. Lawrence River to Lake of the Woods.

As described in the treaty the northern boundary was to be drawn from the point where the forty-fifth parallel struck the St. Lawrence River through the middle of Lakes Ontario, Erie, and Huron,

> thence through Lake Superior northward of the Isles Royal & Phelipeaux, to the Long Lake; then through the middle of said Long Lake, and the water Communication between it and the Lake of the Woods, to the said Lake of the Woods, then through the said Lake to the most Northwestern point thereof, and from thence on a due west Course to the River Mississippi. . . .[1]

The Mississippi was to be the western boundary from the point of intersection west of Lake of the Woods south to the thirty-first parallel, which was believed to be the northern boundary of Spanish claims east of the Mississippi.

When the American peace commissioners left Paris, they were highly pleased with the northern boundary stipulation and totally oblivious to its flaws. And flawed the agreement was, for there was no Isle Phelipeaux in Lake Superior, no Long Lake west of Lake Superior; nor did the Mississippi River lie west of Lake of the Woods. The flaws are understandable: the negotiators were a long way from the fur traders and others who were knowledgeable about the Lake Superior-Lake of the Woods area, and they were hurried, so they relied on the highly reputed Mitchell map of North America which had been drawn nearly thirty years before the Paris deliberations. Mitchell's map was as good as any North American map of the day and far better

1. Hunter Miller, ed., *Treaties and Other International Acts of the United States of America* (Washington, D.C.: Government Printing Office, 1931–1948), 2:97.

than most; nonetheless, it showed all those nonexistent features mentioned in the boundary provisions, as well as other errors. It left the impression that Lake of the Woods was elliptical in shape with a perceptibly narrow northwest end, and that it was the head of the St. Lawrence watershed; and it showed the source of the Mississippi rising in an area on the map covered by an inset, so it was not really located at all. The treaty makers probably believed they were using two uninterrupted water lines for boundaries and closing them in the northwest with a straight line from Lake of the Woods to the Mississippi.

The Revolutionary War boundaries would stand, but they were tested because there were British who believed that Great Britain had been far too generous in the peace settlement. The North West Company, with the aim of discrediting the northern boundary provision of the Treaty of Paris, sent out David Thompson to map Lake of the Woods and locate the headwaters of the Mississippi. The company hoped not only to save Grand Portage, but also to cause the boundary to be shifted far enough southward so that its future extension to the Pacific, which was sure to come, would retain the Columbia River basin for the British fur traders. In 1797–1798, with the aid of Indian guides, Thompson found Turtle Lake (only about ten miles north of where Bemidji now lies) and proclaimed it the source of the Mississippi. Later explorers proved that Thompson had found only the start of the river's northern branch rather than the true source; but his activities did reveal the gap in the boundary, south rather than west of Lake of the Woods. An effort to close that gap was made in 1803 with the negotiating of the King–Hawkesbury line, drawn from the northwest point of Lake of the Woods to Turtle Lake.

When the King–Hawkesbury agreement was presented to President Thomas Jefferson, he was confronted with a dilemma. He had before him also the Louisiana Purchase Treaty, and both documents had to be forwarded to the Senate for consideration. Realizing that the boundaries of the Louisiana Purchase were extremely vague, Jefferson wanted to avoid any action that would perhaps limit American claims to the northern plains. He saw immediately that the King–Hawkesbury line could adversely affect the northern boundary of Louisiana, because the northern source of the Mississippi rather than the northwest point of Lake of the Woods might become the point of departure for a boundary extension. So not until the Louisiana Purchase was secure did Jefferson forward the King–Hawkesbury agreement which the Senate approved, after striking out the article calling for the line by which the northwest boundary gap was to be closed.

Jefferson saw a certain urgency in determining the northern boundary of the Louisiana Purchase, and he found it difficult to believe, despite French insistence, that there had never been a clear definition of it. Finally, he found several sources that seemed to indicate that the forty-ninth parallel had been established as the northern extent of French possession by a commission appointed under the provisions of the Treaty of Utrecht of 1713. Great Britain evidently did not care to prove this was not the case—though Jefferson's citations were erroneous—and finally in 1818 the two countries agreed that the northern boundary would be extended to the continental divide by following the forty-ninth parallel from the point where a due north-south line from the northwest corner of Lake of the Woods touched it. Thus Minnesota's northern boundary was established in principle, though it was years before any of it was marked upon the ground.

The negotiation of the forty-ninth parallel boundary was part of joint efforts by Great Britain and the United States to resolve lingering issues from their two wars. An unsettled boundary was an open door to further troubles, so the Treaty of Ghent, which formally ended the War of 1812, provided for the surveying of the 1783 line. One of the joint boundary commissions was assigned the task of determining the boundary from upstate New York to the northwest corner of Lake of the Woods.

By 1822, after several years of work, the surveyors were ready to move into the Lake Superior area. In that uncharted wilderness they had to determine what was meant by the "Long Lake" mentioned in the peace treaty and where it was located, and they had to fix the northwest point of Lake of the Woods. Mitchell's Long Lake was located in the Pigeon River and appeared to be the middle water course leading from Lake Superior to Lake of the Woods. The American surveyors believed that the boundary should simply be drawn through the Pigeon River since it was obviously Mitchell's "Long Lake," but Anthony Barclay, the British boundary commissioner, advanced the suggestion that the St. Louis River to the south should be the boundary. Ironically, nothing was known at the time of the vast mineral deposits that lay north of the St. Louis River area. In fact, Barclay seems to have advanced this claim so that a more desirable boundary through the water connection between Lakes Huron and Superior might emerge as a compromise. Barclay's tactics drove the American commissioner, Peter B. Porter of Buffalo, New York, to claim the Kaministiquia River to the north as the true Long Lake. After nearly five years of wrangling, the commissioners were finally able to agree that the Pigeon River was "Long Lake," but they still disagreed over the details of a boundary from that river to the northwest point of Lake of the Woods. Barclay wanted the line to follow the traditional canoe route, which because of its numerous portages was partly a land route, but Porter insisted on a truly continuous water route which lay somewhat north of the customary trade route in several places. Finally, in 1827, the boundary commission adjourned without having resolved the boundary from Lake Superior to the northwest corner of Lake of the Woods.

Determining the "true" northwest point of Lake of the Woods was perhaps even more of a challenge than locating the nonexistent Long Lake. In mapping Lake of the Woods, American surveyors became aware of its irregular shape. David Thompson, the principal British surveyor, was equally perplexed: he had identified four possible northwest points. Dissatisfied with Thompson's work, the British Foreign Office hired Johann Ludwig Tiarks, a German astronomer who had previously worked on the New York–Canada boundary, to proceed in secrecy to Lake of the Woods. Tiarks did so, and through scientific measurements determined that the head of the inlet later named Northwest Angle Inlet (which was one of Thompson's original points) was the most northwest point. His measurement preserved British control of the outlet of Lake of the Woods and established the point from which a due south line was to be drawn to the forty-ninth parallel. Tiarks's northwest point left a small portion of Minnesota, the Northwest Angle, separated from the mainland by Lake of the Woods. The Angle proved to be the northernmost point in the contiguous United States and is the inspiration for Minnesota's motto, "L'Etoile du Nord"— Star of the North.

Since the results of the survey had been negated by the dissolution of the boundary commission, the legalization of the northwest point of Lake of the Woods and the boundary from Lake Superior to that point did not occur until the Webster–Ashburton Treaty of 1842. Faced with a New England boundary controversy that threatened to plunge their countries into war, Daniel Webster and Lord Ashburton did not attach great significance to the boundary west of Lake Superior. Consequently, they affirmed without further question Tiarks's most northwest point and fixed the boundary through the Pigeon River and then by the historic traders' route to Lake of the Woods with the stipulation that the Grand Portage Trail remain free and open to subjects of both nations. This treaty ended the diplomatic phase of Minnesota's international boundary, but none of the boundary line east of Lake of the Woods was marked until the early twentieth century and then only after numerous conflicting claims between American and Canadian fishermen, lumbermen, and settlers.

While the United States was establishing its legal boundary west of Lake Superior, it also moved to control the area physically. When the Louisiana Purchase was made Jefferson knew that British fur traders in the area had a great deal of influence over the Indians, and he was determined to see American military posts established as counteractants. In 1805 twenty-six-year-old Zebulon Montgomery Pike, in command of a twenty-man party, was sent from St. Louis to reach the source of the Mississippi. On the way, Pike was to choose sites for army posts, gather intelligence about British traders on the Upper Mississippi, make alliances with the Indians, and if possible effect a truce between the Chippewa and the Sioux.

At Prairie du Chien, Pike engaged two interpreters: Pierre

Rousseau, who could speak to the Menominee and the Chippewa, and Joseph Renville, who was to translate the Sioux language. Pike also crossed to the west bank of the Mississippi and selected ground for a possible military post on a hilltop that later became known, at least locally, as "Pike's Hill." On the first day of fall he reached the mouth of the Minnesota River and camped on an island that was later named for him. There he also met a band of Indians led by Little Crow, grandfather of the Little Crow of Sioux War fame, and in the first American treaty ever concluded with the Sioux acquired title to two parcels of land, one at the mouth of the St. Croix and the other at the mouth of the Minnesota.

Satisfied that he had acquired grounds for an army post, Pike moved upstream until his boats were forced to halt, and he built a wintering post near present day Little Falls. From this rough stockade he hiked in the dead of winter to the trading post of the North West Company on Leech Lake, which was supervised by Hugh McGillis, director of the company's affairs in that district. Pike had the British flag over the post shot down and warned McGillis of possible grave consequences for trespassing on American soil. Then Pike, attempting to carry out his order to find the source of the Mississippi, traveled finally to Upper Red Cedar Lake (later named Cass Lake), and designated it "the upper source of the Mississippi." [2]

Pike returned to St. Louis the following spring to report that he had broken the power of the British traders and had effected a truce between the Chippewa and the Sioux. His accomplishments were not truly that grand, but he did contribute to topographical knowledge of the area, lay the foundations for a future army post, and make the United States presence known fleetingly to the Indians.

British traders were bothered by Pike's expedition; for all they knew, his was just the first of many American military expeditions. But with a wait-and-see attitude, they stayed on American ground. It was a wise enough decision on their part,

2. William Watts Folwell, *A History of Minnesota,* 4 vols., rev. ed. (St. Paul: Minnesota Historical Society, 1956–1969), 1:98.

because the United States was preoccupied with maritime difficulties with Great Britain and a host of frontier Indian problems in the Indiana country (which led to the outbreak of the War of 1812) and so was unable to follow the Pike expedition with the immediate development of armed posts.

Seizing on the war as an opportunity to regain the Northwest, British troops assisted by Indian allies (including the Chippewa and eastern Sioux from the Upper Mississippi) reoccupied such strategic places as Detroit and Mackinac. At the end of the war the situation in the Great Lakes country was not greatly different from what it had been at the end of the Revolutionary War over thirty years before: British traders and their Indian compatriots were firmly in control. But the Treaty of Ghent returned the British traders to the status of trespassers and left their Indian friends in even less desirable circumstances, for the establishment at last of American control presaged the agricultural invasion—something the free-roaming natives had not had to fear from the British.

After ratification of the Treaty of Ghent, American influence spread across the northwest. Military posts were established at Green Bay, Prairie du Chien, and Rock Island, and the American Fur Company headed by John Jacob Astor purchased the North West Company posts in the United States. Astor and his chief lieutenants influenced Congress to pass the Foreign Intercourse Act of 1816, which provided that foreign subjects who had been trading in the United States had to either leave the country or become naturalized. Many of the foreign traders, including the well known Jean Baptiste Faribault and Louis Provençalle, chose naturalization so they could stay with their homes and their families.

Despite these actions British influence in great sections of the border area was still strong several years after the end of the war. Secretary of War John C. Calhoun thus moved to safeguard the Upper Mississippi and the Upper Missouri from the British traders and from possible encroachment by Lord Selkirk's colonists.

Once again a military expedition was launched, this one under the command of Stephen Harriman Long, topographical engineer. In 1817 Long reached the Upper Mississippi and inspected the two tracts of land Pike had purchased from the Sioux. He recommended the construction of a post on a high point overlooking the junction of the Mississippi and Minnesota rivers, which would become the guardian of the entire northern great plains.

While Long was struggling vainly up the Missouri toward another potential site at the mouth of the Yellowstone, Colonel Henry Leavenworth arrived at the juncture of the Mississippi and Minnesota rivers in August 1819. During the next year his dragoons lived miserably in temporary shelters. Leavenworth, believed by his superiors to have dallied too long in starting a permanent fort, was replaced by Colonel Josiah Snelling, a career military officer who had served throughout the War of 1812 and had been present at the disastrous American defense of Detroit.

Because of its commanding view of the river junction, Snelling selected the very site recommended by Long for the post. Its walls, buildings, and blockhouses were constructed of cream-colored limestone quarried from the nearby bluffs, and it was artfully designed to repel attack from any direction. The diamond-shaped enclosure was bastioned by a hexagonal tower on the south corner, a semicircular battery on the east curve, a pentagonal tower on the north corner, and as the last resort for defenders a round tower on the west corner.

Constructing the fort was Snelling's greatest achievement, and in 1825 the War Department renamed it in his honor. Fort Snelling loomed above the wilderness like a medieval fortress, its stone walls and massive towers a symbol of American strength and permanence in an area accustomed to but small and temporary fur posts. The fort was never attacked, but it was maintained as a frontier post nearly to the time of the Civil War. Until the beginnings of St. Paul and St. Anthony, it was the principal center of civilization in Minnesota. Its walls sheltered Minnesota's first hospital, its first school and circulating library. The fort was a lively social center, hosting holiday dances and musical events. Much of Minnesota's Indian history revolved about Fort Snelling as well because it was the headquarters for the St. Peter's Agency established in 1819. The agency was to take care of government payments to the Sioux under the terms of Pike's treaty with them, and it was to aid the Indians in their transition to the white man's way of life.

Because it was at the head of navigation on the Mississippi River, Fort Snelling was commonly visited by both Americans and foreigners who came by steamboat, including the celebrated British novelist Frederick Marryat and the Swedish author Frederika Bremer. President Zachary Taylor in his early career commanded the post for a time, and artist Seth Eastman was several times commander of the fort. Dred Scott, remembered for the Supreme Court case which split the nation in the late 1850s, made his bid for freedom on the basis of his temporary residence in free territory at Fort Snelling.

Even though nearly a century and a half elapsed between Duluth's explorations in Minnesota and the building of Fort Snelling, much of the area was still unexplored when United States troops first arrived. Observers such as Hennepin, Carver, and Pike had left vivid but general descriptions of areas along or near the Mississippi, but the source of that great river had not been determined. Virtually nothing was known about the prairie region or the Red River Valley, and no one had even considered the region's economic potential. There was no real knowledge of the Indian population or natural life, and there was no accurate map of the area. Even such a famed place as the pipestone quarries where the Sioux and other tribes obtained the soft red stone from which they fashioned peace pipes had not been seen by the eyes of the white man.

Of all these challenges none was more alluring than searching for the source of North America's longest river, for it was almost unthinkable that the course of the river first seen by Hernando de Soto nearly three centuries before was not yet fully known. Knowledge of the source was a vital bit of information for map makers and geographers because it was not really possible to draw accurate maps of the United States without it. Fame seemed assured for the man who would discover the source, so Lewis Cass, governor of Michigan Territory, traveled to the Upper Mississippi in 1820. Cass was also superintendent of Indian affairs for Michigan Territory, which then included that part of Minnesota east of the Mississippi, and he made his western trip ostensibly to remind his charges of the change from British to American sovereignty; but he was most interested in the Chippewa who lived along the route that led him through Lake Superior and the Savannah Portage canoe route connecting it and the Mississippi. Cass's party reached Pike's Upper Red Cedar Lake and Cass, like Pike, concluded that it was the Mississippi's true source.

Henry Rowe Schoolcraft, whom Cass had taken along as the expedition's geologist, dutifully reported that Cass had found the Mississippi's "true source"; but he obviously did not believe it, for later on in the same report he noted that two rivers entered the lake, the Turtle and a longer one which he called the "La Beesh" in the language of the voyageurs. The La Beesh, he wrote, was known by the voyageurs to be "the outlet of Lake La Beesh, which lies six days journey, with a canoe, west-northwest of Cassina Lake, and has no inlets." [3] Schoolcraft was content to leave matters as they were, though he was determined to return alone and follow the course of the La Beesh River to its end. It was twelve long years before he could achieve this ambition.

In the meantime, another adventurer came upon the scene— Giacomo Constantino Beltrami, an exiled Italian nobleman who came to Fort Snelling in 1823 on the *Virginia*, the first steamboat on the Upper Mississippi. Beltrami accompanied Long on his expedition through the valleys of the Minnesota and Red rivers, but he quarreled with the commander and left the party at Pembina in a huff to work his way back to Fort Snelling. Beltrami canoed through the area David Thompson had explored before him, and there purportedly discovered a lake which miraculously was both the "most southern sources" of the Red River "and the most northern sources of the Mississippi." [4] Al-

3. Henry R. Schoolcraft, *Narrative Journal of Travels* . . . (Albany: E. & E. Hosford, 1821), p. 251.
4. J. C. Beltrami, *A Pilgrimage in America* (1828; reprint ed., Chicago: Quadrangle Books, 1962), p. 413.

though he believed Lake Julia, as he named it, to be landlocked, Beltrami asserted that its waters filtered through its banks both northward and southward. Beltrami recounted his madcap adventure in *Pilgrimage in America,* a work which captivated its European audience. Years later the Minnesota legislature named a county in the Lake Julia area after him.

After the Cass reconnaissance Schoolcraft was appointed agent to the Chippewa at Sault Ste. Marie. With the assistance of his well-educated wife, who was of Chippewa–British descent, and her numerous Indian relatives he mastered the Chippewa language and recorded tribal legends. He also found time and energy to serve in the Michigan legislature; he helped start the Michigan Historical Society and organized the Algic Society to encourage Indian studies. But he had not forgotten about finding the Mississippi's source. From the Chippewa Schoolcraft learned that the great river started from what they called Elk Lake, and he was assured that with an Indian guide he could proceed directly to it. All he needed was an opportunity to return to the country west of Lake Superior, and that came in 1832 when he received orders to visit the Chippewa living in that region.

Confident that he would find the river's source, Schoolcraft turned his thoughts to naming it. The Chippewa name, while descriptive because the lake's irregular shape resembled elk antlers, would not do. Neither would such commonplace names as Duck, Loon, or Turtle. So, while crossing Lake Superior, Schoolcraft asked his companion, the Reverend William Boutwell, for the Greek or Latin words for true source. Boutwell could not recall his divinity school Greek and the best he could do in Latin was *veritas caput* for "true head." The thought of a "Veritas Caput Lake" was not appealing, but the imaginative Schoolcraft simply struck the first and last syllables of the phrase and by combining the remains coined Itasca. Once he had the name he had only to reach the lake, so he engaged the knowledgeable Chippewa Yellow Head as his guide.

After weeks of traveling Schoolcraft exhilarated at the final approach to the Mississippi's source, noting that every step "seemed to increase the ardor with which we were carried forward." [5] His course led him from Lake Bemidji up the eastern source of the Mississippi, later named the Schoolcraft River, into a swamp. He followed Yellow Head overland

> with the expectation of momentarily reaching the goal of our journey. What had been long sought, at last appeared suddenly. On turning out of a thicket, into the small weedy opening, the cheering sight of a transparent body of water burst upon our view. It was Itasca Lake—the source of the Mississippi.[6]

Schoolcraft spent only a few hours at Lake Itasca, his last as an explorer, but a long career of studying Indian languages, customs, and history lay before him. He made a major contribution to American Indian ethnology by writing a multivolume study on the "history, condition and prospects" of Indians in the United States, and he collected and recorded hundreds of Indian legends. Henry Wadsworth Longfellow drew heavily upon his collections in writing his romantic *Song of Hiawatha*.

The Upper Mississippi area was not mapped adequately until 1836, when Joseph Nicollet, a French émigré, determined the altitude and area of Lake Itasca and mapped it and the surrounding region. Two years later he returned to Minnesota, sponsored by the United States government and accompanied by John C. Frémont. On this trip, he was to determine and record the nature and resources of the land that lay between the Missouri and the Mississippi. Nicollet's findings were published as a federal government document several years later along with his map, which was significant not only as the first accurate and detailed map of Minnesota but also because of its contribution to place-naming. Nicollet admired the Indian facility for capturing the essence of geographical or natural features with their names and usually adopted them in native or translated form. He was also impressed by the thousands of lakes he saw; one particularly watery region stretching from Redwood Falls through Mankato to Faribault inspired him to name it the Undine Region after the

---

5. [Henry R. Schoolcraft], *Schoolcraft's Expedition to Lake Itasca: The Discovery of the Source of the Mississippi*, ed. Philip P. Mason (East Lansing: Michigan State University Press, 1958), p. 35.

6. [Schoolcraft], *Lake Itasca*, p. 35.

Teutonic water nymph. Unfortunately, less learned frontiersmen commonly believed that Undine was the name of a Sioux princess.

Other reports publicized the river valleys and the prairies both at home and abroad. Stephen H. Long was dispatched by the Army in 1823 on a scientific reconnaissance from Fort Snelling which took him up the Minnesota and Red rivers into Canada and across Lake Superior. Long was accompanied by William Hypolitus Keating, who was the diarist for the expedition. Keating had a broad background in not only history, but geology, botany, zoology, and entomology, and he wrote vivid descriptions of the area's terrain, natural life, and Indians in his *Narrative of an Expedition*. . . . This work, which also included reports by other members of the expedition, provided a wealth of new information about the Minnesota and Red river valleys.

Artist George Catlin was the first white man to make known to the world the famous quarries from which Indians for hundreds of years had been taking stone to carve their peace pipes. Catlin in the mid-1830s visited Fort Snelling to paint portraits of the Sioux and from there traveled up the Minnesota River and across the plains to the southwestern part of Minnesota, where he viewed the quarries and painted them. Catlin removed specimens of the stone, which were later analyzed by the Geologist of the United States and given the scientific name catlinite.

George W. Featherstonhaugh was assigned in 1835 to conduct a geological survey of the Minnesota River Valley and specifically to inspect Le Sueur's alleged copper mine. Featherstonhaugh, British-born and middle-aged, had been a gentleman farmer and had started the railroad that grew into the New York Central before going to work for the federal government as a geologist. He wrote an official report of his geological reconnaissance, then returned to England and wrote *Canoe Voyage to the Minnay-Sotor*, the first work to feature the future name of the state. Like many cultured European travelers of his day, Featherstonhaugh depicted frontiersmen as land-hungry barbarians. Most Minnesotans he met, with the exception of his French–Sioux guide and Henry Hastings Sibley, were slashed by his sharp pen.

The fur trade continued as the common thread that ran through the fabric of the region's history, but by the time the Americans gained control it had changed. American fur traders continued the credit system and depended heavily upon Indian fur gatherers, but their center of activity moved west, with their major outfitting points at Mackinac, the gateway to the western Great Lakes, and at St. Louis, the door to both the Upper Mississippi and the Missouri. The American Fur Company realized the advantages of steamboat navigation and pioneered the use of the boats on the Upper Mississippi, the Missouri and the western Great Lakes. The steamboat not only facilitated the fur trade but enabled the American Fur Company to augment its business by transporting supplies and passengers for the Army and the Indian service.

The beaver had been the mainstay of the British fur trade, but by the time the Americans dominated, the beaver was very scarce; in fact, the common animal on the Upper Mississippi by then was the muskrat. Millions of muskrats lived along the lakes and swamps and were comparatively easy to trap. They were attractive to the Indians, too, because muskrat flesh was a regular part of their diet. Thus the "rat" dominated the Minnesota business and it became the medium of exchange between traders and Indians.

The Indians' situation, too, changed with the transition from British to American control. The British had traded with the Indians and used them as allies; but with a growing background of frontier experience, the American government recognized the transitory nature of the fur trade and the inevitable aftermath of settlement, and it tried to prepare the Indians for the future. When Fort Snelling was started, the United States sent Lawrence Taliaferro to serve as agent for the St. Peter's Agency. He was to try to protect the Sioux from exploitation by traders; to end their warring with the Chippewa; and to convert them from hunters to farmers. This stiff, proud Virginian throughout nearly twenty years of service proved to be an exception in a service overridden by corruption and incompetence. He was honest and dedicated, but he was caught in a nearly impossible situation where the traders and the government vied for control of the Indians. The Sioux whom Taliaferro was to serve lived primarily in the Mississippi River Valley, below the Falls of St. Anthony downstream to Prairie du Chien, and in the Minnesota River Valley. The four tribes were divided into two divisions, the Upper and the Lower Sioux, relative to their location along the Minnesota River. The lower tribes, the Mdewakanton and Wahpekute, lived along the Mississippi and on the banks of the Minnesota roughly downstream from present-day Belle Plaine. The Sisseton and Wahpeton, the upper tribes, were generally located upstream from the elbow of the Minnesota River at Mankato to the river's source in Big Stone Lake. These Sioux roamed hundreds of miles from their river villages and claimed part of northern Iowa and the eastern Dakotas. Their northern range was restricted only by the hostile Chippewa, who had forced the Sioux into southern Minnesota in the generation before Jonathan Carver's explorations. During the British period the Chippewa–Sioux wars stalemated and the tribes effected a rough division of territory, although intermittent raiding into each other's domain continued as a way of life.

These raids detracted from the fur trade and made more difficult the attempt to convert the Indians to farming, so the United States sought a formalized boundary between the two tribes. In 1825, a grand conference was held at Prairie du Chien and hundreds of chiefs and headmen from the two tribes were entertained at government expense. Taliaferro appeared with a large delegation of Sioux and Chippewa, and Schoolcraft came with other Chippewa. As part of the treaty, which affected the major tribes from Lake Michigan to the Red River, the Sioux and Chippewa agreed to a boundary from near present-day Chippewa Falls, Wisconsin, that zigzagged northwestward to a point on the Red River near present-day Moorhead. The boundary meant nothing to the Indians; but whether it accomplished the aim of pacifying the Indians or not, it did legally describe tribal lands and thus laid the foundation for future Indian land cessions.

The American Fur Company recognized the boundary line as a sure sign that the Upper Mississippi area would soon be lost to the ax and plow, though the company temporarily strengthened itself by merging with its principal rival, the Columbia Fur

Company, which had cut into the Upper Mississippi and Mississippi trade. Rising costs, the increasing preference for silk rather than beaver hats in Europe, the loss of a vast area to advancing farmers, and his own poor health caused John Jacob Astor to quit the business in 1834. With his withdrawal, the company was divided. One division, headquartered at St. Louis, was sold to the Chouteaus and their associates and the other division went to a group headed by Ramsay Crooks. These were separate companies, and although Crooks legally retained the old firm name, both of them continued to be known as the American Fur Company.

For some years Crooks had anguished over the inefficiency of many of the old traders who were fluent in Indian languages but unschooled in accounting and lacking in business acumen, so when the company became his he moved to revitalize it with young, educated men. With this in mind, he engaged Henry Hastings Sibley and Hercules Dousman to lead the Upper Mississippi trade. Sibley was twenty-three years old when he reached Mendota, across the Minnesota from Fort Snelling, in 1834. He had been given an academy education in his native Detroit, where his father was a judge and community leader. When still in his teens Sibley went to work for trader Robert Stuart at Mackinac and thus came to the attention of Crooks. Perhaps he did not equal Dousman in business savvy, but Sibley handled men well and won the respect of most of his Indian customers.

Sibley at Mendota and Dousman at Prairie du Chien formed a partnership with Old Joe Rolette—a partnership that controlled the trade in an area encompassing most of western Wisconsin and southern Minnesota. In the agreement the area controlled by the Sioux Indians was specially assigned to Sibley, and he, through his Sioux Outfit, had traders located at various stations. Sibley's men worked south of the region controlled by the Northern Outfit led by William Aitkin, who worked out of both La Pointe in the Apostle Islands and Fond du Lac.

Most of Sibley's first associates were inherited from the old American Fur Company. The veteran traders who had started under the North West Company and other British firms included

Jean Baptiste Faribault, who became a close friend and Mendota neighbor of Sibley; Joseph LaFramboise, who traded for a number of years in southwestern Minnesota; Joseph Renville; and Louis Provençalle. Renville, fifty-five when Sibley assumed command, was native to the area. He was born of French–Sioux parentage at the Sioux village of Kaposia south of present St. Paul and served as a leader of Britain's Indian allies during the War of 1812. Following the war he lived for a time in Canada and then after returning to the United States was one of the principal organizers of the Columbia Fur Company. After its merger with the American Fur Company, Renville was assigned the area about Lac qui Parle on the Upper Minnesota, where he built a rude stockade and presided like a feudal baron.

Provençalle, who traded from his post at Traverse des Sioux, the traditional Minnesota River crossing of the Sioux near present-day St. Peter, was known alike to travelers and Indians as Le Blanc, "the white man." Provençalle epitomized the old order. He entered the trade as an illiterate young man and left it as an illiterate old man. His deficiency created some problems in keeping accounts, but he resolved them. Sibley observed that "he kept his Indian credit books by hieroglyphics, having a peculiar figure for each article of merchandise, understood only by himself, and in marking down peltries received from the Indians, he drew the form of the animal, the skin of which was to be represented." As for recording the names of Indian debtors he developed a method "peculiar to himself." Sibley was gratified that the old trader at least "had mastered the mystery of figures sufficiently well to express by them the amount he wished to designate, and the general correctness of his account did not admit to question." [7]

Although he showed remarkable patience and tact with the old traders, Sibley gradually augmented them with young men. So Joseph Renshaw Brown, who had come to Minnesota as a fourteen-year-old drummer boy with the Leavenworth expedition, became a Sibley associate and in time a confidant. In the

7. H. H. Sibley, "Reminiscences: Historical and Personal," in Minnesota Historical Society Collections (St. Paul: The Society, 1872), 1:466–467.

same manner Sibley added to his retinue Norman Kittson, an aggressive Canadian he had first met while working for Stuart at Mackinac. Kittson became the chief trader in the Red River Valley in a business based as much on supplying the settlements near present Winnipeg as it was on the fur trade. Kittson in time turned to transportation on the Red River and moved from it to an extremely profitable association with the young James Jerome Hill. Then near the end of his trading career Sibley engaged Martin McLeod, an avid reader who customarily asked for books with his trade goods, and who later wrote the legislation creating Minnesota's common school system.

Like Astor before them, Crooks, Sibley, and Dousman recognized that the fur trade was nearing an end, but they were not prepared for the suddenness of its decline. The American Fur Company, like most businesses in the nation, was seriously affected by the Panic of 1837; and when one of its major stockholders went bankrupt, Crooks's fortunes plunged. The panic was followed by a lengthy depression in which the outside capital was drawn off into new enterprises such as canals and railroads. As Crooks struggled to save his company, the great fur markets in London and Leipzig were slowed by other business failures. Then, five years after the panic, the Chinese market was lost because of war between China and Great Britain. All of these difficulties coincided with the increasing European reliance on Australian felt and South American nutria pelts. Crooks tried valiantly to cut his losses by reducing operations, but finally in 1842 his American Fur Company went bankrupt.

Other factors contributed to the decline of the fur trade. Pressure from land speculators and Wisconsin territorial officials brought about the Sioux and Chippewa treaties of 1837, by which those tribes gave up most of their lands east of the Mississippi. These treaties were a significant turning point in Minnesota's history, for the ceding of the Sioux lands meant that the fur trade would be replaced by farming, and the Indians, who had previously been so dependent upon the traders, now would become dependent upon the government.

The traders clung to the old business as long as they could, but gradually they turned to other things. Some took up land

and became farmers. Others speculated, engaging in land acquisition or townsite planning. Some entered the lumber business. And some, like Sibley and Brown, emerged as leaders in Minnesota's transition from an unorganized territory to statehood.

4

Minnesota's Quest for Empire

N pushing aside the Indians and breaking the land and building cities, frontier settlers saw themselves fulfilling their destiny. Although they would not have said so—at least in a derogatory sense—they were expansionists philosophically as well as physically; by every thought and action American frontiersmen flung themselves against the challenges of foreign powers, against the untamed land and the Indians.

A distinctive sense of place was a natural outgrowth of frontier expansion. For a host of geographic, economic, political, and cultural reasons, portions of the frontier came to be identified as Ohio, Texas, Kansas, and Minnesota. Such identity was an overriding concern for an area's first settlers. They felt the isolation of the frontier, so their first loyalty was to themselves. In moving to the frontier, they had been inspired by the desire to reject the old and try the new, and their zeal was fired by the belief that in a new land they could form their own territories and states. They had little patience with the thought of government by remote power, and so states rights, a philosophy as old as the federal union, was an important concept to frontiersmen.

From the ratification of the Sioux and Chippewa treaties to the formation of the state of Minnesota, between 1838 and 1858, national expansionism was at a fever pitch—and Minnesotans as a politically identifiable people came into being. Wisconsin Territory was created in 1836, and its leaders assumed that when Wisconsin became a state, it would have the Mississippi River as its western boundary: the Northwest Ordinance of 1787 had specified that not more than five states could be formed out of the Old Northwest, and four states had already been created. When Henry Dodge, territorial governor of Wisconsin, negotiated a treaty with the Chippewa at Fort Snelling in 1837, he envisioned those rich pine forests of the upper St. Croix Valley and all the lands bordering the east side of St. Anthony Falls as Wisconsin lands. What he did not foresee was the tug of war that would occur before the fate of the St. Croix Valley was finally determined.

Among those who impatiently awaited the Indian land cessions was Major Joseph Plympton, commandant of Fort Snelling. Plympton was interested in claiming land for himself, but he had another interest—he wanted to expel civilian squatters from the military reservation. Over the years the land about the fort had become a haven for refugees from Selkirk's Red River colony and for assorted French Canadian drifters. These civilians had become an irksome problem; the traffic in liquor was almost impossible to control, and Plympton complained that they used so much timber that fuel was scarce near the fort and that their cattle and horses grazed at will on military ground. In July 1838, as soon as the treaties had been ratified and public land was available, Plympton banned civilian construction of buildings and cutting of timber on the military reservation. While the trespassers were not forcibly evicted, some of them interpreted the order as an expulsion notice and removed themselves some four miles downstream to public domain well outside the post boundaries. Among those who relocated was Pierre "Pig's Eye" Parrant, who soon became the most notorious character in the straggling settlement. Parrant, about sixty years old, was a onetime voyageur who had lived at Sault Ste. Marie, St. Louis, and Prairie du Chien before moving to Mendota. He had a bad reputation; his conduct was said to be "intemperate and licentious" and his appearance lent credence to the reputation, for he was described as a "coarse, ill-looking, low-browed fellow," who "spoke execrable English." [1] Parrant had only one good eye. His other was "blind, marble-hued, crooked, with a sinister white ring glaring around the pupil," which gave "a kind of piggish expression to his sodden, low features." [2] Application of the name Pig's Eye to the settlement came about quite accidentally. Inspired by Parrant's crooked eye, a customer at his tavern gave "Pig's Eye" as the return address on a letter he was sending. Everyone in the vicinity knew Parrant, and when the response addressed to "Pig's Eye" arrived, it was carried directly to the settlement around Parrant's establishment.

The Roman Catholic bishop of Dubuque soon saw need to send a missionary to the Fort Snelling vicinity. Though Father Lucian Galtier was but twenty-nine years old and barely able to speak English when he arrived in the summer of 1840, he was to change the destiny of Pig's Eye. The priest built a small log-cabin church along the waterfront. With an eye to the future commerce of the place, he chose a site near what would be a suitable steamboat landing for the erection of his church—a church so humble, he said, "that it would well remind one of the stable at Bethlehem." [3] Because of the biblical association of the apostles Peter and Paul and the close proximity of his residence at Mendota—which was then called St. Peter's after the river—Galtier dedicated his chapel to St. Paul.

Galtier's hope that this name, which he believed was recognizable by all Christians, would replace the appalling Pig's Eye came to pass. Because of the chapel the place soon became known as St. Paul's Landing; within a few years after the establishment of a post office in 1846, it was generally known as St. Paul. So the name was changed, but hardly so abruptly as a later wit suggested when he wrote:

Pig's Eye, converted thou shalt be, like SAUL;
Arise, and be, henceforth, SAINT PAUL! [4]

1. J. Fletcher Williams, *A History of the City of Saint Paul and the County of Ramsey, Minnesota,* Minnesota Historical Society Collections (St. Paul: The Society, 1876), 4:65.
2. Williams, *Saint Paul,* p. 85.
3. Williams, *Saint Paul,* p. 111.
4. Quoted in Williams, *Saint Paul,* p. 113.

Under its new name, old Pig's Eye was destined to become a
bustling commercial center and the capital of both the territory
and state of Minnesota. Parrant, perhaps no longer comfortable
in his surroundings, moved several miles downstream to a locality that ever since has been known as Pig's Eye.

St. Paul developed as a trading center at the head of navigation on the Upper Mississippi, but the other early settlements in
the ceded area started as lumber towns. St. Anthony Falls had
long been eyed for its great waterpower potential, and a number
of aspiring claimants fretted through the winter of 1837–1838
awaiting word that the treaties had been ratified. At last, on July
15, 1838, the steamboat *Palmyra* docked at Fort Snelling carrying word that the agreements had gone into effect. Major
Plympton's hopes of claiming the ceded ground on the east side
of the falls were dashed by young Franklin Steele, a storekeeper
at Fort Snelling. Steele, a Pennsylvanian who had already
claimed the falls of the St. Croix, moved with dispatch after the
Palmyra's arrival. Plympton's men reached the falls within a
day after word of the treaties arrived, only to find that Steele
and his men had worked through the night staking a claim to
one of the nation's choicest sites. Steele did not gain legal title
to the claim until it was sold at public auction ten years later.
He then built a dam at the falls and began sawing logs cut from
the Rum River area. Largely because of Steele's activities, the
town of St. Anthony developed.

In the meantime other lumber towns had sprung up in the St.
Croix Valley, where the first sawmill began operating at Marine
on St. Croix in August 1839. Nearby at the head of Lake St.
Croix, the widening of the river, fur trader Joseph Renshaw
Brown had claimed a townsite. He named the place Dakotah
and had visions of an empire, but fortune had a way of eluding
Brown. Other men platted a townsite nearby and before long the
new town, Stillwater, outstripped Dakotah and in time absorbed
it.

The settlers on the Upper Mississippi and the St. Croix were
far removed from most Wisconsinites, who lived south of a line
from Green Bay through Madison to Prairie du Chien, and the
gap was more than geographic. The men of the Upper Missis-

sippi were not the "Badgers" of the lead mines or the wheat farmers of Dane County. Many were lumberjacks direct from the forests of New England. Most had moved to the St. Croix area without even passing through the settled portions of Wisconsin Territory and thus had little sense of identity with its miners and farmers. Instead, they struck up an understandable alliance with the scattering of fur traders who were moving out of that declining trade into townsite speculation and lumbering.

To provide a legal framework for the vast domain stretching from Lake Pepin to the international boundary, the Wisconsin territorial legislature created St. Croix County. The beginning of the county in 1840 was a landmark for the isolated lumbermen and traders. It gave the towns a common bond and provided invaluable experience for the politically conscious who vied for such positions as county commissioner, sheriff, and membership in the territorial House and Council. Joseph R. Brown soon emerged as the area's most prominent politician. He was the county's first representative in the territorial legislature and he won the friendship of key men in Madison. Brown led the formation of a county Democratic organization through which the separatist beliefs of the residents of St. Croix County were propagated. Their relative isolation and their economic uniqueness caused many of these residents to believe that they should be detached from Wisconsin. Thus liberated, they would become the nucleus of a new territory.

The first separation attempt came with Wisconsin's effort to organize as a state in 1846. Morgan Martin, Wisconsin's territorial delegate to Congress, opened the drive for statehood by introducing an enabling bill in the House of Representatives. Martin, basing his arguments on the Northwest Ordinance, preferred a state with the old territorial limits, but most congressmen were of the opinion that a state whose western border followed the Mississippi to its source would be unmanageably large. Expansionists such as Stephen Douglas of Illinois recognized that by restricting Wisconsin they would create the opportunity for the organization of another state roughly equal to it in size out of the remainder of the Northwest. Consequently, the Wisconsin Enabling Act as passed by Congress provided for the present western boundary for the state—a line which for most of its distance follows the St. Croix and Mississippi rivers.

Residents of St. Croix County had mixed feelings about the act. They were unhappy with a boundary that split the St. Croix Valley, but they were pleased that Congress had denied Wisconsin a large portion of the Northwest. The congressional action was not necessarily final, however, because traditionally enabling legislation was considered a recommendation, not a binding action. And so the boundary question was an issue to be considered during the Wisconsin constitutional convention.

In the apportionment for the convention, St. Croix County was accorded one delegate on the basis of its 1419 inhabitants. The voters chose William Holcombe, agent for a lumber company who later became the first lieutenant governor of Minnesota. Holcombe proved to be a highly articulate spokesman for those who wanted to withdraw from Wisconsin and take a fair portion of it with them.

He had visions of a new state northwest of Wisconsin—a lumbering and commercial state centered in the St. Croix Valley, most likely with Stillwater as its capital, which would enjoy the benefits of both the Mississippi River and Lake Superior. Therefore, Holcombe proposed that Wisconsin's northwestern boundary be drawn from a point on the Mississippi below present-day Winona to the western edge of upper Michigan. Such a boundary, he contended, would leave room for another state to be formed out of the Old Northwest. He argued that Wisconsin would otherwise be too large and quite out of proportion to other states; but if a sister state to her northwest were created, sectional interests would be more strongly represented in Congress. Presuming what within a few years came to be called popular sovereignty, Holcombe contended that government to be effective had to be close to the people. A "remote location" over 300 miles from Madison, he argued, "will continue to be as it has been a source of vexation and to a great degree destructive of the very end which a good government has in view." [5]

5. Quoted in Milo M. Quaife, ed., *The Convention of 1846*, State Historical Society of Wisconsin Collections (Madison: The Society, 1919), 17:565.

But the delegates overwhelmingly rejected a proposal that would have denied the state access to Lake Superior and cost it one sixth of the area east of the St. Croix. Holcombe managed one small victory. The constitutional convention finally agreed not to divide the St. Croix Valley and accepted a boundary from Lake Superior to the Mississippi that would lie about fifteen miles east of the St. Croix. But because of several other controversial sections such as liberal women's rights provisions and certain banking stipulations, the document was overwhelmingly rejected in the April 1847 election.

The aspiring secessionists of the St. Croix Valley tried again in the second constitutional convention. George W. Brownell, Holcombe's successor, urged the acceptance of the "Holcombe Amendment"; but the delegates not only rejected it, they instead accepted a resolution advising Congress that Wisconsin preferred a northwestern boundary running from near the mouth of the St. Louis River (present Duluth) to a point on the Mississippi only about fifteen miles upstream from St. Anthony Falls. Such a line would have placed Stillwater, St. Paul, and St. Anthony and half of St. Anthony Falls in Wisconsin and would certainly have fulfilled the St. Croix desire that the valley not be divided.

This preference of the second constitutional convention created a crisis for those who wanted to be left out of Wisconsin. Their only hope of salvation, they believed, was to win a reprieve in Washington. During the first convention, Morgan Martin had proposed the organization of Minnesota Territory in the U.S. House of Representatives. Through he probably had several motives, it was generally believed that he at least used the name Minnesota as a favor to his friend and former colleague in the Wisconsin legislature, Joseph R. Brown. Both Brownell and Holcombe urged the Wisconsin territorial delegate to continue to support their cause, and about 350 men described as residents within the limits of Minnesota Territory (as defined by Martin's proposal) sent a petition to Washington. They asked for a Wisconsin northwestern boundary that was not much less ambitious than Holcombe's original proposal. If such were denied, they prophesied, "the prospects of Minnesota would be forlorn indeed.'' Appealing to the sympathies of Congress, the petitioners wrote that they had

> full confidence that your honorable bodies will consult the wishes of those who are most interested in the solution of this question; and will not do so much violence to the feelings of the people of this region as to place them within the limits of Wisconsin, in utter disregard of their prayers and remonstrances.[6]

The petitioners caused a congressional airing of the boundary question. The long and sharp debate in the House of Representatives jeopardized the admission of Wisconsin for a troubled time in the spring of 1848. Rather than take a partisan stance, the representatives compromised by voting to admit Wisconsin as a state with the northwestern boundary as specified in the enabling act. Thus after two years and thousands of words the subject had come full circle and the state of Wisconsin which came into the union on May 29, 1848, included the eastern portion of the St. Croix Valley.

After the admission of Wisconsin, Brown, Holcombe, and other politicians lamented the condition of those unfortunates who had been left "outside of the United States." Seizing on the fact that Congress had not created a territory west of Wisconsin when the state was formed, they contended that because they no longer benefited from the legal guarantees of the Northwest Ordinance, they had been relegated to the status of an unorganized territory. Minnesota's leaders could have bided their time and within a few years someone would again have proposed a Minnesota Territory, but they were believers in today rather than tomorrow. And so a small group of ambitious young politicians moved. Public demonstrations were organized and Stillwater was the scene of an Independence Day celebration replete with parade and orations. Public meetings were held in St. Paul. Then on August 4, 1848, eighteen recognized leaders met at Stillwater to plan for the area's future. Among them were Henry H. Sibley, Franklin Steele (who was Sibley's

---

6. "Memorial of the Citizens of Minnesota," March 28, 1848, Sen. Misc. Doc. 98, 30th Cong., 1st sess.

brother-in-law), Joseph Brown, and William Holcombe. The group issued a call for a convention to be held at Stillwater on August 26 "to secure an early Territorial organization." [7]

The sixty-one "delegates" who assembled in the courthouse at Stillwater amounted to Minnesota's founding fathers. Although they came by invitation, they were not averse to leaving the impression that they had been elected by their constituencies. All political and personal differences were sacrificed in the interests of securing a territorial organization. In their one-day meeting, chaired by Joseph Brown, they drafted petitions to Congress and President James Polk calling for early territorial organization as a matter of justice and pointing out the difficulties of civil administration in an unorganized territory. In order to represent their case effectively they decided to send a "delegate" to Washington at his own expense. Their choice was Sibley, the most popular Democrat in an area dominated by Democrats. It was generally supposed that if Minnesota Territory were organized while the Democrats controlled the White House, Sibley would be named governor. Furthermore, because of his congenial personality he was expected to win support to Minnesota's cause.

The Stillwater delegates entertained no illusions. They knew that Sibley was not an official delegate from any sort of territory, but merely a spokesman for the area that had come to be known as Minnesota. Would Congress receive such an ambassador without portfolio? The delegates could only hope that Congress would, and they adjourned with the expectation that Sibley would soon make his way to Washington to advance Minnesota's cause.

But some of the region's leaders, notably Holcombe, believed it was vital that any delegate to Congress should claim to represent an organized territory and should be duly elected. Therefore, weeks before the Stillwater Convention the ingenious Holcombe noted that Congress had not repealed the Wisconsin territorial act when the state had been formed. He wondered if

7. "Organizations of Minnesota Territory," in *Minnesota Historical Society Collections* (St. Paul: The Society, 1872), 1:55.

that part of Wisconsin Territory left outside the state did not still exist as Wisconsin Territory. Holcombe's notion was supported by John Catlin, the last secretary of Wisconsin Territory, who insisted that he had retained his position after the formation of the state.

There is no record that Holcombe advanced his interesting theory at the Stillwater Convention. But if he did, it was subverted by the majority opinion that Sibley could simply be a spokesman for the residents of an unorganized area. However, within a matter of days after the Stillwater Convention the delegates began worrying about the legality of Sibley's status. The more they thought about it, the less they believed that a group of unelected men in an unorganized territory could simply choose a delegate. Lack of credentials threatened to doom Sibley's chances in Congress. Suddenly the political leaders were converted to the Holcombe–Catlin view that Wisconsin Territory still existed.

The plot thickened when Catlin, as self-proclaimed acting governor of Wisconsin Territory, moved to Stillwater and issued an election proclamation. All seemed to be going according to plan, but the scheme was threatened when Henry M. Rice, an old fur-trade rival to Sibley, decided to vie for the delegacy. Although Sibley's supporters were worried about Rice, who was very popular among many of the old traders, Sibley won the late October election and was soon on his way to Washington as the elected delegate of the alleged Wisconsin Territory.

Despite his election Sibley was advised by some congressional acquaintances not to introduce himself as the delegate from Wisconsin Territory but merely to act as a lobbyist. But Sibley chose the bolder course and asked to be seated in the House of Representatives where bona fide territorial delegates could participate in all matters except voting. As expected there was some discussion in the house over the existence or nonexistence of Wisconsin Territory, but that body by a two-to-one margin did agree to seat Sibley. Sibley's greatest support came from the West and Northeast and his strongest opposition from Southerners, who were not anxious to facilitate the creation of another free territory.

It soon became apparent that the representatives did not really believe that Wisconsin Territory still existed. One of Sibley's opponents slyly proposed appropriations for the officers of Wisconsin Territory, anticipating that his motion would touch off a lively controversy. It did. Some representatives insisted that the Territory of Wisconsin was real, but eleven others took the floor to contend that it had ceased to exist with the creation of the state. Finally the House ended the charade by defeating the motion. The meaning of the discussion and rejection was clear: Sibley had been seated as a courtesy. The House was willing to give him a podium from which he could work for the organization of Minnesota Territory; but he would have to move with dispatch, for even his strongest supporters did not care to be saddled with the embarrassment of "Wisconsin Territory" for long.

Stephen Douglas, then in the Senate and the emerging champion of westward expansion, again led the move to organize Minnesota Territory. Douglas's support, while beneficial to Sibley's cause, made the Minnesota bill appear like a Democratic Party aim, contrary to Sibley's desire that it be nonpartisan. The Democrats controlled the Senate but the Whigs had a bare majority in the House, and their man, Zachary Taylor, had been elected president in 1848. Since Taylor would not be inaugurated until March 4, 1849, the Whigs naturally chose not to expedite the formation of a Minnesota Territory for which the outgoing Democratic President James Polk could appoint territorial officials.

The Whigs, however, were vulnerable. They wanted the passage of the bill calling for the creation of the Interior Department, which was then pending before Congress. Such a department, they believed, was necessary for the administration of the vast public domain in the Southwest that had been added to the Union as a result of the Mexican War. The creation of this new department would also provide the incoming president with many new positions with which he could reward some of his supporters. Well aware of Whig desires, Douglas authorized Sibley to leak the word that he had enough power in the Senate to block the Interior measure unless the Whigs relented in their opposition to the Minnesota bill. The ploy worked, and in the last hours of the Polk administration the law creating Minnesota Territory was passed.

Since the Minnesota bill was caught up in a political trade-off, no one was particularly concerned about whether the area had the requisite population of 5,000 to be made a territory. Douglas said the region had 8,000 to 10,000 inhabitants, but a sheriff's census taken the following summer showed the actual number was only about 4,500. The territory included those parts of the Dakotas east of the Missouri and White Earth rivers. The white inhabitants, who were probably outnumbered four or five to one by Indians, were concentrated in the area from St. Anthony Falls to Stillwater and about Pembina in the Red River Valley.

Although they had their territory, some Minnesotans continued to fret about losing the area east of the St. Croix to Wisconsin. Nearly a year after the formation of Minnesota Territory the *Minnesota Pioneer* reported that Wisconsinites just east of the St. Croix "are all anxious to be annexed to Minnesota." [8] Despairing of ever changing the boundary, puckish editor James Boyd Goodhue suggested that Minnesotans "who have been carried up into Father Abraham's bosom . . . look down with compassion upon our neighbors across the great gulf of the Saint Croix and pray for their safe deliverance." [9]

The organization of Minnesota Territory was part of the national expansionist urge. Under the gospel of Manifest Destiny the United States had annexed Texas and acquired California and the Southwest as a result of the Mexican War and had won a favorable boundary settlement with Great Britain in the Pacific Northwest. Following the war the mania of Manifest Destiny still hung in the air. It seemed that the destiny of Americans was only partially fulfilled. The Whig administration of Zachary Taylor could not emulate Polk by warring against some foreign power on the continent, but it could stimulate internal expan-

8. *Minnesota Pioneer* (St. Paul), February 13, 1850, p. 3.
9. *Minnesota Pioneer*, March 6, 1850, p. 2.

sion. So the government, responding to popular demands, encouraged the California gold rush, the exodus of settlers to Oregon, the opening of Kansas and Nebraska, and further Indian land cessions in Minnesota. The Indian was to the expansionists nothing more than a deterrent to progress. Only when the tribesmen had been removed or sequestered could the land be truly civilized.

Frontier Minnesotans, like their champion Stephen Douglas, believed in popular sovereignty; they believed, just as the Puritans of Massachusetts and the Wataugans of Tennessee had believed, that the people in a locality should control their own destiny. They demonstrated their dedication to this belief in heated contention over the Wisconsin boundary, and after territorial organization popular will clamored again—this time for the opening of the lands of the Sioux west of the Mississippi.

The "Suland," as it was called in frontier newspapers, was coveted for its agricultural potential. Demands for its cession came from farmers, speculators, townsite promoters, fur traders, half-breeds, and the federal government. The young Pennsylvanian Alexander Ramsey, whom President Taylor appointed as the first governor of Minnesota Territory, understood that one of his first tasks was to acquire the Suland. Since Ramsey was a Whig in an area dominated by Democrats, and since political suicide was not one of his aims, he quickly emerged as a champion of expansion. Ramsey's plans dovetailed neatly with those of the territorial legislature and Henry Sibley, Minnesota's first territorial delegate to Congress. As the leader of the old traders, Sibley had a deep personal stake in a Sioux treaty. Many Sioux were indebted to Sibley's traders, whose only chance of collecting was for the Indians to sell their land.

Despite the general clamor for the Suland and the seeming urgency in negotiating a treaty, the Sioux were not brought to the bargaining table until 1851. Some of the delay was caused by dallying on the part of the Indians, but most resulted from behind-the-scenes maneuvering in naming treaty commissioners. Sibley and his associates realized that their claims stood little chance of being honored without sympathetic commissioners. Not only did the chiefs have to be convinced that the tribes must assume responsibility for numerous individual debts, but the claims of rival traders had to be negated.

Finally the government named as co-commissioners Ramsey and Luke Lea, who was Commissioner of Indian Affairs in Washington, D.C., and the younger brother of army explorer Albert Lea. Sibley had every reason to be satisfied with these appointees. Lea was sympathetic to Sibley's group and Ramsey and Sibley had become good friends. Following the advice of Sibley's traders, Ramsey and Lea decided to make two treaties with the Sioux: one with the Sisseton and Wahpeton and the other with the Mdewakanton and Wahpekute. It was generally anticipated that there would be some Sioux resistance, so common sense dictated that the tribes be divided. There was no point in meeting the assembled four tribes and letting some chiefs think that the Sioux were a mighty nation. The commissioners chose to meet with the Sisseton and Wahpeton first because they were believed to be the more acquiescent. After they had signed, the resistance expected from some of the Lower Sioux would be compromised.

Although some of the Sisseton and Wahpeton did not care to surrender their lands, they thought resistance was futile. Some of the older chiefs who had been at Prairie du Chien in 1825 and had been taken to Washington in 1837 realized the vast numerical superiority of whites, and they also thought they had learned something from the Black Hawk War in which the Army had crushed the last Indian resistance in Wisconsin. The chiefs could not seriously consider refusing to negotiate. Such an action, they believed, would have been desperately reckless and could have led to war and the virtual annihilation of their people. They believed it better to negotiate for adequate compensation and decent reservations. Their stance was understandable in 1851, but before many years had passed some of them regretted their decision.

When Ramsey and Lea met with the Sisseton and Wahpeton chiefs and headmen at Traverse des Sioux in July 1851, the place had a carnival atmosphere. The commissioners came well supplied with provisions and liquor. During the week and a half that the commissioners spent at Traverse des Sioux, editor James Goodhue regularly informed his St. Paul readers of progress. The treaty was also of great interest to a young Baltimore artist, Frank Blackwell Mayer, who traveled from his home to distant Minnesota to witness what he believed would be one of history's greatest moments. Mayer made numerous sketches of the treaty scenes and participants and later produced a large, colorful canvas that captured the pageantry and drama of the signing of the treaty.

Ramsey and Lea struck a good bargain for the government. The Sisseton and Wahpeton ceded all their claims south of the 1825 Sioux–Chippewa boundary for only pennies an acre. At the time the chiefs were satisfied, but they soon realized they had been duped into signing another document in addition to the treaty. When the assembled chiefs were lined up to place their mark on duplicate copies of the treaty some of them happened to notice Joseph R. Brown, an old acquaintance, standing off to the side with a document on an upright barrel. Since they were steered to Brown the Indians dutifully marked the paper, probably thinking it was nothing more than a third copy of the treaty. It was not. Brown had before him what came to be known as the traders' paper, under which the chiefs agreed to use tribal funds to reimburse the fur traders for debts accrued by various individual Indians. Despite vigorous Indian objections, the traders were finally paid from government monies that should have gone to the tribes in payment for the ceded lands. Understandably Indians resented the despicable trick of the traders' paper, and this resentment smoldered for years until it was fired by other causes into the volatile Sioux War of 1862.

After completing the Traverse des Sioux agreement, Ramsey and Lea moved down the Minnesota River to meeting grounds near Mendota to deal with the Mdewakanton and Wahpekute. Although some of the Lower Sioux wanted to resist the commissioners, their chiefs signed an agreement very similar to the Treaty of Traverse des Sioux. In the Treaty of Mendota the Mdewakanton and Wahpekute chiefs agreed to cede all tribal claims to the same tract surrendered by the Upper Sioux, and in a separate agreement some of them acknowledged the traders' claims. The traders could hardly surprise the Lower Sioux with their claims, but they convinced some chiefs that acknowledgment of the claims was required before they could be paid for their land.

The Sioux treaties of 1851 have been controversial since their inception. Indian resentment against the government's pressure tactics, the low purchase price, and the traders' papers were important background causes of what has been generally called the Sioux Uprising. Modern critics, ignoring the frontier context of the treaties, offer alternatives ranging from the suggestion that the Sioux should have been left on the land to the idea that they should have at least been paid a fair market price for it. It would have been extremely difficult for the commissioners to have determined a fair market price, and even if they had, they could not have made such an offer because the Senate would never have approved a document so out of keeping with other Indian treaties of the time. The Sioux chiefs realized far better than later observers that they really had no choice, for the expansionist government was determined to oust them and it had the power to do so either politically or militarily. Unfortunately, there is much truth in the comment of interpreter William L. Quinn that the treaties of Traverse des Sioux and Mendota "were as fair as any Indian treaties." [10] Expansionists looked upon all Indian treaties as nothing more than legal devices which would open the land. Though Ramsey and Lea lived long before Social Darwinism was developed conceptually, they believed it. And the Sioux treaties are not bygones in Minnesota. Minnesota's scholars of the last half-century have regularly criticized the connivance and duplicity of the negotiations, and the presence of a well-organized, vocal American Indian Movement in the Twin Cities has served as a constant reminder of the treaties, which many Indian spokesmen regard as the root of later problems of the Sioux.

The Sioux treaties were not approved by the Senate until June 1852, and because there was some question about the location of the reservations they were not proclaimed by President Mil-

10. Quoted in Folwell, *History of Minnesota,* 1:304.

lard Fillmore until February 24, 1853. These delays did not deter speculators and settlers from invading the Suland. During 1852 promoters platted townsites including Winona, Belle Plaine, and Mankato, and there were said to be about 5000 trespassers in the region between the Lower Minnesota and the Mississippi.

Locating the Sioux reservations was a contentious process. The federal government initially favored removing the Sioux to a reservation along the Missouri River in present-day central South Dakota, but this plan was challenged by Minnesota's frontier politicians. In territorial politics, there was a class of men who thrived on the Indian question, "Moccasinites" to the frontier press. The Minnesota Moccasinites stood for the cession of Indian land, but they did not want the Indians removed from Minnesota. A Missouri River reservation would have meant that St. Louis would have controlled the trade with the Eastern Sioux, while a location on the Minnesota River would assure the trade for St. Paul. The significance of the Indian trade can be appreciated more fully when one considers that the residents of Minnesota Territory were not greatly different from the early colonial planters of Virginia who talked grandly of money, but had very little. There was plenty of land in Minnesota after the Sioux treaties, but there were no exports and the best opportunity to acquire money was from federal payments to the Indians. The Moccasinites, who included many of the old fur traders, realized far better than anyone else that federal payments to the Sioux would soon pass into the hands of local traders.

If the Moccasinites had a high priest it was Henry Mower Rice, the former trader who had challenged Sibley after the Stillwater Convention. Rice had considerable real estate interests in St. Paul and he fancied himself a man who could deal with the Indians, so he was strongly committed to the goal of keeping the Indians within the St. Paul trade area. Rice and his cohorts thought of putting the Sioux on the Upper Minnesota, and it was probably Rice who as territorial delegate maneuvered the movement of the Winnebago from Long Prairie to Blue Earth County rather than to the Missouri River in 1855. The creation of a Winnebago reservation within the Sioux cession and the removal of the white squatters in order to do it can only be explained in light of the determination that the Indians should be supplied from St. Paul.

Keeping the Sioux within the St. Paul trade area was the most important determinant in locating the Sioux reservations, but there were other considerations. Rice and the other traders who had a voice in the selection of reservation sites may even have believed that it was more humane to leave the Sioux on reservations within the ceded area than to remove them from their native soil entirely. The final selection of an area along the Upper Minnesota was probably influenced by the belief that the land along that part of the river was not worth much and would not be in immediate demand. This, however, was a miscalculation, for the rush of settlers into the Suland was so staggering that the Sioux were forced to relinquish the northern half of their reservations in 1858.

During the fall of 1853 the last of the Sioux were moved onto their reservations. Although the Indians had only one government agent to administer to them, there were two reservations physically. Both were long and but ten miles wide on each side of the river. The Upper Sioux Reservation extended from the head of Big Stone Lake to the Yellow Medicine River (several miles southeast of present Granite Falls) and the Lower Sioux ran from the Yellow Medicine to Little Rock Creek (north of Sleepy Eye). Although the army located Fort Ridgely near the eastern end of the Lower Sioux Reservation, the troops made little effort to keep the Indians within its bounds. This policy along with the great length of the reservation gave the Sioux an important tactical advantage in the Sioux War of 1862 because they could sweep out upon white settlers along a broad front.

The Sioux treaties did not satisfy the appetite of the Minnesota expansionists who wanted access to the forest lands of northern Minnesota as well as the farmlands of the south, and within two years of ratification the federal government persuaded the Chippewa to cede vast tracts stretching from Lake Superior to the upper part of the Red River. By the end of the territorial period over four fifths of the future state had been given up by the Sioux and Chippewa. Only the northwest and a north central area remained in tribal hands.

Manifest Destiny abated nationally after the Gadsden Purchase from Mexico in 1853; but in its lingering days it had particular impact in Minnesota, where expansionists overtly strived to annex much of Canada. Annexationist sentiment which peaked in the late 1860s was a natural outgrowth of Minnesota's ties with the Selkirk settlements on the lower Red River—ties that were encouraged by the laxity of the international boundary.

For the last half-century both Canada and the United States have taken pride in the "unguarded boundary" separating their countries. It is ironic that the term is a fairly recent one when much of the boundary (including that in the Red River Valley) was much freer in the years after its establishment than it has been in recent times. Although the forty-ninth parallel boundary was agreed upon diplomatically in 1818, Great Britain and the United States made no effort to survey and mark it until the 1870s. A member of Stephen H. Long's 1823 expedition did determine the point where the line touched the west bank of the Red River, but the single wooden post that was left behind was looked upon as nothing more than a road marker by Canadians and Americans who crossed the boundary with impunity. Without question the natural unity of the Red River Valley prevailed over the artificiality of a boundary that was not even marked upon the ground.

Because of this, when several hundred Selkirkers abandoned their settlements about Winnipeg in the 1820s they found it far easier to move up the Red River and enter the United States than to move to eastern Canada or return to Europe. American fur traders located near Fort Snelling also recognized that they were in a much better position to supply the settlers in the lower Red River area than Canadian or European competitors whose two possible trade routes—one by river from Hudson Bay and the other by the traditional canoe route through the Great Lakes and the border waterways west of Lake Superior—were both slower and more hazardous than routes from Minnesota through the Red River Valley.

American trade to the Red River settlements increased sharply after Norman Kittson became associated with Henry H. Sibley in 1843. Although he was ostensibly a fur trader the en-

terprising Kittson, from his post at Pembina on the North Dakota side of the Red River just south of the border, based much
of his lucrative business on transporting merchandise across
Hudson's Bay Company territory to Canadian customers in the
vicinity of Fort Garry. Kittson and other American traders
moved their goods by Red River carts—contraptions developed
by half-breeds in the Red River Valley. The two-wheel carts
were made entirely without metal. Pulled by a single ox and
driven by one person, they usually traveled in caravans over the
three Red River trails which led from St. Paul to Fort Garry.
These rough-hewn, squeaky carts symbolized Minnesota's
northern movement just as surely as the covered wagon symbolized westward movement in the United States.

Kittson's successful defiance of the Hudson's Bay Company
tightened the bonds between Fort Garry and St. Paul and caused
the isolated Red River settlers to become increasingly dependent
on St. Paul and the United States. Because of this trade orienta-
tion some people on both sides of the border thought American
acquisition of Rupert's Land, as the holdings of the Hudson's
Bay Company in central and western Canada were called,
would be desirable. The Hudson's Bay Company did not know
how to deal with Kittson's challenge and was slow to react.
Consequently, Kittson's free trade during the 1840s led Minnesota expansionists to believe that the Company's days were
numbered and that its vast territory would fall like a ripe plum
into American hands rather than become part of Canada.

Annexationist dreams were first expressed in the early days of
Minnesota Territory, but they were vague and unfocused. Father
Georges-Antoine Belcourt, an American Catholic missionary at
Pembina, suggested just months after Minnesota Territory was
formed that a part of Rupert's Land could easily become part of
the United States if the federal government would only support
its acquisition. Belcourt's sentiments were shared by Rice and
Sibley as well as Alexander Ramsey. As Sibley and Ramsey
were planning the Sioux cession of southern Minnesota they
also strove to develop northwestern Minnesota. Ramsey unsuccessfully sought federal aid to improve the Red River trails and
to build an army post at Pembina, but Sibley secured a congres-

sional appropriation to negotiate a treaty with the Chippewa.

The ink was barely dry on the Sioux treaties of 1851 when Ramsey journeyed to the Red River Valley to treat with the Chippewa. Ramsey persuaded the Chippewa chiefs to sell a block of land abutting the international boundary for only a few cents an acre. The agreement promised to open yet another portion of Minnesota to settlement and to put the added pressure of American land-seekers on Canada's doorstep. However, the grand scheme to open both southern and northwestern Minnesota was aborted in the Senate. Southerners who viewed the rapid settlement of Minnesota as a threat to the delicate sectional balance in the Senate opposed all three Minnesota treaties, and to save the Sioux treaties Sibley had to sacrifice the Chippewa agreement.

This setback and more determined resistance to American traders by the Hudson's Bay Company cooled expansionist ardor somewhat, but Minnesota's dream of expanding across the border was revived and intensified by the writings and speeches of the persuasive James Wickes Taylor. Taylor, who emerged as the chief propagandist of Minnesota's Manifest Destiny, was convinced that interior Canada was destined to become part of the United States even before he moved from his native Ohio to St. Paul in 1857. Taylor and his followers believed that Rupert's Land would be another Oregon. It was destined to become part of the American nation because it lay within the commercial sphere of St. Paul, and Taylor assumed its straggling settlers would be anxious to become part of the United States. With an eye to Rupert's Land, Taylor during pre-statehood days was one of the principal advocates of shaping Minnesota so it bordered on Canada. Much of the support for this idea seems to have been based on the belief that it would give Minnesota a tactical advantage in the future quest for Rupert's Land.

Minnesota's expansionists seized on the Fraser River gold rush to promote their cause. St. Paul newspapers in 1858 likened the discoveries in present British Columbia to those in Australia and glorified the advantages to gold-seekers of a route from St. Paul across Canada to Fraser River. For Minnesotans, Fraser River was more important than the concurrent Pike's

Peak gold rush, because it held not only the promise of individual gains but the opening of a road to empire that might prove to
be for Minnesota and the Northwest what the Santa Fe Trail had
meant to the American Southwest. Taylor and his principal associates, Ramsey and Kittson, organized meetings of a Fraser
River Congress to promote their road plans. Although some
gold seekers trekked from St. Paul to Fraser River the road was
never built, but the Fraser River excitement spurred Minnesota's
reach for Rupert's Land to new heights.

Taylor and his cohorts were greatly frustrated during the Civil
War years when the promises of expansion and economic
growth were checked by the Sioux War. The war's end was
welcomed by these would-be expansionists as an opportunity to
build railroads, settle the land, and pressure Canada for the cession of Rupert's Land. Soon after the war Minnesota's interest
emerged as undisguised imperialism. Before 1865, despite some
talk of annexation, Minnesotans (and St. Paulites especially)
seemed to be much more interested in a commercial alliance
than in annexation; but after the war the expansionists would
settle for nothing less than American ownership of much of
Canada. Taylor, buoyed by his own enthusiasm, called for a
union of the United States and Canada. Under his 1866 proposal
the eastern Canadian provinces would have entered the United
States as states and the remainder of Canada would have become American territories or public domain.

Although Taylor's scheme received much publicity in Canada
and the United States, there was scant Canadian support and not
a great deal more south of the border. Nathaniel Banks of Massachusetts, who was sympathetic to the goals of Irish national-
ism and an ardent Anglophobe, proposed Taylor's plan in the
House of Representatives, but there was only a scattering of
support. Then Alexander Ramsey, who had become a United
States senator, adopted the cause in Congress. Ramsey twice
proposed annexation of Rupert's Land, but like Taylor he soon
realized that time and circumstances were against him. Great
Britain effectively undercut any Canadian desire to defect to the
United States with the Dominion Act of 1867 which gave the
Canadians an unprecedented degree of self-government. Then

during the same year the United States purchased Alaska from Russia, which seemed to indicate to disheartened Minnesotans that the federal government was much more interested in that seemingly worthless region than in Canada. During the congressional debate over funding the Alaska purchase, Minnesota expansionists rallied to its support, for they saw it as an effective way of squeezing Canada between American scissors. Frustrated by lack of congressional enthusiasm, Ramsey and Taylor sought to pressure Congress with a resolution from the Minnesota legislature, and Taylor wrote the resolution which the legislature passed on March 6, 1868. The measure supported the funding of the Alaskan Purchase, expressed its regret that there had been no plebiscite of the settlers in Rupert's Land over the British decision to make it part of Canada, and added that the "cession of northwest British America to the United States, accompanied by the construction of a northern Pacific railroad" would satisfactorily "remove all grounds of controversy between the respective countries." [11]

Congress remained unimpressed. Despite some oratory by Ramsey in the Senate and Ignatius Donnelly in the House, Congress simply could not accept the idea that Minnesota had a natural destiny to control much of Canada. The rejection was a question not so much of philosophy as of time. The utterances of Ramsey and Donnelley would have been well received during the fervor of the Mexican War, but they were strangely out of place with the mood of the Reconstruction era. Their ideas were old, not new, and had been heard many times before in the halls of Congress. American interest in Canada had been evident in both the Revolutionary War and the War of 1812, and Manifest Destiny was as logically applied to Rupert's Land as it had been to Oregon earlier. But Minnesota's Manifest Destiny was just that—it was Minnesota-inspired, Minnesota-promoted, and Minnesota-supported, but it was the beat of a lonely drummer.

Taylor and Ramsey did not give up easily. Without congressional backing they turned to the Grant administration, from

11. Quoted in Russell W. Fridley, "When Minnesota Coveted Canada," *Minnesota History* 41 (Summer 1968):77.

which they elicited private assurances of support, but there was no desire to confront Great Britain over the issue. Finally, in 1870, the expansionists were undone when Canada signaled its determination to govern its own national destiny by organizing the province of Manitoba and sending troops to Winnipeg.

Canada's decisive actions marked an end to Minnesota's long quest for territory. The futile march for empire had run its course, but Ramsey, Taylor, and the other expansionists were proven right in one sense at least. Though they were forced to recognize that Minnesota's physical border had been fixed by its 1858 boundaries, they lived to see a vast economic hinterland added to Minneapolis and St. Paul's sphere of influence as Twin Cities-based railroads edged their way across the northern plains in the 1870s and 1880s.

5

Trials of Statehood

OPULATION gains during the territorial years exceeded the wildest dreams of Minnesota's boosters. The
steady influx following the approval of the Sioux treaties led the
territory's official statistician to estimate the 1855 population at
40,000. The estimate the following year was 100,000, and an
official census taken in 1857 preparatory to statehood showed
150,037 inhabitants. In percentages this was the sharpest period
of growth in the entire history of the state.

The population boom caused territorial officials to launch a
statehood drive in 1856—a campaign nearly two years long, and
one plagued by party politics. Although Minnesota Democrats
and Republicans have had many differences over the years, they
were never further apart than during the transition into statehood. Leading Democrats, including Sibley and Rice, like their
party nationally seemed oblivious to the emotional aspects of
the slavery issue that shattered political harmony during the
1850s. As staunch supporters of Stephen Douglas's popular sovereignty, Minnesota Democrats were not at all prepared for the
spontaneous, angry reaction to the Douglas-sponsored Kansas–
Nebraska Act of 1854.

This act, which left the question of slavery in Kansas and
Nebraska to be settled by the vote of their inhabitants, was challenged vigorously by opponents of slavery and led to the formation of the Republican Party. When the Minnesota Republican

Party was formed during the spring and summer of 1855 its primary aim was opposition to the extension of slavery. Although the only slaves in the territory were those like Dred Scott who were brought into the area as servants, slavery was an issue in all Minnesota political campaigns and legislative sessions until its abolition.

Minnesota's newly formed Republican Party unsuccessfully challenged Rice's reelection bid, then bided its time. Most of the native-born who were moving into the territory were anti-slavery Northerners who also supported the Republican call for homestead or free land legislation, and most immigrants, too, had little sympathy for slavery. By the late territorial period it was just a matter of time until the Republicans would gain political control.

As Republican numbers swelled, political rivalry took on a sectional complexion. The Democrats had their greatest strength in the old commercial and lumbering towns—St. Paul, St. Anthony, and Stillwater—while the Republicans dominated the agricultural southeast. Republicans generally believed that they could control an agricultural state, particularly one long and narrow, running from the Mississippi to the Missouri with a northern boundary that would leave St. Paul and Stillwater barely within it. Democrats generally favored a state whose economy would be based on both agriculture and lumbering, which would stretch from Iowa to the international boundary.

With the future shaping of Minnesota in mind, promoters of southern Minnesota schemed to move the capital from St. Paul to St. Peter in the Minnesota River Valley. A St. Peter capital, they thought, might stimulate the construction of a railroad through southern Minnesota and might also lead to the creation of that long, narrow state in which St. Peter would be the approximate center of population. Though Republicans may have been the prime movers in the scheme, capital removal was not strictly a party issue: some Democrats outside of the larger towns resented St. Paul's eminence, and some were members of the St. Peter Land Company which stood to gain from capital removal.

The St. Peter Land Company, which had been chartered by

the territorial legislature and authorized to construct buildings in Le Sueur and Nicollet counties, included Democratic Governor Willis Gorman among its prominent members. Whether the chartering of the company was part of the plot is not clear, but within months the interests of the land company and other boosters of southern Minnesota joined in a common cause. In February 1857, when statehood appeared imminent. St. Peter advocates proposed a capital removal bill which passed both houses of the territorial legislature. St. Paulites were alarmed over the threatened loss of the capital and took action. Joe Rolette, councilman from Pembina and chairman of the committee on engrossed bills, disappeared with the engrossed removal bill— all the way to a hotel room in St. Paul where he stayed in hiding for a week. The Council's sergeant-at-arms, another St. Paul supporter, conducted a systematic search of all of the wrong places and could not find Rolette. Tradition has it that Rolette dramatically reappeared in the Council chambers as the presiding officer brought the session to its close.

Rolette, who was the mixed blood son of Old Joe Rolette, captured the popular imagination as the man who saved the capital for St. Paul. His prank was actually all in vain, for during his absence another copy of the capital removal bill was passed on to Governor Gorman, who signed it. The act was duly printed as a territorial law, and the St. Peter Land Company, anticipating that the capital would be moved by May 1, 1857, as required by the act, constructed a modest frame capitol in St. Peter. But Gorman was replaced as territorial governor and territorial officials made no effort to move to the new capital. Supporters of the St. Peter Land Company had only one recourse —they went to court. Finally in July 1857 federal district judge Rensselaer R. Nelson ruled that the territorial legislature had exhausted its power of locating when it had named St. Paul the capital, and also that the act signed by Gorman was not a law since it had not been acted on properly. As a result of Judge Nelson's ruling, St. Paul kept the capital and St. Peter's frame building later became the Nicollet County courthouse. Out of its bid for glory grew St. Peter's annual "Capital Days" celebration.

While much public attention was focused on the capital removal sideshow, Minnesota's main act was playing in the halls
of Congress, where Henry Rice had proposed the formation of
the state. Rice's motion of December 24, 1856, which was
prompted by the year's unprecedented population growth,
caused no debate in the House of Representatives although
many Southerners voted against it. However, its introduction in
the Senate by Stephen Douglas touched off a fiery contest between sectional protagonists. Northerners saw the admission of
Minnesota as an opportunity to add two more free senators and
Southerners saw it as a move that would shatter the delicate
sectional balance in the Senate. Although most of the criticism
was based on the polite arguments that statehood was premature
and the population was too sparse, there was some blunt talk.
Senator John B. Thompson of Kentucky argued that new states
cost the federal government too much for roads, canals, forts,
and lighthouses; and he candidly stated that he did not want two
Minnesota senators who would be "arrogant" toward the
South. Holding that Congress was not obligated to form a state
simply because it had a certain population, Thompson proposed
a solution:

> instead of taking into partnership and full fellowship all these
> outside Territories and lost people of God's earth, I would say let us
> take them, if we must do it, and rule them as Great Britain rules
> Affghanistan, Hindostan, and all through the Punjaub, making them
> work for you as you would work a negro on a cotton or sugar
> plantation.[1]

When Thompson voted against statehood for Minnesota, he was
joined by twenty-one other senators, all from the South. Despite
this opposition the Minnesota Enabling Act was passed on February 26, 1857. The act closely followed Rice's preference for a
state encompassing both prairie and forest, bounded on the
south by Iowa, on the east by Wisconsin, on the north by Canada, and on the west by a line from the international boundary
south through the main channel of the Red and Bois des Sioux

---

1. John B. Thompson, "Southern Opposition to Statehood," in *With Various Voices*,
pp. 94–95.

rivers, then through Lakes Traverse and Big Stone, and from the foot of Big Stone Lake by a line due south to the Iowa border.

After the passage of the Enabling Act, Minnesota's road to statehood was very rough. The election of delegates to the constitutional convention was hotly contested with slavery as the burning issue. Through their newspapers and from the stump Democratic candidates lashed out at the "Black Republicans" and decried racial equality. On June 1, 1857, only days before the election, the *St. Paul Pioneer and Democrat* proclaimed the real issue to be "White Supremacy against Negro Equality!"

Both parties claimed victory in the election, and because of a monumental error there was no way to determine who had actually won. The territorial legislature in implementing the Enabling Act misinterpreted the section pertaining to election districts. As a result the voters chose 108 constitutional delegates, or thirty more than was intended under the Enabling Act. Republicans and Democrats alike did not believe that the territorial government could rule on the legality of particular elections, so the matter of thirty disputed seats was left to the constitutional convention.

Shortly after assembling in July 1857 in St. Paul, the convention delegates found that the venomous campaign still divided them. Democrats and Republicans could not agree on the seating of delegates or even on the choice of a presiding officer. The disagreement was so deep-seated that delegates of each party formed their own constitutional convention—each referred to as "the" Minnesota Constitutional Convention. The two conventions met separately for over a month with little thought of reconciliation. If anything, antagonism deepened. The Democratic territorial treasurer even refused to process expense claims of the Republicans.

Each convention kept its own records of proceedings and drafted its own constitution. Both Democrats and Republicans used the constitutions of other states as models and in some cases copied provisions from them, but the delegates in both conventions also debated uniquely Minnesota issues. There was strong minority support for the east–west state but the majority in both groups favored the Enabling Act provision, in part out of fear that any change would jeopardize statehood. Within the Republican convention there was considerable debate over the question of extending suffrage to the blacks. Advocates of black suffrage saw it as a way of protesting the Dred Scott decision, which had been handed down by the Supreme Court only a few months before; but the Republican delegates finally concluded that a black-suffrage provision might cause the defeat of the constitution so they settled for a provision in their draft that the question would be decided by referring it to the voters.

Realizing that the charade had to end sometime, leaders of both conventions formed a compromise committee to reconcile differences between their documents. Considering the volatile background the committee worked reasonably well, although harmony was somewhat disturbed when ex-Governor Gorman broke his cane over the head of Republican Thomas Wilson, who Gorman alleged had provoked the act by swearing at Democratic committee members. The compromise committee agreed that a single document was needed; but rather than write a new draft, they wrote the hundreds of little agreements on words and phrases into the Democratic version of the constitution and then did the same with the Republican constitution. The net result was two documents, both marred by numerous minor errors.

The bitter legacy of the dichotomous constitutional convention carried over into the election of state officers. In October 1857, when Henry Sibley narrowly defeated Alexander Ramsey for the governorship and the Democrats gained control of the legislature, charges of deception and fraud were freely exchanged. Relishing their victory, the Democrats sent their version of the constitution with the Republican changes incorporated to Congress, which had yet to act on the admission of Minnesota.

Congressional approval of Minnesota's statehood hung in the balance for four long months before the state was added to the Union as its thirty-second member on May 11, 1858. Opposition came from both North and South. As the Minnesota question was being considered it was caught up in the Kansas problem, which had plagued Congress intermittently since the

Kansas–Nebraska Act. When the pro-slave Lecompton Constitution was sent to Congress from Kansas, Southerners, arguing
that the next admitted state should be pro-slave, delayed action
on the Minnesota bill until Kansas could be considered. Then
Northerners expressed reservations about admitting Minnesota
to the Union because they feared Minnesota's Democratic congressional delegation would support slavery in Kansas. After
weeks of debate the Kansas issue was compromised, but there
were other roadblocks to Minnesota statehood. Senator John
Sherman of Ohio, probably acting at the urging of Minnesota
Republicans, charged fraud in the delegate election and suggested that it be rerun. Sherman's actions were probably
prompted by his belief that the Republicans (who were on the
upswing in Minnesota) would win a second election, but his
suggestion was rejected.

A last obstacle to statehood was of Minnesota's own creation.
Both the Republican and Democratic conventions had overes-
timated the state's population by about 100,000 people. Therefore, they provided for three representatives and three were duly
elected and sent to Washington to await seating when the statehood act was approved. Minnesota's critics said there should
only be one; other congressmen favored three. They compromised on two, which left the awkward dilemma of the need to
eliminate the extra man. The aspirants agreed to settle the question by drawing lots; William W. Phelps and James M. Cava-
naugh won, and twenty-nine-year-old George L. Becker was
sent home.

By the time statehood was attained, the vibrant optimism of
territorial boom days had been shattered by the Panic of 1857
and the ruinous depression which followed in its wake. Plung-
ing real estate values and countless bankruptcies and foreclosures devastated the frontier economy, which had been based on
the promise of future growth rather than sound money and business. In a desperate effort to counteract the depression, the
young state guaranteed a $5,000,000 loan to railroads so con-
struction could begin.

The railroad loan failed to stem the depression, which continued on into the Civil War years. Governor Ramsey was in

Washington, D.C., seeking aid for the stricken state when news arrived that Fort Sumter had fallen to South Carolina's troops. Ramsey promptly called on Secretary of War Simon Cameron, an old Pennsylvania acquaintance, and offered a thousand Minnesota troops for the Union cause—an action that gave the state the distinction of volunteering the first soldiers for the Civil War. Thousands of Minnesotans followed those first men who were inducted in the spring of 1861, and during the course of the war perhaps as many as 24,000 Minnesotans served in Union forces. They were represented in all major campaigns and played a decisive part in the war's turning point, the Battle of Gettysburg.

During the Civil War, Minnesota's economy and prospects improved even though they were obviously affected by the Sioux War and the severe drought of 1862–1863. The state's 1860 population of 172,022 increased by fifty per cent during the next five years, mainly because the farming area east of the Sioux War front filled in. As thousands of acres of virgin farmland were brought under cultivation, wheat production nearly doubled. Lumbering, greatly affected by the drought and by adverse market conditions, revived sharply in 1865, and even the struggling railroad companies finally emerged from the long shadow of the depression. St. Paul and Minneapolis were connected by a ten-mile track in 1862; and by 1865 the state had two hundred miles of rail and St. Paul was but two years away from being linked to Chicago and points east.

During much of the Civil War Minnesota's attention was focused on the Sioux War of 1862, one of the bloodiest Indian wars in United States history. The panic began in August when Minnesotans learned that reservation Sioux were on the rampage. Stories of Indian atrocities spread like a prairie fire and were matched by calls for vengeance. To most frontiersmen the uprising was without cause, instigated by conscienceless savages. Before the war, Minnesota pioneers were preoccupied with the daily concerns of living—putting in crops, laying by provisions for winter, building houses, putting up fences. If they thought about the Indians at all, it seemed to them that treaties and reservations had taken care of the Indian "problem." Once the Sioux had been placed on their Minnesota River reservations they became the forgotten people of Minnesota. There were a few whites, among them Episcopal Bishop Henry Whipple, who sympathized with the Sioux and complained about government policies—the very policies that later came to be regarded as the underlying causes of the Sioux War.

Smoldering Sioux resentment over the treaties of Traverse des Sioux and Mendota was inflamed in 1858 when the federal government, using a reserve clause in those treaties, forced the Sioux to sell the half of their reservations that lay on the north side of the Minnesota River. Many Sioux saw this move, which was made to satisfy an encroaching finger of speculators and farmers, as a prelude to the loss of the entire reservation and final expulsion from their homeland. Many Sioux were also angered by the government's assimilation policy. Its philosophy was bad enough in itself, but its administration by bureaucrats whose primary qualification was political party service complicated matters. Indians could not really believe that the government cared for their welfare when new political appointees paraded onto the reservations every time a presidential administration changed.

The Sioux Indians were not of one mind regarding government policy. Some, reasoning that resistance was futile, donned white man's clothing, cut their hair short, learned English, converted to Christianity, and began to learn to farm. These "progressives" were derisively labeled "cut-hairs" by the "blanket Sioux" who clung to the old ways and mourned for the time before the white man came. The persistent antagonism between "cut-hair" and "blanket" soon undermined tribal unity, and in desperation the militants began to believe that their only salvation was to expel the whites—something that could not be accomplished at the conference table.

Tribal discontent was further inflamed by several crises of the early 1860s. On one occasion the Sioux charged that they were shortchanged when some questionable traders' claims were deducted from their annuities. Crop failures on reservation land caused severe food shortages; and then, during the summer of 1862, government officials in Washington debated over whether to pay the Sioux with gold or paper money, and the Indians' agent refused to issue food until the money arrived. When some of the starving Indians angrily demanded rations, trader Andrew Myrick, according to Chief Little Crow, responded that "they would eat grass or their own dung." [2]

The hungry Sioux wandered the countryside in search of food. On a hot, dry day in August, four young men found some hens' eggs along a fence row near an Acton farmhouse. One of the young men took the eggs, but a companion warned him that they belonged to a white man. Angered, the first young man threw the eggs on the ground and then dared his comrades to go with him to the white man's farm. Once there, the Indians supposedly asked for liquor. The farmer gave them none and then left, going to a neighbor's place. The Indians followed him there and, after some friendly bantering with the white men, challenged them to a shooting contest. A target was set up, and both sides had discharged their weapons when without warning the Indians, who had already reloaded, fired upon the whites. Three men and one woman were killed, and then, in flight, the young men killed a fifteen-year-old girl.

There had been a time when tribal leaders would have turned these miscreants over to white authorities, but no more. This time, hotheads led by Chief Shakopee called for war. Somehow they persuaded Little Crow to lead them in spite of the fact that he seemed to have recognized that the Sioux stood no chance of winning. One of his companions years later claimed that Little Crow had a plan to sweep the Minnesota River Valley clean of settlers all the way to St. Paul. Whether this was the case or not, the war began with a lashing out against the nearest whites. On August 18, the day after the Acton killings, militant Sioux struck the Lower Sioux Agency like warriors of old. With the element of surprise on their side, the Sioux hostiles (whose hard core probably comprised only about one tenth of the nearly seven thousand Sioux) seized control of the Lower Sioux Agency and nearly annihilated a forty-man relief party from

2. Nathaniel West, *The Ancestry, Life and Times of Hon. Henry Hastings Sibley, LL.D.* (St. Paul: Pioneer Press Publishing Co., 1889), p. 263.

Fort Ridgely in the first day's battle. During a week-long offensive they also devastated many isolated farms and killed dozens of settlers who could offer only feeble resistance, but they failed to take either Fort Ridgely or New Ulm despite sustained attacks on both places.

Governor Ramsey responded to the crisis by naming his old friend Henry Sibley to lead a 1400-man relief expedition from Fort Snelling. Sibley took nine days to make the trip, days which must have seemed interminable to those who cried for help, and then he delayed further at Fort Ridgely trying to marshal his forces. Impatient frontier editors who wanted swift and harsh punishment of the Sioux pilloried Sibley. Jane Grey Swisshelm, the St. Cloud firebrand, cried out in her paper: "For God's sake put some *live* man in command of the force against the Sioux & let Sibley have 100 men or thereabout for his undertaker's corpse." [3] What Sibley's critics did not recognize was that his 1400 men were the rawest of recruits, most with no military experience at all, and that they did not have enough guns or ammunition or even provisions to go around. Sibley had so few horses he had to impress draft animals from farmers during his march from Fort Snelling.

While Sibley at Fort Ridgely tried desperately to make an army out of his ragtag troops, a military burial party was ambushed by Sioux under Chief Mankato at Birch Coulee near present Morton. This skirmish proved to be one of the war's major engagements. Sibley finally moved up the Minnesota Valley on September 18, still hoping to negotiate a settlement. After Little Crow refused to surrender because Sibley could not guarantee amnesty, the opposing sides engaged in the Battle of Wood Lake, the last engagement of the war, on September 23. The "battle," an awkward standoff punctuated by intermittent gunfire, caused Little Crow to retreat out of Minnesota.

Most of the hostile Sioux fled into Dakota Territory or Canada, but Sibley's men rounded up some two thousand Indians and then set to work trying to separate the militant from the nonmilitant. Over a five-week period in the fall a military board

---

3. Quoted in Folwell, *History of Minnesota*, 2:176n.

tried 425 Indians and half-breeds for their alleged participation in the war. The trials were a farce; as many as forty men were tried in a single day with individual trials lasting only a few minutes. Many of the accused were sentenced on the testimony of an informer who had bargained for his own safety. Finally the court convicted 321 men, sentencing all but 18 of them to death. However, Bishop Whipple interceded for the Sioux, and because of his plea President Lincoln ordered that all death sentences except those of accused and convicted murderers or rapists be reduced to jail terms. On December 26, 1862, thirty-eight Sioux were hanged in Mankato.

Even though the Sioux were either imprisoned or dispersed, Minnesotans who lived on the edge of the frontier with the prairies stretching endlessly westward did not really believe that Sibley had vanquished the Indians. There was such widespread fear that the Sioux would return that forts were built and manned by settlers for several years along a rough line from St. Cloud to Hutchinson to Blue Earth. Little Crow did return; but when he did, he was accompanied by only his sixteen-year-old son. On July 3, 1863, the Indian chief was ambushed and killed while picking berries in a swamp near Hutchinson, not many miles from Acton where the war began.

There are those who believe that Little Crow met a kinder fate than many of the peaceful Indians who had raised no hand against the government. Hundreds of Sioux, mostly women and children, were confined in unbelievably crowded quarters at Fort Snelling over the winter of 1862–1863, with much illness and many deaths. In the spring the survivors were herded like cattle onto steamboats and carried over two thousand miles to the desolate Crow Creek reservation on the Missouri River in South Dakota. Their living conditions at Crow Creek were so unbearable that missionary Samuel Hinman bitterly concluded that they would have been better off if they had fought the whites. "Bishop," he tersely wrote to his superior, Henry Whipple, "if I were an Ind[ian] I would never lay down the war-club while I lived." [4]

4. Quoted in William E. Lass, "The Removal from Minnesota of the Sioux and Winnebago Indians," *Minnesota History* 38 (December 1963):364.

This was just the beginning of the dispersal of the Santee Sioux. After several years of subhuman existence the survivors of Crow Creek were moved to yet another reservation, this one near Niobrara, Nebraska. Some who fled from Niobrara established a community at Flandreau, South Dakota. Most of the Sioux had not been apprehended in 1862 and many—both hostile and peaceful—fled into the Dakotas, where reservations were later formed for them in northeastern South Dakota and at Devil's Lake in North Dakota. Other Sioux escaped into Canada, where their descendants remain on small reservations in the prairie provinces. Some Sioux joined their western brethren and lived out their days on the plains of the western Dakotas, Montana, and Wyoming. A few, such as those who benefited from the hospitality of the half-Sioux Alexander Faribault, remained in Minnesota after the Sioux War while others straggled back from the Dakotas and established small communities in the 1880s near Morton, Prior Lake, and Red Wing, where some of their descendants still live.

The effects of the war on the Sioux were calamitous. Though there were few deaths in battle, many died in captivity, and the Indians were so scattered that all hope of tribal unity was gone. Then, with congressional abrogation of the Sioux treaties and the abolition of the Minnesota River reservations, the Santee Sioux formally lost their homeland.

The sudden beginning of the Sioux War and the initial high loss of life made it sensational both in area newspapers and in the East. A tremendous amount of war literature was generated both contemporarily and later. Atrocity stories abounded, and during the harried opening days of the war panic-stricken settlers cried that 800 to 1000 whites had been slaughtered. These figures are still sometimes cited; but in reality, casualties included 413 white civilians, 77 soldiers, and 71 Indians including the 38 who were executed in Mankato. It is no wonder that many Minnesotans believe the Sioux War to be the greatest Indian war in the history of the nation. It was not that, but it certainly is a classic example of the failure of United States Indian policy.

In the fury of the first few days of the Sioux War, the western fringes of Minnesota's frontier were virtually abandoned. Many settlers closeted themselves in homemade stockades and others fled to St. Paul or to Wisconsin. Some of them never returned. Even though the Sioux offensive lasted barely more than a week, fear that the warriors would return lingered through the remainder of the Civil War. The mass execution at Mankato marked the height of the Sioux phobia. Since only those identified as murderers and rapists were to be hanged, the execution should have been a solemn administration of justice, essentially no different from the handling of white criminals in a frontier society. But it was instead an act of vengeance carried out in a gaudy, almost carnival atmosphere. A massive single scaffold was erected and its rope was cut by William Duley, who had lost most of his family in the Lake Shetek Massacre. Hundreds of spectators came from miles around, and when the Sioux dropped to their death the crowd burst into cheers.

The Sioux War was to the Minnesota frontiersmen the end of a barbarous era. The presence of even peaceful Indians had troubled white settlers, for as long as Indians roamed the land, there was the potential for war, and as long as reservations remained, there was land that could not be claimed. When the war came it was sudden and shocking, but it was not really a surprise. The clash between the two civilizations was as inevitable as was the outcome, and the removal of the Indians and the abolition of their reservations, in the minds of the settlers, freed Minnesota at last from the final vestiges of savagery.

Time has cooled emotions, and over several generations the interpretation of the Sioux War has changed. To pioneers it was the "Sioux Uprising," a label in keeping with their view that the Indians were solely to blame. The first historians of the war emphasized atrocities perpetrated by some of the Sioux and overlooked the causes of the Indian discontent. Gradually, however, there has been more and more acceptance of Bishop Whipple's view that the Indians—even though they were the aggressors—were driven to war. Consequently, recent histories, beginning with William Watts Folwell's *History of Minnesota,* have included more dispassionate coverage of the war and its causes.

6

Peopling the Land

FTER the Civil War Minnesota's agricultural frontier closed with a great rush. The state's population, 439,000 in 1870, tripled during the next two decades. This movement of people, unprecedented in terms of raw numbers, hastened the breaking of the prairie as claimants spilled out of the woods into the less hospitable regions in the southwestern and western parts of the state. By the mid-1880s the choicest farmlands had been claimed and would-be farmers who entered Minnesota after that time usually moved into the cutover areas left in the wake of the advancing lumbermen.

It was the cheap, fertile land that drew settlers to Minnesota's frontier—land controlled either by federal or state government or by railroad companies and speculators. After the ratification of the Sioux treaties, the richest portion of Minnesota became part of the federal government's public domain. Until the passage of the Homestead Act in 1862 the United States General Land Office disposed of most of its lands under the Pre-Emption Act, which provided for the cash sale of surveyed government land through district land offices at a minimum price of $1.25 an acre. This 1841 act was designed to protect the pre-emptor or squatter by giving him first option to purchase, but the law worked poorly in frontier regions because it applied only to surveyed land. Very little of the Suland was surveyed prior to the settlers' rush in the 1850s, so thousands of squatters faced the possibility of eviction when the land was sold. The plight of these pre-emptors caused Minnesota's territorial politicians to lobby hard to amend the Pre-Emption Act, and Congress, in 1854, did amend the 1841 law so that squatters on unsurveyed land also were assured of the option to buy. This was a major victory for frontiersmen, but agitation for free land was still widespread. After the Republican Party nationally endorsed the homestead principle, Minnesota Republicans in the late 1850s and early 1860s became particularly vociferous. Even Minnesota Democrats, in spite of the fact that Southerners in their own party were deeply opposed to the free-land principle, joined the chorus. Southern opposition during the pre-Civil War years caused a number of proposals to fail either in Congress or because of presidential veto, but during the Civil War the secession of the Southern states made it possible for a Union congress to pass the Homestead Act at last.

When the act went into effect in Minnesota there was very little settlement west of a line from Blue Earth through New Ulm and Hutchinson to St. Cloud. Minnesota promoters were quick to point out the advantages of the law: any man or woman at least twenty-one who was an American citizen or had begun the naturalization process could obtain 160 acres of land simply by building a suitable dwelling, living on the claim for five years, and paying nominal closing costs. Although homesteads could be claimed only in designated areas because previous land acts remained in effect, the act proved to be very popular in Minnesota. By 1880 over 62,000 claims had been made and nearly one seventh of the state had been homesteaded.

Although the government of Minnesota never had free land to dispose of as the federal government did, it nonetheless had a generous land policy. The state was given federal land to support the common schools, the state university, and railroad construction, and it obtained thousands of additional acres as a result of federal swampland acts. Much of that public land was sold during the frontier period at prices even lower than the federal government's.

Minnesota's prairie homesteaders, like other settlers on the sod-house frontier, had difficulty coping with the treeless environment. Usually the only fuels available were buffalo or cow chips or dried grass. Planting and cultivating trees seemed to be the only answer; so the federal government in 1873 supplemented the Homestead Act with the Timber Culture Act, which required claimants to cultivate 40 acres of trees on their 160-acre claims for five years before they could obtain the land free. Initial response to the new act was poor, but after an 1874 amendment reduced the requirement to only ten acres of trees, many settlers filed "tree claims." By the end of 1880 over a million acres of Minnesota land had been claimed under some 8000 timber claims. Also in 1873, the Minnesota legislature created a bounty system under which farmers were paid $2.00 a year for as long as ten years for each acre of saplings they cultivated. Eight million saplings were planted in 1873; within seven years Minnesotans had planted over 25,000 acres of trees and more than 900 miles of tree rows along public thoroughfares and between farms. Usually the settlers planted thousands of seedlings, so tiny that they were still very small trees when claims were proved. A good number of these trees did not survive, and other stands were cut out after the land became privately owned; but in spite of this many farms in western Minnesota are still sheltered from the sweeping prairie winds by groves planted by those first settlers.

Frontier areas always attract speculators, and in Minnesota the greatest opportunities for them came about because of the existence of military and Indian scrip. The United States had paid bounties to veterans of the Revolutionary War, the War of 1812, and the Mexican War in the form of certificates which entitled the holder to claim 40 to 160 acres of specified public domain. In some instances scrip was also used to pay off government obligations to Indians and half-breeds. By a congressional act of 1852, scrip was made negotiable; since many of the veterans had no intention of moving to the frontier, and since many Indians had no interest in becoming landowners, large amounts of the scrip were sold to merchants, bankers, and speculators, often for next to nothing. The scrip frequently changed hands two or three times before the land was actually claimed, but even then farmers often found it possible to obtain land more cheaply by buying scrip than by paying the going government price. Sometimes speculators were able to amass large amounts of scrip and redeem it for parcels of land running to thousands of acres.

Despite Minnesota's bountiful land, the region was regarded as an American Siberia. Though the steamboats plied the Mississippi to St. Paul, they were slow and unreliable, and when the river froze Minnesota was virtually isolated. Understandably, the completion of a railroad to Rock Island, Illinois, about 350 miles downstream from St. Paul, in the summer of 1854 was welcomed. The railroad contractors sponsored "The Great Railroad Excursion" in which hundreds of guests (including ex-president Millard Fillmore) were taken by rail to Rock Island and then by steamboat to St. Paul. The excursion dramatized the end of Minnesota's extreme remoteness, for now St. Paul was at best but thirty hours from Chicago and four days from major eastern cities.

The generation after the Civil War was the age of the railroad in Minnesota. The line to Rock Island inspired territorial politicians to work hard for their own railways, and their efforts were rewarded by a congressional land grant in 1856. The grant was to help finance four major railroads radiating out from St. Paul, but the railroad companies were barely organized when the Panic of 1857 hit. Even the state's $5,000,000 loan was not enough to stimulate rapid construction of the lines. Not until late in the Civil War, after the companies were reorganized and refinanced, did the tempo of construction pick up. Finally, in 1867, St. Paul and Chicago were connected by rail.

Minnesota prospered as settlers rode the lines, goods began to flow, and the railroads continued to expand. Then, in 1873, a second frontier panic struck, but its impact was not so disastrous as that of the Panic of 1857. The railroad companies recouped rapidly: by 1880 there were over 3000 miles of track in the state and all the main lines had been laid.

The railroad companies were interested in settling the frontier—not just because they stood to profit from transporting passengers and produce, but because they had to sell their federal grants of land to help defray construction costs. Major companies such as the Northern Pacific and James J. Hill's St. Paul and Pacific had immigrants' guides written and printed in English, German, and the Scandinavian languages. These guides were distributed by the hundreds. What immigrant would not have been attracted to a Minnesota described in the following manner?

> The whole surface of the State is literally begemmed with innumerable lakes. . . . Their picturesque beauty and loveliness, with their pebbly bottoms, transparent waters, wooded shores and sylvan associations, must be seen to be fully appreciated.
>
> There is no Western State better supplied with forests. . . . The assertion that the climate of Minnesota is one of the healthiest in the world, may be broadly and confidently made. . . .[1]

The railroads had agents in principal European cities and American and Canadian ports of entry. They made cooperative arrangements with steamship lines to offer group rates to colonists, they helped the immigrant make transfers at railroad centers like Chicago and Milwaukee, and they established reception houses in Minnesota. Railroad cooperation in moving whole colonies led to the establishment of communities such as Ghent, Adrian, and Mountain Lake. Sometimes the companies even platted their own towns along the tracks and carried settlers to them—towns like Willmar, Litchfield, and DeGraff.

Railroad lands, given companies by the federal government to encourage and fund construction, had to compete with the federal government's free land. To be competitive, the railroads sold land in Minnesota's prime farming belt for $3.00 to $5.00 an acre, and often a buyer needed only to make a down payment and several annual installment payments with no interest charges. The generosity of the railroads' land policies won them much good will among settlers, but this was soon lost when the farmers became victims of the companies' freight practices.

The railroads were not Minnesota's only promoters. Everyone who had something to gain joined the chorus—mercantile firms and land companies, religious organizations, municipal and

1. Quoted in Harold F. Peterson, "Early Minnesota Railroads and the Quest for Settlers," *Minnesota History* 13 (March 1932):34.

state agents, and the newspapers. Perhaps Minnesota's most ardent booster was James Madison Goodhue, founder of the *Minnesota Pioneer*, the area's first newspaper. Goodhue came to St. Paul when the territory was only a few weeks old and with his first issue dedicated himself to promoting Minnesota's image. He answered questions from readers outside of Minnesota in his columns, he carried articles designed to encourage further settlement, he eulogized, he editorialized. And most important, he sent his papers to the major newspapers in the East so that his comments were copied and widely circulated.

A common frontier promotional gambit was to compare an opening area to other sections of the country, and so Goodhue extolled the "salubrity" of Minnesota's climate and lambasted the "bilious" regions south of Minnesota:

> Although we have in Minnesota, immense tracts of land as rich as the best soils in which the victims of agues and bilious fevers find sure and early graves along the sluggish streams of Iowa and Illinois, we have, universally, a pure, bracing, wholesome atmosphere, and *Health* standing up manfully under the burden of daily toil—sound livers and firm muscles. In Minnesota, honest Toil is not compelled to hobble about through harvest time upon such miserable crutches as calomel and quinine. . . . Never has a case of fever and ague originated here; and except for the use of invalids who come up, pale as a procession of the ghost of Banquo and its attendants, from the damp plains of the South, which like cemeteries open their black jaws and swallow, in their very youth, the generations of livid wretches who have been lured there by the *one idea* of fertility; except for these invalids, who fly from those charnel-houses to recruit their health in this land of cataracts and pine forests, and dry, wholesome atmosphere, there is no use for quinine, or Morrison's pills, or Rowand's Tonic mixture, or any of the anti-bilious nostrums of our times, the sale of which, in some of the towns south of us, constitutes a large share of their commerce.[2]

There were even full-length books written extolling Minnesota, like the many editions of John Wesley Bond's *Min-*

2. *Minnesota Pioneer*, June 5, 1851, quoted in Mary Wheelhouse Berthel, *Horns of Thunder: The Life and Times of James M. Goodhue Including Selections from His Writings* (St. Paul: Minnesota Historical Society, 1948), pp. 86–87.

nesota and Its Resources, Ephraim S. Seymour's *Minnesota, the New England of the West,* and William G. LeDuc's *Minnesota Year Books,* but Minnesota's government did not consider all of these private efforts enough, so it, too, joined in the boosterism.

In 1853, the territory sent LeDuc to New York City to display Minnesota products at the Crystal Palace World's Fair. LeDuc was not permitted to display the buffalo he had brought, but his exhibit of crops and vegetables attracted much attention. LeDuc returned from New York convinced that the territory's best hope for rapid settlement lay in attracting foreign immigrants, and he urged official action toward this end. Governor Willis Gorman listened to LeDuc, and at Gorman's suggestion the territorial legislature in 1855 passed an act providing for a Commissioner of Emigration. Gorman named Eugene Burnand, who was well educated and fluent in several languages, to the position. Burnand set up a New York office from which he met immigrant ships, distributed literature, and advertised Minnesota in newspapers and publications of immigrant groups. Burnand emphasized and was especially successful in the recruitment of Germans. Official promotion was discontinued for lack of funds, but in 1867 the Minnesota legislature revived its activity by creating a Board of Immigration. By then state officials believed that the most fertile ground for attracting settlers was the Scandinavian countries, and appropriately they named Hans Mattson, a Swedish immigrant, as commissioner. Mattson had settled at the village of Vasa in the early years of Minnesota Territory and then had served as an officer in a Minnesota unit during the Civil War. "Colonel" Mattson wrote dozens of immigrant tracts and had them translated into the languages of northern Europe. He also made recruitment trips to Sweden and other European countries, and years later in his book *Reminiscences: The Story of An Emigrant,* he wrote that on his first trip, he found himself "besieged by people who wished to accompany me back to America in the spring." [3]

In spite of all of the official and commercial boosterism,

3. Hans Mattson, *Reminiscences: The Story of an Emigrant* (St. Paul: D. D. Merrill Co., 1892), p. 110.

perhaps Minnesota's best publicity was the thousands of "America letters" sent back to the "old country" by new Minnesotans. These writers were usually not well-to-do proprietors who would profit by attracting more settlers, but ordinary people who had found new hope and prosperity in a far-off land. Some of the immigrant letter-writers revealed a resentment of life, customs, and institutions in the "old country" and a great pride in things American. One Swedish immigrant, for example, wrote home that

> No one need worry about my circumstances in America, because I am living on God's noble and free soil, neither am I a slave of others. On the contrary, I am my own master, like the other creatures of God. I have now been on American soil for two and a half years and I have not been compelled to pay a penny for the privilege of living. Neither is my cap worn out from lifting it in the presence of gentlemen. There is no class distinction here between high and low, rich and poor, no make-believe, no "title sickness" or artificial ceremonies, but everything is quiet and peaceful and everybody lives in peace and prosperity. . . .[4]

Historian George M. Stephenson observed that in Sweden the

> 'America letters' fell like leaves from the land of Canaan. They were not only read and pondered by the simple and credulous individuals to whom they were addressed, and discussed in larger groups in homes and at markets and fairs and in crowds assembled at parish churches, but they were also broadcast through the newspapers, which unwittingly or not, infected parish after parish with the 'America fever'. . . . The result was that the most fanciful stories were circulated about the wonderful country across the Atlantic—a land of milk and honey.[5]

Minnesota's publicity featured numerous claims about the salubrity of the climate. These claims, which originated with the first territorial promoters, were meant to counteract the widespread belief that Minnesota was another Siberia. The climate was not only invigorating, Minnesotans said, but health-giving

4. Quoted in George M. Stephenson, "When America was the Land of Canaan," *Minnesota History* 10 (September 1929):247.

5. Stephenson, "Land of Canaan," p. 238.

as well. Surprisingly, the claim developed into far more than its first advocates could possibly have foreseen, for Minnesota, from the early 1850s to about the mid-1870s, experienced a tremendous influx of settlers attracted by the alleged restorative properties of its climate.

Salubrious Minnesota became the haven for those afflicted with malaria and tuberculosis, or consumption as it was then called. The belief that a cool climate would help the afflicted was buttressed by testimonials from individuals who came to Minnesota. One visitor in the 1860s said he had been cured of consumption merely by residing in Minnesota for a time, and he reported that "Minnesota all the year round is one vast hospital. All her cities and towns, and many of her farm houses, are crowded with those fleeing from the approach of the dread destroyer." [6] Minnesota's reputation was further enhanced by the publication of two books in the early 1870s. Ledyard Bill, a New York businessman who had spent a winter in Florida and had earlier written about that state's advantages to health-seekers, wrote a work entitled *Minnesota: Its Character and Climate . . .* and in it concluded that two types of climate, very hot and very cold, would provide the most relief for consumptives. When he compared the best examples of each, Florida and Minnesota, Bill gave his final approval to Minnesota. The other book, by the more partisan Brewer Mattocks, a St. Paul doctor, included an attack on the undesirability of Florida and other southern states as refuges for health seekers. Mattocks's claims for Minnesota's healthfulness were most dramatic. For example, he advised a young consumptive to move to Minnesota because it was

> greatly favored in having a society superior to most of the new States, because many families of wealth and high social position are obliged to live in our State on account of ill health, rather than the necessity of again commencing life. Most of our large business men and professional men in St. Paul sought our climate for health.[7]

6. Quoted in Helen Clapesattle, "When Minnesota was Florida's Rival," *Minnesota History* 35 (March 1957):215.

7. Brewer Mattocks, *Minnesota as a Home for Invalids* (Philadelphia: J. B. Lippincott Co., 1871), p. 147.

Whether Minnesota could prove her climate was restorative or not, the fact is that many people did move to the state in the belief that it would improve their health, including such prominent figures as Doctor W. W. Mayo, father of the Drs. Mayo of Rochester's Mayo Clinic; journalists Henry A. Castle and Joseph A. Wheelock; politicians James B. Wakefield of Indiana, who became a congressman from Minnesota, and Stephen Miller, who became governor of Minnesota; minister and novelist Edward Eggleston; and Dr. Mattocks himself.

While most newcomers to Minnesota sought farmland, thousands of others were attracted by lumbering and iron mining and urban industry. Lumbering peaked during the 1890s at the very time that the opening of the Mesabi Iron Range provided other opportunities for unskilled workers. Many native-born Americans and European immigrants during the 1870s and 1880s moved directly to the Twin Cities, where the major industries were flour milling and sawmilling. During this twenty-year period the population of Minneapolis swelled from 13,066 to 164,738 and that of St. Paul from 20,030 to 133,156.

The great influx of population into Minnesota was part of two major nineteenth-century movements—westward movement within the United States and an international westward movement of Europeans to the United States. The frontier beckoned to those who were discontented with their lot in life, and improved transportation, particularly rail and steam transportation, made movement easier. Many of the native-born Americans moved west because of soil exhaustion; others because of rising land costs, encroaching industry and urbanization, or high property taxes. Many of the Europeans who came were fleeing from poverty, social inequality, political discrimination and persecution, and religious intolerance. Others, fairly well to do in their homelands, had dreams of becoming yet wealthier in the United States.

The native-born Americans who moved to Minnesota came principally from New England, New York, and the Great Lakes states. The New Englanders or Yankees, which included those who moved directly from New England as well as those of Yankee stock from other regions, were an especially important group, wielding much influence in politics, business, and society. The first large movement of New Englanders into Minnesota came with the beginning of lumbering in the St. Croix River Valley. Yankees provided know-how and capital, and their impact on lumbering was visible as long as there were virgin forests. Isaac Staples, lumber baron of the St. Croix Valley, was a Yankee, as was Dorilus Morrison, the first mayor of Minneapolis and a ranking lumber entrepreneur after the Civil War. In the business world there were the Crosbys, the Pillsburys, and the Washburns of flour-milling fame, all of New England stock, as was Franklin Steele, the area's first millionaire. In politics, the Yankee roster of well-known Minnesotans was long: Sibley and Rice were Yankees, and seven of the state's first eleven governors were of New England ancestry. During the period before 1890, about a third of Minnesota's major administrative officers and supreme court justices were natives of New England.

New Englanders were prominent in the field of education also in Minnesota's early years. William Watts Folwell, the first president of the University of Minnesota, was a New Englander, and Carleton College in Northfield was started by Yankees with its greatest financial boost coming from the Massachusetts benefactor after whom it was named. New Englanders exerted considerable influence in establishing the public school system and one of them, Harriet Bishop, is recognized as the founder of Minnesota's first school.

The movement of European immigrants into Minnesota roughly parallels the national pattern. The first settlers were primarily from western and northern Europe—principally from Germany and Ireland—and generally moved to rural frontier areas. The Germans and Irish continued to arrive in Minnesota in significant numbers through the 1860s and 1870s. Although some Scandinavians came at the same time, their migration generally came later, from about 1870 to 1900. Rural Minnesota also attracted some eastern European settlers such as Czechs, Bohemians, and Ukrainians.

Despite Minnesota's widely accepted Scandinavian image, the state's largest single immigrant group was the Germans. On the eve of World War I slightly over seventy per cent of Minnesota's population was foreign born or native born who had at least one foreign-born parent. Of this number over one fourth were Germans. To this day, Minnesotans of German extraction are the state's ranking ethnic group. The heaviest concentrations of Germans are in the southern and east central counties. New Ulm was established by two distinct German groups during the territorial period; since its founding it has had a marked cohesiveness that can be related to the utopian socialist philosophy of some of its founders, the existence of an active Turner Society, and the presence of a freethinker element. The height of freethinker dominance came in the 1890s with the erection of a mighty statue to Hermann, the Teutonic God of War. Though "Herman the German" is taken for granted by many of the present residents, his presence atop the high ground overlooking the city is a unique symbol of the community's onetime psyche.

Religious preference of the German immigrants ranged from Lutheranism, Catholicism, and Pietism through freethinking, and generally each area occupied by Germans tended to be dominantly of one faith. Thus New Ulm had its freethinkers, while Catholics were the most populous group in heavily German St. Cloud and Shakopee. Most of the Germans came as fairly well-to-do land-seekers, and a common belief developed that they had a particular talent for selecting the best farmlands. Perhaps in some cases they were able to acquire the best land, but it is now generally recognized that they created the best farms through hard work and a passion for neatness and order.

By the sheer weight of their numbers, the Germans have had an impact on all aspects of Minnesota's development. They have had their colonists like William Pfaender of New Ulm, their missionaries like Father Francis Pierz of St. Cloud, their business leaders like lumber magnate Frederick Weyerhaeuser, but they have made relatively few contributions to Minnesota politics: this may have been in part because of the German phobia of the two world wars, but even before World War I Germans did not produce major political leaders.

Minnesota's Scandinavian tradition arises from its large number of Norwegians, Swedes, and Danes. Collectively, these groups far outnumber the Germans. The federal census of 1890 showed slightly over 100,000 Norwegians of foreign birth in Minnesota and slightly under 100,000 foreign-born Swedes, an order reversed since 1900, but only 14,000 Danes. Although similar in certain cultural traits and points of origin, the three Scandinavian nationalities are distinctive. Consequently they have tended to settle not as Scandinavian communities, but rather as Norwegian, Swedish, or Danish. Urbanization and internal migration have altered the pattern of frontier settlement, but there are still identifiable Norwegian, Swedish, and Danish areas. The heaviest concentrations of Norwegians are in the southeastern counties, the upper Minnesota River Valley adjacent to South Dakota, and the Red River Valley, while the Swedes are most prevalent in the area between the St. Croix and the Mississippi and the region west of Minneapolis. The Danish immigrants settled primarily in Freeborn County near Albert Lea and in Lincoln County on the South Dakota border.

As numbers of Scandinavians were naturalized they soon replaced New Englanders as the foremost political group. Initially they tended to be drawn into the dominant Republican Party and did not participate in the protest movements. When Knute Nelson, the first of the Scandinavian governors, was inaugurated in 1893 Minnesota's period of Yankee governors came to an end and Scandinavians usually captured the governorship after that time. Of the twenty-two governors since Nelson all but five have been of Scandinavian extraction. Rudy Perpich, who followed Wendell Anderson as governor in 1976 when the latter went to the U.S. Senate, is the first non-Scandinavian governor since Harold Stassen resigned in 1943. Scandinavians have also been heavily represented in the state legislature and in Minnesota's congressional membership. When so many of Minnesota's politicians bear Scandinavian names, it is no wonder that the national impression is that Minnesota is almost completely Scandinavian despite the fact that the other ethnic groups combined outnumber them.

Although Scandinavians were generally well assimilated by the third generation, they have tended to perpetuate their customs and, in some rural areas, even their languages. Lutheranism is the dominant religion among the Norwegians and Swedes, and the churches were often leaders in establishing educational institutions in Minnesota—institutions such as Augsburg College in Minneapolis, Concordia in Moorhead, St. Olaf in Northfield, and Gustavus Adolphus in St. Peter.

The Irish follow the Germans, Swedes, and Norwegians as Minnesota's fourth largest immigrant group. The first Irish influx into Minnesota followed the disastrous potato famine of the 1850s which drove millions of Irishmen from the Emerald Isle. Some of the Irish movement into Minnesota Territory was encouraged by James Shields, an individual who later earned the unique distinction of having served as a United States senator from three states (including Minnesota). Before becoming a major figure in Minnesota politics, Shields persuaded numerous Irish landseekers to take up claims in Rice County near the community of Shieldsville.

After the Civil War, Irish immigration to Minnesota was encouraged by various colonization efforts. Particularly notable in this endeavor was the Catholic Colonization Bureau, whose guiding spirit was Bishop John Ireland of St. Paul. Ireland led the way in starting ten Catholic colonies during the period 1876–1881 on railroad lands in western Minnesota, among them the Irish communities of DeGraff, Clontarf, Graceville, Currie, Avoca, and Adrian. Although the Irish were well represented in the rural areas of southern and western Minnesota, their heaviest concentration was in St. Paul, which came to be known as an "Irish town" in spite of the fact that the Germans outnumbered the Irish.

Canadians were in Minnesota even before the area had a political identity. During the time that the upper Mississippi region was within the trade area of Montreal, hundreds of Canadian fur traders worked in the area that is now Minnesota. Such noteworthies as William Morrison, Joseph Renville, and Norman Kittson had both Minnesota and Canadian careers. Some of the earliest squatters about Fort Snelling were French Canadians. Pierre Parrant was notorious, but there were more reputable citizens such as Louis Robert, who became one of the most important community leaders in the early history of St. Paul. Without doubt Canada's foremost contribution to Minnesota's citizenry was James J. Hill, who came to St. Paul as an eighteen-year-old in 1856 and then went on to earn his reputation as the "Empire Builder" for his part in organizing the Great Northern Railroad. In the age of railroad giants Hill was the only one who resided in Minnesota. His mansion still stands on Summit Avenue in St. Paul, a symbol of the Gilded Age.

In Minnesota, Canadian immigrants are usually believed to be French Canadian or English Canadian, but actually, since the Canadians are a national rather than an ethnic group, their numbers include Icelanders, Ukranians, Scottish, Scotch-Irish, and many other European nationalities. The greatest number of Canadians occurs in the Mesabi Range towns and in the Twin Cities, and there are still identifiable French Canadian settlements such as Gentilly in the Red River Valley.

Southern Minnesota's farming frontier might be considered a melting pot within the Minnesota melting pot, for virtually every ethnic group from western Europe was represented, as were some groups of eastern Europeans. There were English, such as those who started a colony at Fairmont in the 1870s; Belgians who moved to Ghent, one of the communities started by Bishop Ireland; Dutch who settled most heavily in the southwestern part of the state about Edgerton and Worthington and at Hollandale south of Owatonna. The Welsh who moved on from Ohio and Pennsylvania into Minnesota Territory took up farmland around Lake Crystal, Judson, and Cambria. There were even a number of Swiss and Austrians who moved to the southern Minnesota frontier. The eastern Europeans, though few in numbers in southern Minnesota, included Poles, who first moved to Winona to work in its sawmills; German Mennonites, who moved as a group from southern Russia to Mountain Lake; and Bohemians, who peopled the Silver Lake and New Prague areas.

By the time the heaviest wave of immigration from southern and eastern Europe reached the United States, Minnesota's agricultural frontier was nearly closed, and so for those latecomers the greatest opportunities were in the Twin Cities, Duluth, and the towns of the Mesabi Iron Range. The Mesabi Range especially became a mosaic of eastern Europeans. Every small group that was within the old Holy Roman Empire or the kingdom of Austria-Hungary which was formed in 1867 was represented on the Mesabi. The Mesabi hungered for thousands of unskilled workers to extract the ore from the open pits, so during the 1890s and early twentieth century the streets of places like Virginia, Hibbing, and Chisholm were filled with Finns, Ukrainians, Yugoslavs, Ruthenians, Italians, Bulgarians, Hungarians, and many others. At the turn of the century nearly half of the Mesabi's people were foreign born; ten years later at the height of the Mesabi boom there were thirty-five identifiable ethnic groups on the Range.

Ethnic rivalry on the Range, with its inevitable social stratification and discrimination, led to street fights and knifings. The Range had an unsavory political reputation too, because of the Socialist leanings of many of the "Red" Finns who had fled from the Russian Empire. Gradually, however, mechanization reduced the size of the work force, dispersing some of the ethnic groups and thus hastening the process of assimilation. The ethnic diversity still remains—people of the Range are still conscious of their Italian or Yugoslav or Finnish origins, but more in the sense of a distinction that identifies but does not divide them.

About ninety-eight per cent of the nearly four million Minnesotans today are of European stock. The other two per cent of the population are primarily black, Indian, and chicano. Minnesota's 35,000 black citizens are located primarily in the Twin Cities and Duluth, but Minnesota's first blacks (including the famous George Bonga) were fur traders. During the Civil War other blacks came to St. Paul as steamboat laborers, but the major movement occurred after World War I as part of the northern shift of blacks that led to huge black populations in Chicago and Detroit.

Minnesota's Indian element, which numbered 23,000 in the 1970 census, is naturally dominated by the Chippewa and Sioux. Although there are still Sioux communities in rural southern Minnesota and Chippewa reservations in northern Minnesota, the Indian population has shifted drastically since 1960.

Today the majority of Minnesota's Indians live in Minneapolis and St. Paul. The development of the urban Indian community must be attributed to the lack of opportunity in rural areas rather than to the attractions of the cities. This movement coincided with a new Indian self-consciousness, and the Twin Cities have become one of the main centers of the American Indian Movement.

Minnesota's chicano population, which in 1970 included over 4,000 permanent residents and perhaps as many as 12,000 transients, resulted mainly from the state's need for seasonal harvest workers. Even before the turn of the century, some Minnesota sugar beet farmers recruited Mexican laborers, and the World War I labor shortage intensified the hiring of Mexicans to work not only in the beet fields but in the vegetable and potato fields and the canning plants. The largest permanent chicano settlement is in St. Paul, but there are chicanos represented also in the Red River Valley communities and the canning towns of southern Minnesota such as St. James, Fairmont, Le Sueur, and Owatonna.

Urbanization has unavoidably altered the original patterns of settlement in Minnesota, so much so that the largest representation of any given ethnic group is likely to be in the metropolitan area. Nonetheless, the ethnic heritage remains. Minnesota's calendar abounds in ethnic observations—Kolacky Days in New Prague, Polka Days in New Ulm, Robert Burns Day in Mapleton, and St. Patrick's Day in St. Paul. The Swedes across the state observe St. Lucia's Day, *Svenskarnes Dag;* Norwegians, *Syttende Mai;* and St. Paul sponsors an annual Festival of Nations. It is possible, of course, to single out particular ethnic contributions—the Germans to the art of brewing, the Danes to the development of the dairy co-operatives, the Scandinavians generally to education. But the greatest impact Minnesota's broad ethnic base has had may simply be that Minnesotans have a heightened awareness of the diversity that has created both Minnesota as a state and the nation as a whole.

7

Three Frontiers

$\mathcal{M}$INNESOTA was blessed with three frontiers that attracted distinct types of pioneers: lumbermen who reaped the waiting harvest in the vast coniferous forests; farmers who claimed the fertile soil of the west and south; and miners, both big businessmen and common laborers, who extracted the iron from the northern ranges. Although geography molded the economic diversity of the land, to a large degree time and circumstance governed the rapidity with which these frontiers developed.

In the second half of the nineteenth century great changes were wrought by the Industrial Revolution. These changes, especially improved transportation, major advances in technology, and the restructuring of the old economic and social orders, all contributed to Minnesota's headlong rush from frontier to modern state. Because of the vast undeveloped resources at their command, Minnesotans were able to apply technological advances and make significant contributions to the new order. Huge quantities of Minnesota's high-grade lumber were used to build cities and railroads, enough ore was extracted from the ranges to make Minnesota the ranking iron-ore producer in the nation, and Minnesota revolutionized the flour-milling industry.

The pioneer farmers who moved into Minnesota Territory knew of railroads, since many of them had come by rail at least part of the way to the frontier, and they knew that eventually they would come to rely on railroads to transport their produce. But they also knew that it took time to break the virgin land and produce paying crops and were prepared for those lean subsistence years. Most of these pioneer farmers realized, too, that it took time to learn the land's vagaries. The elements were immutable; man was powerless to lengthen the growing season, and so he had to adapt his crops, his animals, and himself to the conditions imposed by nature.

Thousands of those first pioneers had been inspired by visions of Minnesota as a veritable wilderness garden, and initially they did harvest wild fruits, berries, and nuts and hunted, trapped, and fished to fill their larders. But these people had come to farm, and as soon as they could break a bit of ground, they planted. Because they did not know what Minnesota's soil and growing season would produce, they tried a little of everything. At first the farm products were used by the farmers themselves or else bartered at the local markets, but all the while they were searching for a fast-growing, profitable cash crop that could be exported.

In 1859 nearly a third of the total grain produced was corn, followed closely by potatoes, wheat, and oats. That same year, Minnesotans also harvested orchard products, hops, flax fiber, hemp, nearly 40,000 pounds of tobacco, and over 3,000 pounds of rice. Even silk cocoons and wine from cultured grapes were reported in the agricultural census. Ironically, most farmers who had money during that depression year earned it by digging and selling the wild ginseng root which abounded throughout the Big Woods and adjacent deciduous forest areas. The root, much in demand in China where it was prized for its purported medicinal properties, remained an important Minnesota export during the early Civil War years and was lauded by many as Minnesota's salvation during those lean times.

In the late 1850s wheat was produced in sufficient quantities so that some was exported, and more and more farmers became convinced that wheat was where prosperity lay. By 1860, production more than doubled and for the first time wheat became the state's ranking crop. Production accelerated throughout the Civil War and afterward, until by 1870 Minnesota was the twelfth-ranking wheat producer in the United States. Within another decade, it had moved into fifth place. In 1868 a writer for *Harper's Magazine,* ignoring both other states and other crops in Minnesota, declared that "Minnesota is pre-eminently the wheat growing State of the Union. . . . Owing to the peculiarity of her climate and soil, she is the best adapted of any of the States to the raising of this staple. Wheat is in fact almost her exclusive object of production. None farm here except for this." [1]

Wheat was never Minnesota's only crop, but it was clearly king during the 1860s and 1870s. The high point in its relative importance was reached in 1878 when nearly seventy per cent of all the state's tilled land was planted with wheat. Production continued to rise until 1902, and the censuses of both 1890 and 1900 showed Minnesota to be the nation's leading wheat producer. But millions of acres of the state's frontier land were opened and the percentage of wheat in relation to other crops declined. The record year in terms of bushels of wheat harvested was 1902, but by that time only thirty per cent of the state's cultivated land was in wheat.

Today pictures of vast fields of golden wheat are associated with the Great Plains and it is difficult to envision southeastern Minnesota with its timbered areas, dairy farms, and corn fields as a wheat belt; but throughout the frontier era in the northern United States wheat was the traditional staple crop because in comparison with other crops it demanded less soil preparation and cultivation. In fact, it usually could be planted profitably the first year after the tough prairie sod was broken.

Many Minnesota farmers tried corn at first, but they soon found that the heavy, root-packed prairie ground required repeated workings before the soil was mellow enough for corn's deep roots. The farmers who sowed wheat rather than corn, having come from milder climates, tended at first to plant the varieties of winter wheat that they were accustomed to raising.

1. G. W. Schatzel, "The Wheat Fields of Minnesota," in *With Various Voices,* p. 143.

Hard experiences with winter kill, however, very rapidly caused them to shift to spring wheat that could be planted in April and harvested in late July to mid-August. Although the land was not being used intensively, it did not matter to farmers because frontier land was plentiful and cheap; besides, there was a cash market for wheat, which there was not for other Minnesota grains in the 1860s and 1870s. Minnesota's wheat boom also coincided with advances in farm mechanization which made it possible for farmers to handle larger and larger acreages during the short harvest season.

Though vast acres of fertile, cheap land lay waiting to be cultivated, frontier farmers were inhibited by a limited capacity to work the land. Many of Minnesota's first wheat farmers cut grain with a cradle scythe. A good man working long days with such a scythe could cut only two to two and one half acres a day, and then there remained the laborious work of raking the grain, tying it into bundles, shocking it, and finally threshing it. Needless to say, the fields of the man who harvested in this manner were very small. There were mechanical reapers in existence; the first was invented by Cyrus McCormick in 1831, and during the 1850s it was improved with the addition of a self-rake. Some of these improved reapers were in use in Minnesota by the early 1860s, but what farmers really wanted was a machine that would tie the grain into bundles as well as cut it and rake it.

The development of such a binder was a real challenge. First it was necessary to invent a mechanical device that could tie knots, and then to find a suitable material to use for binding. A wire binder was perfected and patented in 1874 and immediately put to wide use, but just as immediately problems developed. Cattle and other animals were injured or killed by bits of wire buried in straw stacks, and wire in the harvested grain so damaged millstones that wheat containing wire particles was docked on the market. The twine binder, which finally reached the market sometime after 1875, remained the principal machine for cutting wheat and other small grains until the popularization of the combine. With a twine binder pulled by three or four horses, an operator could cut from ten to fifteen acres a day. At last the agonizingly slow task of raking loose grain and tying it by hand was eliminated.

While binding technology was being improved, so were threshing machines. In the 1860s, the most used thresher was a small machine powered by horses that walked on a treadmill, but during the 1870s steam threshers became a common sight. The first steam-powered machines were turned by small stationary steam engines whose furnaces burned wood, coal, or sometimes even straw, but a glimpse of better things to come was provided with the exhibit of a steam tractor at the Minnesota state fair in 1879.

These manifestations of the Industrial Revolution were the leavening in the rapid growth of Minnesota's three frontiers. After more than a decade of experimentation, wheat emerged as the sought-after cash crop, and its emergence coincided with improved methods of harvesting and with expanding railroad networks so that the tremendous yields could be marketed widely. Then, as the lumber frontier and the iron ranges boomed after the Civil War, they provided huge markets for wheat and other produce from the southern Minnesota agricultural frontier. The wheat farmer, the flour miller, and the lumberman had a common meeting place in Minneapolis, which, because it lay just south of the great coniferous forest and just north of the principal wheat area, was both a sawmilling and a flour-milling city. Minneapolis was in the 1870s, as the metropolitan area is today, the meeting place of east and west, of urban and rural, of industry and agriculture.

Until the early 1870s Minneapolis was just one of Minnesota's many flour-milling centers. During the 1860s the number of mills in Minnesota leaped from 81 to 507, most of them small-capacity mills that ground flour in return for a share. Most were water-powered, like the famous Archibald Mill at Dundas on the Cannon River, but some were steam-powered and there were even some of the Dutch windmill type, including the Seppman Mill near Mankato. Although the mills were found throughout the wheat area in the southern part of the state, the

greatest concentration was in the Cannon River towns—
Faribault, Dundas, and Northfield.

But there were also thirteen mills clustered around the Falls
of St. Anthony by 1870; and Minneapolis had the advantages of
not only bountiful waterpower, but a growing home market
because of its increasing urban population. These advantages
were sufficient to attract Cadwallader Washburn, a New Englander who had made a fortune in Wisconsin lumber and had
served as governor of that state. Washburn brought capital and
business acumen into flour milling along with the ambition that
was necessary to make it more than a local concern, and he led
the way in the development of the new technology which revolutionized flour milling.

Like all Minnesota millers, Washburn was confronted with
the problem of satisfactorily grinding spring wheat. Traditionally winter wheat had commanded higher prices than spring
wheat because it was softer and yielded white flour, much preferred by consumers, with much less processing than spring
wheat. But Minnesota was a spring-wheat area, so millers had
to work with a very hard grain that had a brittle bran coat.
When ground between the grist stones, all four parts of the
wheat kernel—the outer or bran coat, the thin layer of gluten
cells, the starchy interior which comprised most of the kernel,
and the embryo—were crushed together. Spring wheat crushed
in this fashion yielded an undesirable product. The bran flecks
made the flour dark and speckled, hence unappetizing to most
consumers, and the oily embryos caused the flour to turn rancid
rather quickly, which greatly inhibited storing and marketing.
With winter wheat, even though the soft gluten layer was
usually ground fine, the bran coats tended to stay whole and
could be sifted out, but with spring wheat the hard gluten layer
often broke into coarse particles that tended to separate from the
flour along with the bran. This was particularly distressing since
the gluten was not only the most nutritious part of the kernel but
also that element in the flour that enabled the baked product to
rise. Because spring wheat was richer in gluten, millers realized
that it had the potential to produce better flour than winter

wheat, but they had to find some way of grinding the gluten and the starch together and eliminating the bran. Hence by the late 1860s there was considerable talk about the need for a "middlings purifier"—middlings being the name given to the gluten and bran waste, which was sometimes ground into a course, dark, but very rich flour.

Some millers at Winona, Hastings, and Dundas discovered that they could produce superior flour by cracking the kernels instead of crushing them and then grinding the middlings after laboriously sifting out the bran, but this method was slow and not adaptable to large-scale production. Alexander Faribault, in the town of Faribault, pursued the idea of purifying the middlings by machine. Faribault brought a young French engineer, Edmund La Croix, to his mill to experiment with a purifier. La Croix and his brother were familiar with purifiers that had been used experimentally in France as early as 1860, and they built one for Faribault's mill in 1868 and used it for two years before the mill was destroyed by a flood.

Word of La Croix's device leaked out, and George Christian, who formed a partnership with Washburn in 1870, hired La Croix to perfect a purifier for Washburn's Minneapolis mill. La Croix and Christian worked on their project in secret. The Frenchman spent most of his time locked in a room at the mill, and by the spring of 1871 his completed machine was installed. Although inspired by earlier French models La Croix developed a unique device with moving sieves which were covered by an air blast that separated the bran coats from the middlings. The middlings, which at that point had only been cracked, not crushed, were then ground again, resulting in a fine, white flour rich in protein.

Flour milling changed dramatically with the advent of the "New Process" flour from Washburn's mills in 1871. For the first time it was possible to mass-produce high-grade white flour from spring wheat, and for the first time in history spring wheat was more in demand than winter wheat. Not only was spring wheat flour more nutritious, but about twelve and one half per cent more bread could be made from any given quantity of the

"New Process" flour; and the demand for Minneapolis flour soared.

The ability to produce "New Process" flour, also known as "Patent" flour because it was advertised as having resulted from a patented process, quickly spread to all Minneapolis millers. La Croix left Washburn and Christian and installed a purifier for a rival, and then the company's head miller, who had worked with La Croix, joined the Pillsbury Company. Millers reaped unprecedented returns from the "New Process" flour. Christian noted that "our profits the first year of the 'New Process' . . . were fifty cents a barrel, the second year they averaged a dollar a barrel, the third year two dollars, and the fourth year anywhere from four to four and [one] half dollars a barrel." [2] Washburn and Christian netted profits of $650,000 from a single mill over a three-year period. Because of the "New Process," flour milling became Minnesota's first big business and the demand for Minneapolis flour stimulated great expansion in the 1870s and 1880s.

Although the middlings purifier was an essential first step in modernizing flour milling, it added to the grist-milling process when millers were already plagued by fast wearing of the sandstone millstones. Not only was it costly and time-consuming to replace the stones, but as they wore down a fine grit was mixed with the flour, so Minneapolis millers looked about for some way of eliminating the stones. Because of their experience with the middlings purifier they looked to Europe for inspiration, and they found that many millers were replacing stones with rollers. Christian experimented with rollers as early as 1873 and within a few years many mills were using a combination of stones and rollers —stones to crack the wheat and rollers to refine it. But there were problems in how to arrange the rollers and questions as to whether porcelain or corrugated iron or steel was the best roller material. When Washburn and his new partner, John

2. Quoted in Charles Byron Kuhlmann, *The Development of the Flour-Milling Industry in the United States with Special Reference to the Industry in Minneapolis* (Boston: Houghton Mifflin Co., 1929), p. 119.

Crosby, learned that Hungarian millers who worked with wheat similar to Minnesota's were the leading developers of roller mills, they decided to send an agent to Budapest to learn Hungarian trade secrets. William de la Barre, a young Austrian engineer, found that when the Budapest "mill owners learned that I was from the United States, and particularly from Minneapolis, the doors of the mills were closed against me." [3] The enterprising de la Barre finally made arrangements with a Hungarian miller to visit a mill for a number of nights so he could study the practical application of its roller mills.

Upon de la Barre's return Washburn and Crosby completely equipped one of their mills with the "Hungarian method" of interspaced steel rollers which ground wheat into as many as eleven different grades of flour. The gradual reduction method (as it came to be called) soon completely replaced grist stones because the rollers could do more work with less power; they lasted much longer than the stones and were said to have increased flour yields.

The new technology exemplified by the middlings purifier and the gradual reduction process caused Minneapolis to rapidly emerge as the country's leading milling center. The genius of Washburn and the men he gathered around him did not lie in invention, but rather in the capacity of men like the La Croixs, Christian, and de la Barre to learn from others.

From 1870 to 1890 Minneapolis flour production rose from about 200,000 barrels annually to 7,000,000. Most of the capital and business experience behind flour-milling came from former lumbermen such as Cadwallader Washburn and his brother William D., Governor John S. Pillsbury, and Dorilus Morrison. Without the lumbering frontier so close, it is unlikely that Minneapolis would have had the capital to finance the new flour mills. As flour-milling expanded, the millers promoted railroads westward, not only to market flour but to tap the wheat lands of the distant Dakota and Montana prairies. With the extension of the Northern Pacific and the Great Northern through

3. Quoted in William G. Edgar, *The Medal of Gold: A Story of Industrial Achievement* (Minneapolis: The Bellman Co., 1925) pp. 106–107.

western Minnesota and North Dakota and the construction of the Milwaukee Road into South Dakota, Minneapolis was able to draw on a great wheat frontier at the very time that the importance of wheat as a crop in Minnesota was declining. Looking eastward, millers led by William D. Washburn promoted a shorter route to the markets in the United States and Europe through the construction of a railroad to Sault Ste. Marie in Upper Michigan. When the line was completed in 1887 it not only reduced shipping costs but freed the millers from the dominance of Chicago based railroads. Largely because of the combined interests of millers and lumbermen, Minneapolis emerged as the most important railroad center northwest of Chicago.

By 1890 Minneapolis claimed to be the world's leading wheat market, and its buyers were exporting wheat as well as selling to local millers. In its marketing role Minneapolis became the center for great grain storage facilities and the headquarters for the companies that operated railroad line elevators. Flour milling also stimulated banking in Minneapolis. Millers had to buy wheat for cash during the short harvest season and then store it until it was needed. This holding operation demanded great amounts of capital; as the leading millers became active in organizing banks, the city became a major financial center. All this activity contributed to the city's growth and made a very broad hinterland dependent upon it: thousands of farmers or their suppliers who ultimately sold wheat in Minneapolis tended to look to the "Mill City" as the source of farm machinery and other manufactured products and capital.

Flour milling also spurred related manufacturing in Minneapolis. In the early years flour was generally marketed in barrels, so numerous cooperage firms sprang into being. Later, when cloth and paper bags replaced the barrels, the city became an important manufacturing center for these products and by the mid-1920s only St. Louis surpassed Minneapolis in the production of bags. Flour milling also ultimately stimulated allied food businesses. During the early twentieth century the increasing popularity of durum wheat flour, which was better suited for macaroni and spaghetti products than for bread, caused these businesses to develop in Minneapolis; during the 1890s various cereal manufacturers were attracted because of the availability of the needed raw materials.

By the 1870s much of the Minnesota land that had been planted to wheat year after year was nearly exhausted, and crop rotation seemed the most feasible way to improve it. At the same time, wheat farmers found land values rising simply because the country was becoming settled. Increased occupancy drove the original frontier prices of a few dollars an acre to $40 or more in just a few years. The wheat farmer could afford to cultivate a staple crop on cheap land, but increasingly expensive land accompanied by rising property taxes forced him to look for ways to use his ground during more of the year in order to realize larger returns.

There were other problems, too—stem rust, discriminatory railroad rates, questionable elevator practices, and insects. Wheat farmers, or anyone who raised crops to sell, had to sell immediately after the harvest and so were especially vulnerable to railroad rate fixing. In order to meet increased costs, many farmers tried to produce more, which only forced many to mortgage their farms to buy more machinery. Wheat farmers complained that they were also bilked by the grading and weighing done by the elevator companies controlled by railroads and millers.

In the midst of these concerns Minnesota farmers were ravaged by the great "Grasshopper Plague." For five successive summers waves of "hoppers" (actually Rocky Mountain locusts) swept over most of western and southern Minnesota. They chewed wheat to ground level, sometimes denuded trees, and even ate the paint from buildings. Stories of the Grasshopper Plague contain a certain grim humor. One oft-repeated tale was about the farmer who abandoned his horses to an advancing horde only to return later to find two of the gargantuan hoppers pitching horseshoes to decide which one got to eat the farmer. In desperation farmers devised tar traps which were pulled through the fields, but they were more a gesture of defiance than an effective destroyer. In 1877 the state of Minnesota offered bounties for the insects and their eggs and Governor John Pillsbury finally proclaimed April 26, 1877, a day of prayer and fasting in the hope that it would help lift the plague from the land. At last by 1878 the locust cycle had run its course, but many people believed they would return, and in part because of that belief wheat farmers looked to new ventures such as dairying which seemed to promise more insurance than a staple crop.

Although wheat persisted after 1880 in much of southwestern Minnesota and in the Red River Valley, where it was well suited to the valley's bonanza farms, there was a decided shift to diversification in the older farming sections of southeastern Minnesota. Finally, over a period of about thirty years, nearly all of the old wheat lands were diversified. This trend, hailed by its advocates as Minnesota's road to economic salvation, was characterized by an increasing emphasis on scientific agriculture. The old cross breeds were replaced with purebred livestock, farmers engaged in systematic crop rotation, and crops and animals suited to Minnesota's rigorous climate were developed. Dairying in particular emerged during the diversification movement, and during the 1880s and 1890s Minnesota became one of the leading dairy states, a status it has enjoyed since. Minnesota's pioneer dairymen exhibited their products throughout the United States, and their prize-winning displays along with displays of Minnesota wheat and flour at the Pan-American Exposition in Buffalo, New York, in 1901 earned the Gopher State yet another nickname—"the Bread and Butter state," a reference still heard on occasion today.

Dairying during the 1880s was aided by a number of developments, including the silo, the cream separator, and the Babcock milk fat test. This test provided a simple method of measuring the richness of milk, and it encouraged better feeding practices and the search for better milk producers. The growing concept of year-round dairying, however, necessitated changing the habits of the farmers. Traditional spring calving caused the market for dairy products to be depressed during the summer and fall because of the milk surplus and to be almost inactive during the winter when cows were dry. The solution, said Oren C. Gregg of Marshall, was to breed some of the cows to calve in the fall. Gregg, as superintendent of the University of Minnesota's Farmers' Institutes, traveled throughout the farming sections of the state urging farmers to accept his advice. His zeal caused some local wits to suggest that his middle initial stood for "cow," but Gregg is still remembered in Minnesota history as the "Father of Winter Dairying."

Winter dairying was only part of the answer. Dairymen still had much to learn about cattle breeds and feeding, and Theophilus L. Haecker, who came to the University of Minnesota Agriculture School in 1891, did more than any other individual to make Minnesota dairying scientific. He determined the most effective diets for milk cows, and he developed judging standards for the selection and breeding of cows. He also wrestled with the problem of the best type of animal for Minnesota's climate and finally concluded that the Holstein (now the commonest breed by far in Minnesota) was the most productive. Haecker also strove to improve the marketing of dairy products. After visiting the dairy co-ops organized by Danish immigrants of Clark's Grove near Albert Lea, Haecker concluded that this form of business, owned and managed by its own members, was very efficient, and his advocacy helped popularize the movement. By the 1930s the idea of participant-owned businesses had spread from dairying to elevator companies and other aspects of farm marketing and to such ventures as rural electrification projects. The co-op movement in Minnesota grew beyond Haecker's greatest expectations. In 1921 hundreds of co-ops united to form the Minnesota Cooperative Creameries Association, which began marketing its products under the "Land O Lakes" brand. The brand name was later given to the co-op, and since its inception Land O Lakes has been nationally famous.

Although the influence of scientists such as Haecker advanced dairying, one of its greatest boosts was given by private experimentation of Wendelin Grimm, a farmer. When Grimm moved to Carver County to farm in the late 1850s he carried with him some "everlasting clover" seed from his native Germany. He planted the seed and then carefully saved seeds from the plants that survived the winters, developing a hardy variety of alfalfa which proved to be a superlative cattle feed. Grimm did not brag about his accomplishment. Instead, he fed his own animals and said nothing. One of his neighbors recalled that Grimm's cattle were fat during the summer of 1863, a notorious drought year when corn was scarce. When the neighbor asked where Grimm had obtained his corn the response was: *"Kein Körnchen, nur ewiger Klee"* —"not one kernel, only everlasting clover." [4] Grimm's close neighbors imitated him, but as late as 1900 alfalfa was virtually nonexistent in Minnesota outside of Carver County. Then some of Grimm's seed was called to the attention of the University of Minnesota Agriculture School. During the decade from 1910 to 1920 Grimm Alfalfa finally emerged as a ranking forage crop, with a more than twenty-fold increase from the roughly two thousand acres planted in 1910.

Adaptation was also the key in developing other Minnesota crops. Peter M. Gideon did for apples what Grimm did for alfalfa. After moving to a farm on Lake Minnetonka in 1853 Gideon spent more than forty years experimenting with fruit that would thrive in spite of Minnesota's winters. His greatest accomplishment was the "Wealthy" apple, named after his wife, the former Wealthy Hall. Although apples grow fairly well throughout most of southern Minnesota, the area about La Crescent in the southeastern corner of the state has emerged as the state's apple center.

While Minnesota's farmers were struggling to adapt their crops to the land, its lumbermen were harvesting a crop that nature had planted centuries before. The common frontier references to the coniferous forest zone as the "pineries" belied the region's complexity, for most of that forest was actually made up of spruce, balsam fir, tamarack, white cedar, and jack pine intermingled with large stands of deciduous trees such as scrub oak, maple, birch, and aspen. Some of the coveted white pine was found in every county east of the Mississippi, but the richest stands were in an arc that swung southwestward from Duluth through the Snake River area and then westward across the Rum River south of Mille Lacs Lake before turning north and following the Mississippi to about Leech Lake. Within this

---

4. Quoted in Everett E. Edwards and Horace H. Russell, "Wendelin Grimm and Alfalfa," *Minnesota History* 19 (March 1938):22.

arc, the best white pine lands were in Carlton County near present Cloquet.

Even within its favorite habitat the white pine did not exist as a continuous forest. Stands of it were usually scattered among other trees, a circumstance which hindered cutting operations, for as long as there was white pine the lumbermen wanted nothing else. As they ferreted out the prized pine they destroyed thousands of other trees and, more seriously, increased the dangers of forest fires by abandoning their waste among the trees they bypassed in their unrelenting pursuit.

In the eyes of the lumberman, the white pine was without fault. It was a large tree, usually 120 to 160 feet tall with a diameter of two and a half to three feet at its base, and sometimes it reached heights of 200 feet with a five-foot base. Its wood was strong, odorless, and so soft and straight-grained that usable boards could be split off with a broadax. Its lightness gave it a buoyancy in streams where hardwoods would have sunk, and its lumber was comparatively long lasting. Because of these virtues the tree had been prized since colonial times, when it was cut in New England for ships' masts for the Royal Navy and for merchant vessels. Later generations of lumbermen followed the trail of the white pine, felling it along Michigan and Wisconsin streams before they reached Minnesota.

Although the lumbering frontier generally moved from New England westward, it did so rather haphazardly. Before railroads, lumbermen were almost completely dependent on river transportation for their logs. As long as there was white pine to the west they found it much easier to leapfrog to virgin forests along a navigable stream than to haul logs from the interior to the rivers. Thus New England lumbermen became interested in the forests of the upper St. Croix even though millions of acres of white pine remained in Michigan and Wisconsin.

The desire to open the pine lands on the upper St. Croix was one of the reasons for the Chippewa and Sioux treaties of 1837. In fact, even before the treaties had been ratified eager Yankee lumbermen had staked claims along the St. Croix. The first sawmilling town was Marine on St. Croix, but it was soon surpassed by Stillwater. The lumber that supplied Stillwater's mills generally came from the Snake River, a Minnesota tributary to the St. Croix. The town's first market was downstream to St. Louis and to intervening points like Hannibal, Missouri, and Clinton and other river towns in Iowa. In the beginning, Marine on St. Croix and Stillwater lumbermen marketed only cut lumber; but as the pace of harvesting picked up and as demand increased, they began selling rafts of whole logs which were sawed after they reached their destinations. Before 1851 Stillwater's market was small and almost entirely downriver, but after the Sioux treaties the territorial population boom created an immediate and heavy home demand for Minnesota pine lumber.

Stillwater dominated antebellum lumbering, but it had its rivals. St. Anthony Falls became a booming lumber center drawing on the pineries along the Rum River, and both Stillwater and St. Anthony were challenged by Winona, which lay further from the pine forests but closer to the ready market in the rich farm belt of southern Minnesota. Winona, on the banks of the Mississippi, deserved its title as the gateway to the west, for the nearest stream navigable by steamboats to the west of Winona was the Minnesota River, with its elbow at Mankato 120 miles distant. Much of that intervening space could easily be supplied by wagon from Winona; but Stillwater, upstream from Winona and with no access to the Minnesota River, could not touch the southern Minnesota market, and St. Anthony lumbermen who traded up the Minnesota to St. Peter and Mankato were severely hampered by the seasonal nature of steamboating. Because of this, Winona controlled the sale of lumber in well over half of the area between the Mississippi and Minnesota rivers.

Winona's first sawmill was started in 1855, the same year that John Laird and his brothers began marketing lumber bought from mills along the St. Croix and Chippewa rivers in Wisconsin. Two years later the Lairds, who had been joined by their cousins, James and Matthew Norton, opened their own mill at Winona and began processing logs floated down from Minnesota and Wisconsin streams. The cousins later organized the business as Laird, Norton Company and it ultimately became one of the largest lumbering companies in the entire Upper Mis-

sissippi region, though Winona was never quite able to over-
come the lead of Stillwater and St. Anthony.

Logs and lumber were the major exports of territorial Minnesota; in fact until about 1860 lumbering surpassed agriculture
as Minnesota's most lucrative business. The 1860 census
showed commercial lumbering in three Minnesota counties—
Hennepin, where St. Anthony Falls was located; Washington,
with mills at Stillwater and Marine on St. Croix; and Winona.
Washington County produced an estimated $400,000 worth of
lumber, while Hennepin and Winona counties had about one
half and one fourth of that respectively. While lumbering was
the state's foremost economic activity, even after two decades
of harvesting it was still a fairly small business. In terms of cutting, the forests had barely been touched. Coupled with sparse
population and the fallacious belief that the white pine belt
stretched all the way from the Snake and Rum rivers to Canada,
the slow pace of development helped create the myth of the in-
exhaustible forests.

James Madison Goodhue promoted Minnesota Territory by
prophesying that "centuries will hardly exhaust the pineries
above us," [5] and an early St. Anthony mill manager was convinced that the Run River pineries alone would supply seventy
mills for seventy years. These men would not have believed that
nearly all of Minnesota's white pine would be gone in seventy
years. In 1871 Hans Mattson, trying to attract immigrants, proclaimed that "the great forests will for hundreds of years furnish
work for loggers at the same time that sawmills and other factories using lumber will need large numbers of workers. . . ." [6]
Those who tried to stimulate lumbering did not seem to realize
that even when pines of all types were counted—including the
lowly jack pine—less than one fifth of Minnesota's total forest
area was pine.

During the quarter-century following the Civil War, Min-

5. *Minnesota Pioneer*, April 8, 1852, as quoted in Berthel, *Horns of Thunder*,
p. 81.

6. Quoted in Agnes M. Larson, *History of the White Pine Industry in Minnesota*
(Minneapolis: University of Minnesota Press, 1949), p. 70.

nesota lumbering truly became a big business. In 1857, the last year of territorial status, the log cut was about 100,000,000 board feet; the yield of 1869 was more than double that amount and production again doubled during both the 1870s and the 1880s. In 1889 over one billion board feet were harvested and Minnesota had risen from fourteenth to fourth in rank as a lumber state.

Postwar expansion was spurred by the rapid settlement of the treeless Great Plains states, which looked to Minnesota for building materials; by the construction of a railroad network; and by the sharp population rise in Minnesota. As Minnesota's prairies were being occupied by wheat farmers in the 1870s and 1880s so also were much of the enormous grasslands of Kansas, Nebraska, the Dakotas, and Montana. Most of the prairie homesteaders first lived in sod shanties or tarpaper shacks, but these were conditions they tolerated only until they had the wherewithal to buy pine lumber and build more substantial dwellings. Minnesota became both the supplier of the pine and the recipient of the wheat produced by the prairie settlers. Not only was Minnesota's pine used for the construction of thousands of farm buildings on the plains; it also built hundreds of towns and cities that sprang up on America's last frontier—cities like Miles City, Bismarck, Sioux Falls, Omaha, Wichita. Even the railroads that carried the pine to the settlers depended on lumbermen for ties and other construction materials to extend their lines west.

Despite the advent of Minnesota railroads, much of the state's lumber and some of its logs were floated down the Mississippi—mainly to St. Louis—until the early twentieth century. In 1882, a record year, St. Louis received over 160 million board feet of white pine lumber from the Upper Mississippi. Much of this was used locally, but the city was also the chief emporium for a broad trade area that stretched to distant New Mexico.

Increased demand after the Civil War turned Minneapolis into the greatest sawmilling center in Minnesota and, in time, in the nation and the world. Minneapolis on the west bank of the Mississippi and St. Anthony on the east merged in 1872, so the story of lumbering in Minneapolis is really a continuation of the

St. Anthony saga. As lumbermen moved beyond the Rum River and further up the Mississippi, Minneapolis remained the natural destination for logs floated downstream.

Because of its railroads Minneapolis developed outlets in all directions. The completion of the St. Paul and Sioux City line in 1872 through the Minnesota River Valley to Mankato and then by way of St. James and Worthington through southwestern Minnesota opened parts of Minnesota and northwestern Iowa and gave Minneapolis vital connections with Sioux City, Omaha, Kansas City, and points west. In most years well over half of the line's tonnage consisted of westbound lumber and eastbound wheat. Other sections of southern Minnesota fell within Minneapolis's sphere with the construction of the Iowa and Minnesota Railroad and the Minneapolis and St. Louis line, which was completed through Waseca and Albert Lea to connections at the Iowa boundary in 1877. Minneapolis reached out into the Red River Valley, North Dakota, and parts of Montana by way of the St. Paul and Pacific, the line later called the Great Northern, which was finally extended to the west coast in 1893 by James J. Hill.

During the 1880s Minneapolis businessmen led by William D. Washburn constructed yet another important railroad—the Minneapolis, St. Paul and Sault Ste. Marie. Washburn's primary goal was to bypass Chicago and give Minneapolis flour a direct market to the eastern states, but Washburn was a lumberman as well as a miller and clearly recognized the interdependence of the two industries in Minneapolis. He knew that the Soo Line would open new markets for Minneapolis flour and would give the city direct access to some of the finest forests in Minnesota and Wisconsin—forests that Minneapolis could not have tapped with river transportation.

During the twenty years from 1870 to 1890 Minnesota's population shot from 438,000 to nearly 1,300,000, and Minneapolis became the undisputed metropolitan center. Most of the towns and cities in western Minnesota were started during this time, most were built with Minneapolis lumber, and it was to Minneapolis mills that those prairie farmers sent their wheat. As the city was earning an international reputation as the "Mill City" because of flour manufacturing, many of its residents called it the "Sawdust Town." In 1870 there were 207 sawmills in Minnesota, but Minneapolis alone had thirteen clustered about St. Anthony Falls. Minneapolis sawmills increased in number as well as in size, but they still had difficulty meeting the demands of both the Twin Cities and the prairie hinterlands, so Minneapolis distributors imported lumber by river and by rail from other Minnesota and Wisconsin mills.

The city fed upon itself—the flour milling, the railroads, and the lumbering swelled the city's population of nearly 47,000 in 1880 to more than triple that during the next decade, when Minneapolis and St. Paul combined showed a growth of over a quarter of a million. To the immense housing needs of these people was added industrial construction—more flour mills, huge grain terminals, warehouses, and more sawmills. While Minneapolis had plenty of sawdust, it also had miles of muddy walkways much of the year which were improved by laying boardwalks. During 1887 the city used 6,000,000 feet of lumber to construct sixty-seven miles of boardwalk. Because the mills handled almost exclusively white pine, these boardwalks were probably made with some of the world's finest lumber.

There was still lumbering business enough left for Minneapolis's principal rivals, and both Stillwater and Winona grew also during the 1870s and 1880s. Stillwater continued to be a main supplier of both logs and lumber for points on the Mississippi and through her own rail connections supplied some of the western market, while Winona sawmillers cemented their hold on their trade area to the west by the extension of the Winona and St. Peter Railroad through Rochester, Owatonna, and Waseca and extended their business yet further when the line was pushed across Minnesota and eastern South Dakota to the Missouri River in the early 1880s.

Duluth became a lumber town when it was liberated from its isolation by the completion of a railroad to St. Paul in 1870. But even more important to the development of the quiet village on the shores of Lake Superior was its selection by Jay Cooke as the starting point for his great transcontinental railroad. As the Northern Pacific pushed westward, lumber from thousands of white pine was shipped from the Duluth area for its ties, trestles, and bridges. In 1871 the line was completed to Moorhead on the Red River and the next year it reached the Missouri River, where the town of Bismarck sprang up. The Panic of 1873 halted the line at Bismarck for six years, but when construction resumed, new markets for Duluth and Minneapolis lumber were opened along its route through western North Dakota and the Yellowstone River Valley of Montana.

The railroad which was so important in the marketing of Minnesota's lumber was the most conspicuous symbol of the state's abrupt entry into the new world of technology, but the actual process of lumbering was also affected by the Industrial Revolution. Lumbering, however, was not revolutionized overnight like flour milling through the development of a spectacular new process. Increased demand following the Civil War stimulated a series of technological innovations, and those in turn helped bring production to a peak—a peak which in turn contributed to the rapid denuding of the pine forests and the abrupt decline of frontier lumbering in Minnesota.

Lumbermen, like farmers and millers, looked for new devices and methods that would increase their speed, efficiency, and production. The urge to move faster became more pressing as the trees along navigable streams were cut away and the length of the haul from lumber camps to assembly points on a river or railroad became longer. The Yankees who made up Minnesota's first generation of lumberjacks called upon their New England experience, and they cut trees during the winter months when frozen ground and snow facilitated dragging them to a river bank. Then with the opening of navigation the logs were guided by teams of men called "river pigs" to places like Stillwater or Minneapolis where they were either milled or formed into rafts for downstream markets.

Later lumbermen continued this pattern of cutting during the winter and moving logs to market during the navigation season, but their nearly frenetic efforts to keep apace of the burgeoning market led to important changes. During the 1870s and 1880s lumbermen turned to the peavey and the cant hook, and they used spar lines to load log sleighs and railroad cars. The yoke-shaped go-devil which could carry but a single log was replaced by the dray, a heavy sleigh capable of hauling thousands of board feet of logs in a single load. Lumbermen also began using horses instead of the plodding oxen and they learned to ice their roads. During the 1890s ice roads became yet more sophisticated as a special rutting device was developed which cut tracks for the sleigh runners in the haul roads and made it necessary to ice only the ruts rather than the entire surface of the road. The use of steam tractors on farms led lumbermen to believe that some type of machine could be developed for use in the forest, and by the late 1880s there was some experimentation in the logging areas with steam traction engines. Though these steam loggers (which had both sled runners and caterpillar-like tracks) were used to some extent, they were never very popular because of their high price and operating costs. Then, as the movement away from the rivers accelerated, narrow-gauge lumbering railroads came into widespread use in the 1890s and early twentieth century. All of these advances in the practical aspects of cutting occurred at a most auspicious time. Up to this point, sawmilling had been a navigation season business because the logs had to be moved through mill ponds, but the development of the "warm water pond" in which an agitator kept the water from freezing enabled mills to saw year round, and the cutting of timber proceeded at a yet more rapacious rate.

The high point came in 1899 when Minnesota's production of over two billion board feet made it the third-ranking lumber state, the highest position it ever attained. The 1899 production, which was roughly double that of ten years earlier, declined gradually until about 1905, and Minnesota dropped to fifth position. Then production plummeted quickly as dozens of Minnesota mills closed and entrepreneurs shifted to the Pacific Northwest. By the early 1920s Minnesota lumber yards depended primarily on Pacific Northwest imports. Finally the large white pine mill at Virginia closed in 1929 and the last major log drive on Rainy Lake, the scene of some of the last extensive cutting of virgin timber in Minnesota, took place five years later.

The leveling of the forests was far more sudden and ultimately more calamitous than most of the participants anticipated. Lumbermen knew that the virgin forests were going to disappear, but they simply went on doing what they had always done. Lumber was the stuff out of which cities and fortunes were made, and when technological improvements enabled men to cut and mill faster, they did. Most lumbermen were spurred by increased competition, especially after Michigan lumberers swarmed into Minnesota in the 1890s following the depletion of Michigan's white pine. As they battled each other for a larger share of the white pine market they also feared competition from the yellow pine of the South and Douglas fir and western pine of the Pacific Northwest, so they increased production merely to retain their relative share of the market. They were also influenced by Minnesota's sorry record of disastrous forest fires like the awful Hinckley fire of 1894 and the Chisholm fire of 1908. These and hundreds of lesser fires meant the loss of thousands of acres of Minnesota's coniferous forests. It has been estimated, in fact, that more of Minnesota's forest was lost to fire than was cut by lumbermen, and the ruinous conflagrations were seized upon as an excuse to cut faster before more timber was lost to the flames. An unusual marketing situation stimulated cutting, too. The opening of the Vermilion and Mesabi iron ranges created heavy local demand for white pine as thousands of buildings were flung up during the iron ore boom. As this was occurring there was an increased market for Minnesota's pine in the east because Michigan and Wisconsin production had slackened. Lumbermen also cut rapidly in order to lower their property tax liability because the taxes were lower on cutover land than on timbered land. Lumbermen justified the denuding of the forest, too, by telling themselves that they were the cutting edge of another farmers' frontier—that they were helping to pave the way for cultivation of the land. This sentiment was so strong in lumbering areas during the 1890s and early 1900s that conservation efforts were usually criticized as nothing more than deterrents to agricultural development. As one looks at the rocky, rugged terrain in much of northern Minnesota today, it is difficult to see how they could have so deluded themselves.

Frontier lumbering was of brief duration, but it affected Minnesota in a multitude of ways. Lumbering helped populate Minnesota by providing employment for thousands of men; it provided inexpensive building materials for farms, and for towns and cities. Pioneer lumbermen lent their considerable influence to the formation of Minnesota Territory, and they participated in the drive for Sioux land cessions in southern Minnesota which expanded agricultural development that in turn provided foodstuffs for the lumber camps. A number of virgin areas in central, eastern, and northern Minnesota were opened up because of lumbering. Sawmilling was the first industry of places like Stillwater, St. Cloud, Little Falls, Brainerd, Duluth, and Virginia. Lumbering and sawmilling were the most important businesses of frontier Bemidji and International Falls, and lumbering ranked next to flour milling as the major industry in Minneapolis for almost forty years.

Lumbering provided the first major accumulation of capital in Minnesota—capital that was used to start or to encourage other businesses. Lumbering capital promoted banking, railroad construction, and flour milling. Virtually all of the early important banks in Stillwater, Minneapolis, and Duluth were organized by lumbermen. Some lumbermen (such as Dorilus Morrison, who was also a banker) lent capital to railroads, and the millions of dollars needed to modernize flour milling came from such former lumber barons as John Pillsbury and Cadwallader Washburn.

Lumbermen actively supported charitable, educational, and cultural institutions. William H. Laird assisted Carleton College, the Pillsburys generously donated funds to the University of Minnesota during the 1800s when state support was niggardly, and the Weyerhaeuser family assisted Macalester College in St. Paul, the Forestry School of Yale University, and many other institutions. Amherst H. Wilder of St. Paul, who had investments in lumbering, provided for a charitable foundation which is very active yet today, and Thomas B. Walker, using his personal collection of paintings and sculpture as a base, established the Walker Art Gallery in Minneapolis.

Minnesota politics and government were conditioned by lumbering. The state through the office of the surveyor general provided a registration service for log brands and in its efforts to stimulate frontier expansion sold quantities of state lands to lumbermen at minimum prices. Liberal, permissive state legislation also facilitated the construction of numerous dams which were needed to raise water levels for moving logs. Some individuals associated with lumbering were politically active. Franklin Steele was a power behind the throne in the early Democratic Party in Minnesota. William Holcombe, the Stillwater lumberman active in the formation of Minnesota, served as the state's first lieutenant governor, Dorilus Morrison was the first mayor of Minneapolis, and David Marston Clough served as state governor from 1895 to 1899.

The entrepreneurs of lumbering left a Minnesota legacy, but so, too, did the lumberjacks who labored in the rough and rugged camps and by night regaled themselves with tall tales traditional to the lumbering industry. They told stories about strange forest creatures like the monkey-like agropelter that killed unwary lumberjacks by flinging hefty branches down on them; the hugag, a moose-like animal with jointless legs who slept by leaning on trees; and the sidehill gouger, a fascinating gopher-like beast which had shorter legs on its uphill side and so was committed to a life of moving around hills in the same direction. Interestingly, the lumberjacks talked little and perhaps not at all about the best-known folk hero of lumbering—Paul Bunyan. Paul is, to a large degree, the creation of various twentieth-century imaginations.

Extensive interviewing by Minnesota's foremost historian of lumbering, Agnes Larson, failed to uncover a single person who during the time he had worked in the Minnesota lumber camps had heard of Paul. The plethora of Bunyan literature began with the publication of an article in the Detroit, Michigan, *News-Tribune* of July 24, 1910. This first story, written by James McGillivray, contained some of the larger-than-life aspects of a genuine American folk hero; but such embellishments as Paul's blue ox, Babe, whose footsteps formed lakes and who could drink a river dry in one gulp, were added later and say far more for the American fascination with gargantuanism than for frontier knowledge of Paul Bunyan. During the twenty years following the appearance of McGillivray's story dozens of Bunyan tales and books were published, and the impression left was that they were tales directly from lumber camps.

Nonetheless, Paul has captured the American imagination and has a particular place in Minnesota lore because many of the Bunyan tales have Minnesota settings. The legend is further fed by the large statue of Paul that stands on the lake shore at Bemidji and by the Paul Bunyan Center at Brainerd which features a massive concrete Paul who greets thousands of children by name every year.

Throughout the 1880s, despite age-old rumors of mineral wealth and confirmed findings of iron ore, there was little speculation about the potential for iron mining in northern Minnesota. Yet barely more than a quarter-century after the first ore was taken from the Soudan Mine near Lake Vermilion in 1884, the Vermilion Range was fully developed, the Mesabi Range had become the largest iron ore producer in the nation, and the Cuyuna Range was opened. The discovery of the Vermilion Range in the 1880s and the Mesabi in the 1890s caused a boom unprecedented in the history of Minnesota's frontier. As thousands of iron-seekers and attendant businesses were drawn to the new-found riches, towns sprang up on the Vermilion and Mesabi with a spontaneity common to gold rushes. In just a few years places like Tower, Ely, Virginia, Hibbing, Mountain Iron, and Chisholm mushroomed from straggling camps to small cities, and Duluth, the emporium of a vast mining and lumbering region, rapidly changed from a small, isolated frontier town to a minor metropolis.

Tales of the valuable minerals of Lake Superior date as far back as the era of the French voyageurs. The French learned about copper in Upper Michigan from Indians who had used it for centuries, and they assumed that the region held vast, unknown mineral wealth. Although the French made no effort to develop Lake Superior mines, their belief that the land was mineral laden was perpetuated by the British and passed on to the Americans. The United States through Lewis Cass, governor of Michigan Territory and territorial superintendent of Indian affairs, reserved mineral rights in northern Minnesota in an 1826 treaty with the Chippewa even though there was no proof of the existence of copper or iron or anything else. The old beliefs were given yet more substance when Daniel Webster, writing under the name of President John Tyler, defended the Webster–Ashburton Treaty on the grounds that the region between the St. Louis and Pigeon rivers, later known as the Arrowhead Region, had valuable mineral deposits. Although Webster was propagandizing, his message proved to be that of a seer when members of a United States Geological Survey team reported the discovery of iron ore near Gunflint Lake in 1850.

This find caused Governor Alexander Ramsey to urge further investigation of the territory's mineral potential. Later territorial and state governors also encouraged such investigation, and finally in 1865 the legislature appropriated funds to hire a state geologist who was to reconnoiter the Vermilion Range. Henry H. Eames was hired for the task, and he and his brother Richard brought back far better news than anyone had expected. Eames had not found significant iron deposits, but he had discovered mineral-bearing quartz, which the chief assayer of the federal mint in Philadelphia determined would yield $25.63 in gold and $4.42 in silver to the short ton.

Eames's find created an immediate sensation. Rumors of gold at Oronoco on the Zumbro River in Olmsted County in 1858 had attracted gold-seekers who were soon disappointed. Others left the state for the Pike's Peak and Fraser River gold fields. When the news of Eames's discovery was circulated, it reached an audience that wanted to believe, and the Vermilion Lake Gold Rush of 1865–1866 was on. As the hopeful beat a path to Vermilion Lake a wagon road was opened from Duluth, and a town of several hundred with all the trappings of the western gold rush towns sprang up. All that was lacking was gold. None of the would-be miners found gold-bearing quartz, and the rush ended as suddenly as it had begun. The spot where Eames had found gold was never determined.

Although the Vermilion gold rush was a bust, it had significant implications. The improved road made the area more accessible and some of the prospectors, including George Stuntz of Duluth, came away convinced that valuable iron ore deposits lay near Vermilion Lake. Stuntz, who had at one time been a United States government surveyor, had started a trading post along the Duluth harbor in 1852. Five years later the town was formed by a union of little settlements, and Stuntz believed that it was destined to become the commercial center of the northwest. The opening in 1855 of a canal through the troublesome Sault Ste. Marie connecting Lakes Superior and Huron brightened Duluth's prospects, and the growth of the city seemed further assured when it became the eastern terminus of the Northern Pacific. But Stuntz and fellow promoter George Stone envisioned Duluth as more than a shipper of wheat and lumber. They believed that its development—and for that matter the development of the whole of northern Minnesota—depended on mining and marketing iron ore.

But they were men of little means. They knew that unlike a gold prospector with a pan who might strike it rich and be able to walk out with his find, the aspiring iron miner had to think of sinking shafts, of managing large crews of experienced miners, of constructing railroads from mine to lake and then building ore docks to facilitate loading into Great Lakes ships. Stuntz and Stone were superficially familiar with the problems of iron mining because the Marquette Range of Upper Michigan had been producing ore since the 1840s. It was in fact this Michigan success that stimulated the search for ore west of Lake Superior. With a knowledge of the existence of ore on the Vermilion Range and some understanding of the complexity of mining and marketing ore, but without funds, Stuntz and Stone could only turn to the capitalists.

Their selection of Charlemagne Tower was logical. Tower was an attorney for various Pennsylvania iron mining companies and the agent for a number of eastern investors. He was intrigued by the specimens of ore shown to him by Stone, but before committing himself to an investment of several million dollars he needed further proof. So Tower and another sponsor,

Samuel A. Munson of Utica, New York, commissioned a private geological reconnaissance of the Vermilion Range. On two occasions, in 1875 and in 1880, Professor Albert Chester of Hamilton College, New York, was guided over the Vermilion by the knowledgeable Stuntz. Chester was impressed by outcroppings of iron-bearing rock and by formations that resembled those of Michigan's Marquette Range, so he strongly recommended to Tower that the range be developed. In the course of his investigations Chester was led over the eastern part of the Mesabi Range, but he saw nothing noteworthy. If Chester had had more time and more curiosity Tower might have been in a position to exploit what eventually proved to be the richest range of all.

After Chester's second expedition Tower, along with his son Charlemagne Tower, Jr., and Stone and Stuntz, organized the Minnesota Iron Company. Through Stone, who was then a member of the Minnesota legislsture, Tower made it clear that he expected concessions from the state to encourage his venture. The state legislature approved a measure under which the Minnesota Iron Company would be taxed only a penny a ton on all ore mined or shipped. Although this seemed much too generous to later critics who railed about eastern exploitation of Minnesota, it was understandable at a time when the young frontier state hungrily sought any type of industrial development. Once the tax question had been resolved, Tower and his associates opened the Soudan Mine on the south side of Vermilion Lake.

Although the first ore was found near the surface, it soon became apparent that most of the hard ore was in a vertical formation which would have to be mined by underground methods. This necessitated the importation of skilled miners, so Tower hired Cornishmen and Swedes from the Marquette Range and put them to work on the Soudan Mine. To move the ore from the mine to Lake Superior, Tower sought the shortest possible route: from Lake Vermilion to Agate Bay, where the town of Two Harbors was established. Once a seventy-mile track was completed and ore docks had been readied at Two Harbors, the first ore moved out from the Soudan Mine in July of 1884.

Tower's operations were supervised by Charlemagne Tower,

Jr., who moved to Minnesota and lived for a time in Tower, the mining town near Vermilion Lake named for his father. The younger Tower was the principal agent in encouraging further exploration and development by the Minnesota Iron Company. His father, who did more than any other single individual to develop Minnesota iron mining, never set foot in the state.

During its second full season of mining in 1886, the Minnesota Iron Company exported over 300,000 tons of ore. This large quantity and the richness of the hematite (which sometimes ran to about sixty-five per cent iron) attracted hundreds of prospectors who combed the breadth of the Vermilion Range. During 1887 particularly, Duluth was buoyed by excitement as hundreds of professionals and amateurs sought ore deposits. Important finds were made northeast of Vermilion Lake, where Ely was started as a mining town and where the significant Chandler Mine was developed.

The Vermilion Range excitement of 1887 quickened interest in the Mesabi Range, which had been bypassed by Tower and his associates even though their railroad cut into some interesting-looking red earth. Even before iron ore was discovered on the Mesabi it was known as "The Range" because of its hilly eastern portions which rose hundreds of feet above the adjacent flat terrain. The Chippewa Indians knew the hills as the Missabe, their name for the sleeping giant who in their tradition had once roamed the area and now reposed in his eternal grave under the hills. The Mesabi Range fooled Chester and others because its formations were not like those of the Marquette and Vermilion ranges. Trained geologists such as Chester entered the area seeking hard ore-bearing rocks rather than soft iron ore, and their very depth of knowledge caused them to overlook the obvious because it was so unexpected.

However, there were men who believed that iron ore lay in the sleeping giant. Of these men Lewis Merritt, one of the pioneer settlers of Duluth, was the best known and the most determined. Merritt was a veteran timber cruiser and his faith was unfettered by professional knowledge. He insisted the Mesabi held iron ore—an insistence that he passed on to his seven sons. The Merritts were the first to find Mesabi ore, but they were not

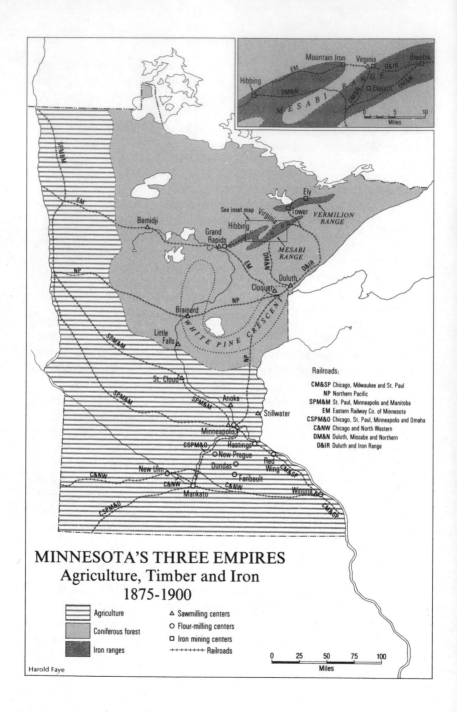

Railroads:

CM&SP Chicago, Milwaukee and St. Paul
NP Northern Pacific
SPM&M St. Paul, Minneapolis and Manitoba
EM Eastern Railway Co. of Minnesota
CSPM&O Chicago, St. Paul, Minneapolis and Omaha
C&NW Chicago and North Western
DM&N Duluth, Missabe and Northern
D&IR Duluth and Iron Range

MINNESOTA'S THREE EMPIRES
Agriculture, Timber and Iron
1875-1900

▨ Agriculture	△ Sawmilling centers
▨ Coniferous forest	○ Flour-milling centers
▨ Iron ranges	□ Iron mining centers
	+++++ Railroads

Harold Faye

0   25   50   75   100
Miles

alone in the search, for by the late 1880s hundreds of ore prospectors ranged over the Mesabi hills. On November 16, 1890,
Captain J. A. Nichols, who worked for the Merritts, uncovered
soft red ore just under the surface of the ground. The joyous
Merritts had the rare opportunity of naming a place in the wilderness that would become world renowned. The discoverer of
the Soudan mine had wishfully named it after the African Soudan after spending his first winter in Minnesota, but the Merritts
were not cynical and did not fancy themselves clever. They
chose the simple and descriptive name Mountain Iron. In 1891,
with the discovery of the Biwabik mines about ten miles east of
where Virginia was later established, their stake in the Mesabi
seemed assured.

Hoping to duplicate the "luck" of the Merritts, perhaps as
many as 15,000 prospectors spread over the range in 1892.
Duluth relived the hectic days of the 1887 Vermilion rush. The
Mesabi was ballyhooed in the Duluth press and the outfitting of
ore-seekers again became a major business. It was soon evident
that the rich ore did not exist throughout the Mesabi, but rather
occurred in comparatively small pockets along the range. The
task was to find the pockets. Although there were thousands
who failed, instant success came to some men such as Frank
Hibbing, who struck it rich at the place where he started his
town. Such successes attracted many knowledgeable and
wealthy men who wanted a part of the Mesabi. They included a
number of experienced Michigan iron miners such as John
Munro Longyear, whose cousin Edmund J. Longyear traveled
the length of the Mesabi taking thousands of core samples with
diamond-bit drills. The Longyears were prospecting for the
Pillsbury family, who had bought quantities of Range lands for
lumber during the great land sale at Duluth in 1882, and for
many years managed their Mesabi interests. Among those
drawn to the Mesabi in 1892 was Henry Oliver, a Pittsburgh
steel magnate. Oliver visited the Mesabi on his way home from
the Republican National Convention in Minneapolis and was instantly impressed. Recognizing the vast potential of soft ore that
could be taken from the surface, he began buying and leasing
land on the Mesabi. He was but the first of the steel barons to

become interested in the Mesabi, and it was not long until he and his kind had gained control of the great Mesabi Range.

Flushed by their initial successes in finding ore, the Merritts—with neither capital nor experience in big business—aspired to control Mesabi iron mining. They were able to acquire sizable land holdings inexpensively because the state, in its efforts to stimulate mining, leased the Merritts 141 quarter sections, charging only $100 each for a fifty-year lease. Encouraged by this easy acquisition, the Merritts began to think about marketing the ore. As experienced lumbermen they knew something about the problems of moving heavy goods long distances, so from the start they thought about a railroad from the Mesabi to Lake Superior and about ore docks on the lake. Their original plan was to build a railroad line which would join the established Duluth and Winnipeg Railroad at Brookston, about twenty-five miles west of Duluth. The Duluth and Winnipeg, in return for the guaranteed ore shipments, agreed to construct a large number of ore cars. The Merritts built their railroad—the Duluth, Missabe and Northern—and shipped ore from Mountain Iron to Superior, Wisconsin, in October of 1892. Their hopes were buoyed by this first shipment from the Mesabi, but they were disappointed when the Duluth and Winnipeg Railroad failed to live up to its agreement to construct the ore cars.

Undaunted by this setback, the Merritts decided to construct their own ore cars and to extend their own railroad all the way to Duluth. Perhaps they would have succeeded if the Panic of 1893 had not caught them in a precarious overextension. To meet construction costs and salaries the Merritts had to put stock of the Duluth, Missabe and Iron Range Railroad on the market. John D. Rockefeller bought about half a million dollars' worth. When the Merritts again could not meet their obligations they approached Rockefeller through agents about his possible interest in advancing more credit.

Rockefeller made the loan, but only with some rather unusual stipulations. The brothers had to agree to form a combination with Rockefeller in which they assumed an interest in some of his Michigan and Caribbean mining ventures, and he in turn acquired a controlling interest in their Mesabi properties. The

Merritts had an option to buy back the Mesabi interests within a year, but all except one refused to exercise it because by then they had had problems that led them to charge Rockefeller with fraud and misrepresentation. Although they won a judgment in a lower court, the opinion was reversed by the United States Court of Appeals in St. Louis. Ultimately, Rockefeller made a settlement with the Merritt family in return for their dropping of charges. Years later, in 1911, a United States Senate committee while investigating alleged monopolies investigated the Rockefeller–Merritt affair. The investigation did not show any wrongdoing on Rockefeller's part but revealed instead the naivete of the Merritts and the shrewd acumen of Rockefeller.

The Merritts are heroes in Minnesota because they pursued their dream. They found the Mesabi ore when geologists passed over it; and though they lacked capital, experience, and skill, they dared to challenge the nation's industrial giants. When brother Lon died on May 9, 1926, he had a reported worth of only $2,450; but he was a symbol of the free-spirited prospectors of Minnesota's mining frontier, and it was he who was used as the model for the figure of the prospector that is carved into the base of the statue of Governor John A. Johnson that stands today on the state capitol grounds.

Rockefeller's venture following the Oliver entry into the Mesabi Range solidified the pattern of control by absentee landlords. At the same time that Rockefeller interested himself in Minnesota iron ore, two of Oliver's Pittsburgh colleagues, Andrew Carnegie and Henry Frick, also bought or leased Mesabi lands. When the Oliver-Frick-Carnegie interests were merged in 1901 into United States Steel, a combination engineered by J. P. Morgan, Minnesota's iron lands passed almost entirely into the Oliver Division of the gigantic corporation.

James J. Hill provided the exception to the rule that Mesabi lands were controlled by major out-of-state businesses. Hill became involved in the Mesabi quite inadvertently. In 1897 he was persuaded to purchase the bankrupt Duluth and Winnipeg Railroad, and the railroad proved to have a land grant that included some ore lands on the Mesabi. Then somewhat later he acquired a Mesabi Range logging railroad. In both instances

Hill was primarily interested in adding to his railroad network, but he may also have sensed the potential value of the railroad lands even though iron ore had not yet been discovered on them. In 1906, after many ore discoveries on his holdings, Hill formed the Great Northern Iron Ore Properties. This corporation leased its lands to United States Steel and by the end of 1914 had been paid royalties of over $30,000,000.

The Mesabi was very different from other Lake Superior iron ranges because its ore was soft like soil, and it lay close to the surface in horizontal beds. There was no need to dig deep underground mines and extract the ore from hard rock; instead the miners could simply scrape away the topsoil, which in places was only a few feet deep, and scoop out the ore-bearing earth. Strip mining became the pattern on the Mesabi. There were some small underground mines, but even many of these were converted to open pits when the advantages of that method were proven. Veteran miners like the Cornishmen who first worked the deep Vermilion mines ridiculed the so-called mining of the Mesabi. It may not have been mining in the traditional sense, but there was no scoffing about its effectiveness. The steam shovels which were first used in 1894 could move thousands of tons each day. Largely because of the introduction of the open-pit process, the Mesabi Range in 1894 assumed first place in production among the Lake Superior ranges. A decade later there were 111 open pit mines on the Mesabi and the cumulative Mesabi ore production had surpassed that of its closest rival, the Marquette Range, which had been mined for sixty years.

Although the soft ore of the Mesabi was plentiful and easy to extract, it did present problems for the steel-makers because it was dusty and did not burn well in the Bessemer furnaces. For these reasons, the ore for its first several years was not so much in demand as was the hard ore from other ranges. However, as improvements in the furnaces were made the Mesabi ore became easier to handle and its softness was no longer an issue.

The Mesabi Range was like many of America's last frontiers. It opened during the Industrial Revolution, and the application of the new technology transformed it almost overnight—the forests were cut or burned over, towns sprang up along the narrow spine of the Mesabi from Babbitt in the east to Grand Rapids in the west, and gaping chasms appeared as the heavy ore was gouged from the face of the land. Within a decade after the Merritts opened Mountain Iron, the uncertainty of exploration and experimentation had been replaced by systematic extraction and marketing of ore by major capitalists. By the turn of the century, the Mesabi had become the greatest source of iron in the United States and Minnesota had become the ranking iron producer in the nation.

The taming of the Vermilion and Mesabi ranges coincided with the final days of Minnesota's agricultural frontier and the lumbermen's rapacious assault on the coniferous forests. By the turn of the century, there was but little undeveloped or unexploited land left in the state, and the patterns had been established that were to dictate Minnesota's future character and prospects.

8

A Legacy of Protest Politics

$\mathcal{S}$INCE Hubert Humphrey was first elected to the United States Senate in 1948 he more than anyone else has called national attention to Minnesota's Democratic-Farmer-Labor Party, which for over three decades was the only major state political party in the nation to call itself something other than Democratic or Republican. The party has some Democratic origins, but it also has a distinctiveness derived principally from its Farmer-Labor traits, the roots of which lie buried deep in Minnesota's long tradition of protest politics.

Henry H. Sibley, the state's first governor, was a Democrat, but after he completed his term in 1859 there was an unbroken reign of Republican governors for the next forty years. Even the election of John Lind in 1898 and John A. Johnson six years later did not seriously erode Republican control. Their election is attributable primarily to their personal qualities and their Scandinavian backgrounds as well as to petty squabbling between the Republican rivals at the time. Republicans still firmly controlled the legislature through the Lind and Johnson years, and Republican presidential candidates carried Minnesota regularly until 1912 when Theodore Roosevelt, the Progressive candidate, swept the state. Franklin D. Roosevelt in 1932 was the first Democratic presidential candidate to win Minnesota's electoral votes. But despite this impressive record, Minnesota's Republicans were not without opposition; almost continually after the mid-1870s they were buffeted from the left by agrarian reformers who attacked them as the party of big business, hard money, and the protective tariff.

Frontier Minnesota was a natural seedbed for agrarian discontent. The wheat farmers whose hopes had been buoyed by the lure of cheap, productive land and the promise of the good life were soon disillusioned. The Industrial Revolution seemed to promise much, but the railroads that made the markets more accessible charged high and discriminatory rates and the farmers were also at the mercy of elevator companies (often controlled by railroads and flour millers) which cut into farm profits through fraudulent weighing and grading of wheat. The high cost of farm machinery, another of the blessings of the Industrial Revolution, drove many farmers into debt and increasing farm tenancy drove them to the money lenders, who were usually agents of eastern capital. To meet rising costs the wheat farmers did the only seemingly logical thing—they produced more. Their critics said they over-produced—that that was the root of the "farm problem." Throughout the long era of discontent farmers refused to accept this reasoning. In their view they were being victimized by the giants of the new industrial world—the railroads, the millers and the eastern money cartels.

During the heightening of the agrarian revolt in the 1890s thousands of farmers agreed with the admonishment of Populist Mary Lease of Kansas that they should "raise less corn and more Hell." [1] During the dry years, at least, those were easy things to do. But farmers had groped for solutions long before they organized the Populist Party in the early 1890s.

The first farm spokesman in the troubled period following the Civil War was Minnesota's Oliver H. Kelley. In 1849 Kelley moved from Boston, Massachusetts, to a farm near what became the town of Elk River. In 1864 he was appointed a clerk in the U.S. Department of Agriculture. Then, early in 1866, he was sent to study the agricultural resources of the war-torn Southern states. Kelley returned to Washington convinced that

1. Quoted in John D. Hicks, *The Populist Revolt: A History of the Farmers' Alliance and the People's Party* (1931; Lincoln: University of Nebraska Press, 1961), p. 160.

the depressed conditions of rural America would be improved through cooperative farm associations—associations that might even become national in scope. He and a few associates organized the "National Grange of the Patrons of Husbandry" in Washington late in 1867, but lack of interest in the new organization caused Kelley to return to Minnesota with the hope of forming Granges in his home state. With the assistance of Daniel A. Robertson, a well-known public figure and former editor of the *Minnesota Democrat,* then the state's best-known newspaper, Kelley organized the North Star Grange at St. Paul in 1868.

Patterned along Masonic lines, the Grange emphasized secret rites and brotherhood. The association as Kelley envisioned it would unite the farmers and encourage them to study new farming methods, engage in cooperative buying and selling, and attempt to influence legislation. Kelley and other Grangers insisted that they were not a political party; Kelley was above politics, believing that highly principled men acting in unison would somehow prevail.

Agrarian grievances against Minnesota railroads, particularly the Winona and St. Peter line, stimulated the rapid formation of Grange lodges. The Minnesota State Grange was organized in 1869 and by the end of the next year there were nearly fifty active local Granges in the state. The highest Minnesota Grange membership was reached in 1874, just a year after Congress chartered the National Grange.

After the organization of the Minnesota State Grange the reformers concentrated most of their efforts on railroad freight rate regulation. Inspired by Illinois laws, Minnesota Grangers pushed for similar measures. Governor Horace Austin was sympathetic to their demands, as were many legislators, and with strong bipartisan support the first of Minnesota's Granger laws was passed in 1871. It established the office of railroad commissioner and it specified rates which could not be adjusted except by legislative act. As expected, the railroads ignored the law, which caused its supporters not only to file a lawsuit against the Winona and St. Peter Railroad but also to work for yet stronger legislation.

During their efforts to get the railroad act enforced many Grangers learned that it was not enough to lobby for railroad regulation: they needed their own political arm. Many agreed with the assessment of Ignatius Donnelly that the Grange was like "a gun that will do everything but shoot." [2] Donnelly spearheaded the drive to weld the Grangers into a potent political force. He began his long championship of agrarian causes when he helped organize a lodge at Hastings in January 1873, but his conversion to the Grange creed was questioned by many from the start. Throughout his career he was hounded by critics who charged that he was neither a farmer nor a particular friend of farmers, but instead had associated himself with political dissent simply to further his own ambitions.

By the time he became a Grange organizer Donnelly was well known in Minnesota. A native of Philadelphia, he had come to the territory as a townsite speculator during the flush times of the mid-1850s. With glowing optimism he and his partners platted Nininger; but Donnelly was much sobered and considerably poorer when the Panic of 1857 sent real estate values tumbling. He had gotten involved in politics, too, and as one of the bright young men in the Republican Party he was nominated for the lieutenant governorship in 1859 on the ticket with Alexander Ramsey. He and Ramsey were swept into office on the Republican tide and at age twenty-eight he started his elective political career. Donnelly moved from the lieutenant governorship to the U.S. House of Representatives in 1863. During three terms in Congress he was a regular Republican, but partially because of personal ambitions he broke with Ramsey, then the boss of the state Republican organization. This move lost him much support in his own party, so after failing in an 1868 re-election bid he turned to lecturing and through this avenue campaigned actively for the Liberal Republican Party in the 1872 presidential campaign.

Donnelly's experience, speaking ability, and facile mind assured his rapid emergence in Granger ranks. During 1873 when

2. Quoted in Martin Ridge, *Ignatius Donnelly: The Portrait of a Politician* (Chicago: University of Chicago Press, 1962), p. 150.

the Grangers urged further railroad regulation they were up-staged by Republican gubernatorial candidate Cushman K. Davis, who was widely known throughout the state for his anti-railroad stance. With Davis's nomination there was little chance that the Grangers could dominate the Republican Party, so Don-nelly schemed to form a political arm of the state Grange. De-spite opposition from some Grangers who contended that politi-cal organization violated Grange principles, Donnelly and his supporters met at Owatonna in September, 1873 and formed the Anti-Monopoly Party, which soon came to be known as the Anti-Monopoly Independent Party. As an advocate of the rights of the little man against the big corporations, the party urged railroad regulation and monetary reform.

Aided by the Panic of 1873, which hurt Republican candi-dates, Donnelly was elected to the state senate as an Anti-Monopolist. Angry debtor farmers also carried many other Anti-Monopolists into the legislature, and with Donnelly as the leader of a coalition of Anti-Monopolists and Democrats the re-formers pushed through a second Granger law. This act of 1874 provided for a board of three railroad commissioners with power to hold hearings, establish rates, and force railroads into re-ceivership; railroad cases were to be given priority in the state courts.

The reformists soon realized that they had achieved a hollow victory. Because railroads had been so adversely affected by the panic, the railroad commissioners did not enforce the 1874 law and usually rubberstamped existing freight rates. In 1875, be-cause it was generally believed that the stringent act was imped-ing the railroads in particular and the entire economy in general, the 1874 law was repealed, and Minnesota was left with a single railroad commissioner whose only real duty was the gathering of information about railroads.

Despite the repeal, the state supreme court upheld the consti-tutionality of the 1871 law; and in 1876 the U.S. Supreme Court, acting on an Illinois case, also ruled that states could reg-ulate railroads. Ten years later when the Supreme Court re-versed itself Congress was moved to revive an idea that had first been advanced by U.S. Senator William Windom of Minnesota in 1874. Windom, widely recognized as a financial genius and later Secretary of the Treasury under Garfield and Harrison, had suggested some type of federal railroad regulation. Windom was not a crusader; instead he seemed to have realized that federal regulation would simply have the effect of guaranteeing a reasonable profit to the railroads. Whatever Windom's motives may have been at the time that he suggested federal regulation, the creation of the Interstate Commerce Commission in 1887 was welcomed by dissident farmers.

The Panic of 1873 marked the eclipse of the Grange. Its vitality was undermined by sympathy for the railroads and the 1876 Supreme Court ruling undercut its basic reason for existing, since the courts henceforth had the power to control the railroads. Although the Grange was waning, its offspring, the Anti-Monopoly Party, was flourishing. By 1876, the party had turned its attention almost entirely to the money problem and was becoming increasingly identified with the National Greenback movement. Next to the railroads, the money question was the most pressing matter to debtor farmers. They protested vigorously at paying off debts with currency that was increasing in value; they much preferred an inflationary money that permitted them to fulfill their obligations with currency that was worth less on the dollar than at the time they had borrowed. The period of the 1870s through the 1890s was deflationary, and farmers strongly urged currency reform.

The first reform impulse was to continue printing and circulating greenbacks, which had been issued during the Civil War to conserve the Union's gold. But hard-money men dominated by eastern bankers urged retirement of the paper money and a reliance on gold. The Greenback movement, known in its early years as the Ohio Idea, was well enough organized by 1876 to hold a national convention in Indianapolis. Donnelly attended and during the next several years was one of the Greenbackers' chief spokesmen in Minnesota and the nation. In 1878 he ran as a Greenback candidate for Congress but was defeated by William D. Washburn. The Greenback Party, although it made a respectable showing in the congressional elections of 1878, succumbed, like the Anti-Monopoly Party before it, to the winds of change. Vast silver discoveries in Colorado in the mid-1870s assured a surplus of that metal, and when Congress accepted limited coinage of silver in 1878 the old Greenbackers and the farmers who wanted cheap money became silver advocates.

The silver movement was nurtured through the 1880s by a new farm organization, the Farmers Alliance, which was started in New York in 1877 by Grangers who wanted a political voice. During 1880 Milton George, the Chicago editor of the *Western Rural,* popularized the Alliance movement and the next year the first state Alliance was organized in Nebraska and local chapters were formed in Minnesota. By 1882 the Alliance, with about 100,000 members nationally, had really become two organizations—the Southern Alliance and the Northern Alliance—a division primarily caused by the race issue. In Minnesota as elsewhere Alliance popularity rose and fell in relation to the farm economy. Good crops and acceptable market prices caused the Alliance to decline in 1883–1884, but during the winter of 1884–1885 it revived sharply when wheat prices fell. An overall decline in farm incomes in the mid-1880s, however, strengthened the Alliance until Minnesota had 438 local units in 1886 when the first state convention was held.

Nationally, the Alliance stressed the old educational and economic goals of the Grange. The Minnesota Alliance achieved one of its aims in 1885 when the state legislature created the Railroad and Warehouse Commission, which, among other things, was to inspect scales at the terminal elevators in Minneapolis, St. Paul, and Duluth. The law, while welcome, did not go far enough to satisfy the delegates to the 1886 convention, who called for state inspection of local elevator scales as well. The delegates also urged state-imposed reductions of rail rates, regulation of railroad monopolies, and making the use of free railroad passes by state officials a crime.

Alliance delegates clearly saw themselves as representatives of the common man who was being victimized by plutocrats; they maintained in their platform "that there are really but two parties in this State to-day—the people and their plunderers. The only issue is: Shall the people keep the fruits of their own

industry, or shall the thieves carry them away?" [3] Believing
they were exploited, the farm agitators sought an alliance with
organized labor. The labor movement in the Twin Cities was
headed by the Knights of Labor, which had grown dramatically
with the modernization of flour milling, and the Minnesota Alliance arranged its first state convention as a joint meeting with
the Minnesota Knights of Labor. The two groups drew up separate platforms, with labor demanding an income-tax law, a state
bureau of labor statistics, and prohibition of child labor. Representatives of agriculture and labor talked about a formal political
tie and discussed the creation of a Farm and Labor Party; but the
party was never formally organized because farmers and la
borers believed their aims could better be accomplished through
the Republican Party, which adopted their demands and added
them to its platform.

The Alliance and the Knights of Labor were pleased with the
prospects of achieving their goals through Minnesota's major
party, but Republican betrayal of their interests in 1886 and
again in 1888 caused them to think more and more about organizing another third party—a party devoted solely to representing the farmers and laborers. And Ignatius Donnelly again came
to the fore. After his Greenback experience Donnelly had embarked on a literary career in which he wrote knowingly
although unconvincingly about a variety of popular subjects. His books made Donnelly a literary figure of note, and
with his new-found reputation as the "Sage of Nininger" he became a popular lecturer. But throughout his literary phase Donnelly never abandoned the urge to return to Congress, so in
1889 after twenty years of detachment from the Republican
Party he attempted to win its endorsement for United States
senator. Again he was frustrated by the supporters of William
D. Washburn, who Donnelly thought had defeated him by
fraudulent means in both the congressional race of 1878 and the

3. Quoted in Rhoda R. Gilman, *Minnesota: Political Maverick,* component of *Minnesota Politics and Government: A History Resource Unit* (St. Paul: Minnesota Historical Society, 1975), p. 26.

senatorial contest. The embittered Donnelly, convinced that Washburn epitomized the evils of politics, wrote *Caesar's Column*, his last major work. The story told of a Ugandan who visited New York City in 1988 only to find that the legacy of corrupt politics had reduced the once proud American democracy to a mob-ridden society. Fearing that its decadence might spread, the Ugandan convinced his countrymen to convert their nation into a Utopian Socialist republic, which within a few years became a blissful earthly paradise.

In the real world of politics, Donnelly not only had lost to Washburn but had estranged many Alliance members who questioned his sincerity after his trafficking with the Republicans. In 1890 when the Minnesota Alliance ran its own candidates, Donnelly, who aspired to the gubernatorial nomination, was passed over in favor of Sidney Owen, the popular editor of a farm journal. Donnelly survived the rebuke and became one of the leaders in uniting the Northern and Southern alliances into the Populist Party. When the "People's Party" held its national convention at Omaha in the summer of 1892, it drew up a reformist platform calling for measures such as a graduated income tax and public ownership of railroads and utilities, and Donnelly wrote a stirring preamble to it. Appealing to the disillusioned and the disaffected, he urged major reforms because "from the same prolific womb of governmental injustice we breed the two great classes—tramps and millionaires." [4]

Whatever aspirations Donnelly had to be the party's presidential nominee were dashed when the Populists turned to the less colorful but less controversial James Weaver of Iowa. Donnelly had to fight hard even to become the Populist gubernatorial candidate in his home state. During the ensuing campaign he challenged Republican candidate Knute Nelson to debate. As the front runner, Nelson, a former congressman who was very popular with farmers and who had been courted earlier by the Alliance, saw no need for such debate. Theodore Christianson, a rather shrewd political observer and a three-term governor of

4. "Populist Party Platform," in Henry Steele Commager, ed., *Documents of American History*, 2 vols., 7th ed. (New York: Appleton-Century-Crofts, 1963), 1:593.

Minnesota from 1925 to 1931, noted later that "the people came to hear and applaud [Donnelly] . . . but in November they voted for Knute Nelson." [5] Donnelly finished a weak third in the gubernatorial contest and only two dozen Populists were elected to the state legislature.

Although the Populists hardly dominated, their interests were served nonetheless when the legislature provided for state licensing of all grain elevators on public rights-of-way and appropriated funds for the construction of a state-owned grain terminal elevator in Duluth. The latter measure, which seemed too socialistic to many conservatives, was declared unconstitutional by the state supreme court, which held that the state's constitution forbade the contracting of debts for internal improvements. Nelson, however, succeeded in enhancing his standing with some of the political dissidents by proposing a public works program to help solve unemployment after the Panic of 1893.

The panic, which seemed to underscore the evils of the old system and the inability or even unwillingness of the major parties to assist the common man, helped the Populists in the 1894 elections. Nationally the party's vote was over forty per cent higher than it had been in 1892, and in Minnesota the Populists temporarily became the state's second-ranking party. Knute Nelson, the incumbent Republican governor, was more popular than ever and easily won re-election; but Sidney Owen, the Populist candidate, finished well ahead of Democrat George L. Becker, who as a former railroad agent was vulnerable to the charge that he represented a special business which was opposed to the interests of farmers.

After the election the Populists anticipated continued success, but they failed to reckon with the free-silver sentiment within the Democratic Party. When William Jennings Bryan led the Democrats on the silver crusade of 1896, the Populists suffered the fate common to third parties—their platform was absorbed by a major party. In 1896 Minnesota Populists accepted the inevitable and like their counterparts in many other states agreed to a "Fusionist" ticket composed of Populists, Silver Democrats, and Silver Republicans. John Lind, a Silver Republican and the Fusionist gubernatorial candidate, narrowly lost to the Republican nominee. Lind, a former congressman from New Ulm who was extremely popular with farmers and Scandinavians, won the governorship in 1898, but by that time he was in reality a Democrat and the Populist Party as such was dead.

When compared to a number of western states, including some that were carried by the Populists in the presidential election of 1892, Minnesota's Populist gains were modest. The party never captured the governorship; it sent only two men to the U.S. House of Representatives and it never controlled the legislature. But in Minnesota, as elsewhere, the Populist era paved the way for the progressive movement, a broader and yet more profound criticism of American institutions and practices.

Carl Chrislock, in writing about Minnesota progressivism, observed that "the inauguration of Governor John Lind on January 2, 1899, heralded the progressive era in Minnesota." [6] In his opening message Lind suggested a series of sweeping reforms. He called for an increase in railroad taxes and the creation of a state tax commission to study alternatives to the onerously high property taxes. Lind also suggested the creation of a supervisory state board of control to make state institutions more fiscally responsible, and he asked that consideration be given to ideas such as the direct primary, initiative, referendum, and recall. Faced with a hostile legislature, Lind accomplished none of his major goals, but subsequent developments gave him a significance not apparent at the time. During the twelve years after Lind left office, Minnesota was profoundly affected by the tone he set. Minnesota's conversion to progressivism was not so rapid as that of neighboring Wisconsin, which won a national reputation for sweeping reforms under Governor Robert La Follette, a progressive Republican, but in time the reform urge in

6. Carl H. Chrislock, *The Progressive Era in Minnesota 1899–1918* (St. Paul: Minnesota Historical Society, 1971), p. 9.

Minnesota became broadly based and transcended party lines.

The muscle in Minnesota's progressivism came from the small towns, whose citizenry, like the surrounding farmers, resented railroads, banks, and the Twin Cities. These rural residents saw rampant industrialization and urbanization as threats to the traditional agrarian America, so they cried out against the evils of big business. Progressivism's appeal in the Twin Cities was narrower; metropolitan business interests were attracted to tariff reforms which promised to help them economically and there was popular support for such ideas as direct primaries, but there was no general reaction against the increasing power of big urban business.

Although the thrust of progressivism finally affected all aspects of corporate business and political reform, the fear of railroad domination was particularly strong in the minds of Minnesotans. In late 1901 when it became publicly known that railroad barons James J. Hill and Edward Harriman with the assistance of J. P. Morgan had formed the Northern Securities Company, a merger of the Northern Pacific, Great Northern, and Chicago and Burlington railroads, there was an angry public response. In an age when railroads were the only effective means of transportation this merger created a virtual transportation monopoly in Minnesota. The fact that Hill was party to the merger did little to assuage the ire of Minnesotans.

Even if he had been otherwise inclined, Governor Samuel Van Sant had little choice other than to challenge the Northern Securities Company. Within days after its formation he ordered his attorney general to bring suit in the name of the state against it for violating a Minnesota statute forbidding construction of parallel rail lines by the same company. Van Sant also spearheaded a widely publicized conference of the governors of Minnesota, South Dakota, Montana, Idaho, and Washington at which the merger was condemned. President Theodore Roosevelt instructed the Justice Department to proceed against the company; and as a result of the federal suit the Northern Securities Company was ordered dissolved and Roosevelt had taken his first important step in earning his reputation as the "trust-buster."

The anti-railroad crusade was continued during the administration of Van Sant's successor, John A. Johnson, with the passage of a new law forbidding the issuance of free railroad passes. By the time of Johnson's governorship, the public mood for reform had deepened. Most big businesses were under attack and there was a loud demand for more democratic, more responsive government. Johnson, although he was much more conservative than the later common impression, epitomized the type of leadership needed in an age when responsiveness and openness in government were the expectation. The first native governor, Johnson was born to Swedish immigrant parents in a St. Peter log cabin and left school when he was thirteen years old. He read widely and worked in a general store and as a supply clerk before buying an interest in the *Saint Peter Herald* when he was twenty-five. His political start was inauspicious: he was defeated in a bid for a seat in the state House of Representatives in 1888 and for the state Senate six years later. He was elected to the Senate in 1898 but again defeated in 1902. By the time he ran for governor as a Democrat in 1904 he had, in the words of Theodore Christianson, "left no important legislation on the statute books of the state, had done no outstanding committee work and had in no way distinguished himself. But by his affable nature he had won many friends among Republican as well as Democratic members." [7]

By strength of character and personality and also because of a power struggle among rival Republicans, Johnson won the governorship in 1904 even though Theodore Roosevelt swamped his Democratic opponent in the presidential election and all other state elective offices were won by Republicans. The handsome, gentlemanly Johnson appealed to many voters with his characteristic openness. When asked by a reporter what he had to say about reports that his father had been a drunkard, Johnson replied simply: "Nothing—it is true." [8] To answer the taunt that his mother had taken in washing he responded: "Took in washing? Yes, she did—until I was old enough to go out and

7. Christianson, *Minnesota,* 2:287.
8. Quoted in Christianson, *Minnesota,* 2:291.

earn something. But she never took in any washing after that.'' [9] Criticized by both right and left, Johnson appealed magnetically to Minnesota's electorate throughout his administration. He was re-elected in 1906 and again in 1908, when he was the only successful Democratic candidate for state executive office.

As governor, Johnson recommended the nomination and election of nonpartisan judges, a state income tax, and more stringent railroad regulation, and he was the first governor to suggest a Minnesota workmen's compensation law. However, most of his reform effort was aimed at curbing fraudulent practices of insurance companies operating in the state. At Johnson's instigation President Theodore Roosevelt called for a conference of the states to adopt uniform insurance regulation. As permanent chairman of the conference Johnson attracted national attention when twenty-two states passed laws regulating insurance companies in keeping with the recommendations of one of the conference's committees. As part of the crusade Johnson became active in the International Policyholders' Committee, a reform group based in Boston. Through his association with this group he became a popular banquet speaker and as early as 1905 the group's leader, Boston multimillionaire Thomas Lawson, heralded Johnson as a presidential possibility.

Johnson's supporters saw him as a viable conservative alternative to the liberal William Jennings Bryan, and he was nominated for the presidency as a favorite-son candidate in 1908 at the Democratic national convention. Although Johnson garnered few votes and Bryan easily captured the nomination, it was obvious that his supporters were thinking ahead to 1912. Some believe that he could have been the Democratic presidential candidate in 1912. His sudden death on September 21, 1909, ended a career of great achievement but yet greater promise.

Johnson himself was a moderate reformer. The real flowering of progressivism in the state came during the administration of Johnson's successor, Republican Adolph Eberhart, a man of limited vision whose reform impulse was stimulated late during

9. Quoted in Christianson, *Minnesota,* 2:291.

his administration only by the political instinct to survive. Many members of Eberhart's own party, including United States Senator Moses Clapp and Congressman Charles Lindbergh, were leaders in the insurgency against the Republican old guard and President William Howard Taft. After Eberhart witnessed the involvement of Minnesota's Republican congressmen in the overthrow of conservative leadership in the House of Representatives, the defeat in 1910 of the only Minnesota congressman who supported Taft's opposition to tariff reform, and the rising progressive tide in Minnesota and the nation, he became very interested in reform.

By 1912 Eberhart's problem was twofold: he had alienated many liberals in his own party by his lack of reform zeal, and since he had completed Johnson's third term and served a full term of his own many of his opponents complained that he was actually seeking a (not unprecedented) third term. So Eberhart convened a short special session to consider a host of reforms in the summer of 1912. In less than two weeks the legislature approved amendments to the federal constitution calling for an income tax and direct election of United States senators, extended the direct primary to state offices, and provided for fair political campaign practices. The *Minneapolis Journal* pronounced the session to be "in many ways . . . the most memorable in the history of the state. In thirteen days the legislature has completely revolutionized the state's present political system. . . ."

> The special session of the legislature has sounded the death knell of the old party convention system. And with the convention system will go, if the supporters of the statewide primary bill and the corrupt practices act are right, the paid political worker, the hanger-on at elections, the perennial follower of the man who seeks office. . . .[10]

Eberhart's conversion (even if for only tactical reasons) and the success of the special session followed by the victory in Minnesota of Progressive Party presidential candidate Theodore

10. *Minneapolis Journal,* June 18, 1912, as quoted in Gilman, *Minnesota: Political Maverick,* p. 35.

Roosevelt stimulated yet more reforms. The 1913 legislature extended the nonpartisan principle beyond judgeships to include such local posts as county coroner and surveyor and, with very little deliberation, even forbade party designation for state legislators. The extension of the nonpartisan principle to the legislature was a most curious event in Minnesota history. Some thought it was the epitome of democratic reform, but the law evidently passed primarily because of the influence of liquor lobbyists who believed dry laws could be forestalled by obfuscating party lines. The legislature remained officially nonpartisan for sixty years, thereby adding to Minnesota's independent and even maverick tradition, but, in actuality, the conservative caucus was predominantly Republican and the liberal caucus was composed mostly of opposition groups.

Minnesota and the nation drifted from their progressive preoccupations into concern with European affairs and involvement in World War I. Fears of an uncertain loyalty from many in Minnesota's large German element caused the state legislature to create a Public Safety Commission, which among other things was to control seditious activity, ensure compliance with the national military draft, and take steps to conserve food, fuel, and other essentials for the war effort. Unfortunately the commission, which was dominated by ultraconservatives, became a virtual government in its own right, employing its own agents and constabulary. Arbitrarily assuming powers and responding vigorously to the worst fears of super-patriots, the commission clashed with officials of New Ulm and Brown County over alleged draft evasion and attempted to squelch political dissent, which the commission thought detracted from the war effort.

One object of the commission's wrath was the newly formed Nonpartisan League, which had spread into Minnesota from its North Dakota origin. The League was yet another organization intended to represent the embattled farmers. Its founder, Arthur C. Townley, was inspired by both the Socialists and a radical farm group, the American Society of Equity, that had espoused great political and economic power for farmers after its formation in 1902. Townley, a native of Browns Valley, Minnesota, had taught school before moving to Beach, North Dakota, where he joined his brother in a large flax farming operation. As the "Flax King of North Dakota" Townley's prospects were promising, but like many staple-crop farmers he found himself irretrievably in debt because of one poor crop. After his 1913 disaster Townley began actively planning a new organization that would truly represent farm interests. Townley himself was not a Socialist and he personally believed that Socialism (at least under that name) would not be acceptable to farmers, but he thought some key Socialist ideas were sound and could be achieved under the banner of a major party.

Townley formed the Farmers Nonpartisan League in February 1915, not to create a new party but to dominate an existing one which would have a broader respectability and base. Recognizing that the Republican Party was dominant in North Dakota, Townley and his supporters sought to control it. Through a massive recruitment effort in 1915–1916 the Nonpartisan League actually did gain control of the North Dakota Republican Party and won the governorship and control of the legislature in the 1916 elections. Since some of its aims, such as state-owned and -operated grain terminals, packing plants, and flour mills, were frankly socialistic the League appeared to be the most radical protest group spawned by the half-century of farm discontent. It officially supported American involvement in World War I, but it called for tight government control of wartime profiteering and some of its more radical members believed the thesis of Bolshevik leader Vladimir Lenin—that the war was nothing more than a power struggle between rival imperialists. The League's lukewarm enthusiasm for World War I made it extremely suspect to the Public Safety Commission, which in a fit of zealous patriotism tarred the League's supporters and German-Americans with the same brush, thereby creating a rather strange fellowship.

After the League moved its national headquarters to St. Paul early in 1917, its Minnesota membership rose sharply. From the start Townley and his principal aides realized that Minnesota, unlike North Dakota, was both agrarian and industrial and that the League would have to enlist the support of both farmers and organized labor. The support for the League from labor, wheat farmers, and German-Americans was sufficiently strong to encourage Townley to attempt to dominate the Minnesota Republican Party, but incumbent Republican Governor Joseph A. A. Burnquist, a strong supporter of the Public Safety Commission, rejected all League overtures. The League then challenged Burnquist in the 1918 Republican primary with former congressman Charles A. Lindbergh, a dedicated opponent of American involvement in the war. After Burnquist defeated Lindbergh the League entered an opposition candidate in the general election. When the Minnesota attorney general ruled that the candidate had to have a party label, League officials designated him the candidate of the Farmer-Labor Party.

Although the name was first used in 1918, the party was not officially formed until four years later. Townley himself never abandoned his original notion that the League should be a nonpartisan influence group. But like other founders in history, Townley had to accept the fact that his creation grew beyond his expectations. David H. Evans, the League's gubernatorial candidate in 1918, finished well behind Burnquist but well ahead of the Democratic candidate—meaning that almost overnight the League had become Minnesota's second-ranking political group. This rank was reaffirmed in the 1920 state elections and the League, even though it was accused of advocating "atheism, communism and free love," continued to gain in strength because of the postwar agricultural depression.

Those who did not take the League seriously enough—and there were many—were rudely awakened in 1922 when League candidate Henrik Shipstead, a Glenwood dentist, upset incumbent United States Senator Frank Billings Kellogg. Kellogg, who had won national stature for prosecuting anti-monopoly cases for the federal government, had returned to Minnesota long enough in 1916 to become the first elected senator in the state's history. However, he courted defeat when he failed to detect and respond to the feelings of angry farmers and laborers.

Kellogg went on to be Secretary of State in the Coolidge administration and was awarded the Nobel Peace Prize in 1929 for his part in initiating the Kellogg–Briand Peace Pact, while Shipstead came to epitomize Midwestern isolationism. After serving

three full terms as a Farmer-Laborite senator, Shipstead returned
to the Republican fold in 1940 and was elected to a fourth term.
He was never converted to the internationalism of World War
II; in 1945 he was one of only two American senators who
voted against approval of the United Nations charter. Finally, in
the Republican primary of 1946, he was defeated smashingly,
his isolationism no longer appreciated.

The depth of the Farmer-Labor strength had become very evident with Shipstead's surprising win over Kellogg in 1922. In
1923, when Senator Knute Nelson died, Magnus Johnson challenged Republican Governor Jacob Preus in a special election
for the remainder of Nelson's term. The earthy, robust Johnson,
who purportedly delighted farm audiences by standing on a ma-
nure spreader and proclaiming that that was the first time he had
ever stood on a Republican platform, was castigated by the opposition as a "dirt farmer." Although he was short on both
manners and syntax and, his enemies said, intellectual capacity,
Johnson—as a friend of the farmers—was victorious. With his
victory the Farmer-Labor Party controlled both Senate seats.

Although Minnesota, like most of the Midwest, was detri-
mentally affected by the agricultural depression that persisted
through the 1920s, the Farmer-Labor Party did not benefit at the
state level. The party temporarily held both Senate seats, and
two of its members in the House of Representatives contributed
significantly to the activities of the farm bloc. But in the struggle for control of the governorship, the party prevailed only
after the great crash of 1929.

The stock market plunge and subsequent depression which
embarrassed the old orders in both Washington and St. Paul
opened the way for the emergence of one of the most colorful
and controversial figures in Minnesota's history—Floyd B.
Olson. As Minnesota's New Deal governor, Olson attracted national attention as a speaker, as an advocate of change, and as a
potential vice presidential and even presidential candidate.

Olson is often compared to John A. Johnson: both were Scandinavians, both came from humble backgrounds, both were
magnetic speakers, both were men of the people who seemed to
have the interests of the common man at heart, and both died

during the height of their careers. But Olson was the rougher gem. Sometimes coarse and ribald, he often offended while Johnson was unfailingly gracious. Johnson typified the age of consensus politics in which reformist sentiment crossed party lines and political independence was in vogue, but Olson was a product of political partisanship. He represented a new liberal group that urged its reforms with evangelistic fervor. Olson also lived in a harsher age than Johnson: the disaffection of the progressive era was mild compared to the bitterness of the New Deal years, when it seemed to many that the old system had at last failed utterly. Olson, unlike Johnson, continually had to seek a balance between political extremes ranging from those of his ultra-liberal supporters to those of his arch-enemies who saw him as a homegrown Red.

Olson, whom biographer George H. Mayer portrayed as "more rebel than radical," was conditioned by his upbringing in the slums of north Minneapolis. Continual contact with the poor and struggling imbued him with a life-long sympathy for the underdog. As a young man he labored in Alaska and up and down the West Coast before returning to Minnesota and working his way through law school. After serving as county attorney of Hennepin County he became the Farmer Labor gubernatorial candidate in 1924, only to be defeated by Republican Theodore L. Christianson in a campaign marked by charges that Olson was in league with the Communists. He learned from his defeat and earned public acceptance through his vigilant prosecution of political graft and his compassionate attitude toward petty offenders.

With this background he went into the governorship with a commitment to reform, but with strong opposition from conservatives who dominated the legislature during his first term. Although Olson's situation improved with increasing Farmer-Labor strength during his second and third terms, he never enjoyed a truly supportive legislature. Nonetheless, he successfully championed some major changes—the acceptance of a graduated state income tax, the banning of yellow dog contracts and injunctions, and the postponement of farm mortgage foreclosures.

A master of rhetoric with immense crowd appeal, Olson spoke for the poor farmers and laborers. To them he seemed a beacon of hope, but he also polarized opinion—he tended to be greatly loved or greatly hated. Through his advocacy of the rights of labor and his efforts to aid the state's farmers he earned a national reputation as the country's most liberal governor, but in an age when people desperately cried for a solution it was beyond the power of any one man to offer one. To the opposition he was too socialistic and to many in his own party he was not liberal enough. After he pursued a middle course in the bloody Minneapolis truckers' strike of 1934 and failed to push vigorously the socialistic 1934 platform of his own party, which advocated public ownership of banks, factories, mines, transportation, and utilities, Olson came under increasing attack and was more open than ever before to charges that he was pragmatic but little else. He certainly was not a doctrinaire liberal, and he resisted efforts to propagate the third-party faith nationally. Olson's posture was one of cooperation with Franklin Roosevelt and the New Deal, and his disinterest in a national third party in 1936 was dictated by his desire not to undercut Roosevelt's strength in Minnesota.

In 1936 Olson fully expected that he would be elected to the United States Senate and that his party would continue to control the governorship; but during the campaign he died from cancer, an event that deeply affected his party and the immediate political history of the state. Perhaps partly because of his untimely death, he became something of a legendary figure.

Like many of the protest movements before it, the Farmer-Labor Party rose quickly, peaked during a time of troubles, and then plunged rapidly into public disfavor. Olson's successor, Elmer Benson, earned the distinction in 1936 of winning the governorship by the largest plurality in Minnesota's history and then two years later lost it by another record margin. Benson fell victim to the patronage excesses of his party, his unswerving dedication to liberal causes, and his unwillingness or inability to dissociate himself from Minnesota's small group of Communist agitators. Benson, who in the minds of many was the gravedigger of the Farmer-Labor Party, has naturally been compared to Olson. Carl Chrislock notes that

> the marked difference between Olson and Benson is aptly expressed
> in an often-repeated tale, possibly apocryphal but nevertheless
> illuminating. It tells of a businessman discussing militant Farmer-
> Labor rhetoric shortly after the 1936 election. He complained that
> "Floyd Olson used to say these things; but this son of a bitch
> [Benson] *believes* them." [11]

Benson's fall was not all of his own doing. The Republicans of 1938 were not the conservatives who had battled Olson; they were led by Harold Stassen, a bright, articulate, progressive young lawyer who preached the gospel of "enlightened capitalism," his answer to the socialism of the Farmer-Laborites. Stassen, only thirty-one when he won the governorship, had risen through the party's ranks on the strength of his leadership in the Young Republican League, which supported many of the New Deal measures. After Stassen surprised Republicans by winning the primary, he waged an extremely effective campaign in which he pledged to rid Minnesota of Communism and corruption in government.

During his first term, the nation's then youngest governor effected a major reorganization of state government and instituted a state civil service system. He seemed to be an ideal administrator—a moderate reformer in the spirit of the old progressives and perhaps a Republican answer to Roosevelt's New Deal. Stassen was put on center stage in 1940 when he delivered the keynote address at the Republican National Convention and then successfully led the floor fight for the nomination of Wendell Wilkie. After this national exposure he was twice re-elected governor of Minnesota, only to resign in 1943 to enlist in the navy. At President Truman's invitation he served as a member of the United States delegation to the San Francisco conference in 1945 that drafted the permanent United Nations charter. Then in 1948 he began his never-ending quest for the White House.

11. Chrislock, *Progressive Era*, p. 196.

He was undone by Thomas Dewey in the Oregon primary, but from his position as president of the University of Pennsylvania he entered the lists again four years later. Ironically it was the large write-in vote for Dwight Eisenhower in Minnesota's primary that ruined Stassen in 1952. He later served as special presidential assistant for disarmament in the Eisenhower administration and then, following defeats in his bids for governor of Pennsylvania and mayor of Philadelphia, in 1964 he resumed his fruitless quest for the presidency of the United States.

Unfortunately, his lingering presidential ambitions, which in 1976 especially seemed like nothing more than a wistful bid for attention, have beclouded his earlier accomplishments, particularly as governor of Minnesota. Not only did he lead a Republican resurgence in Minnesota that carried into the mid-1950s, but his reforms set the tone for his Republican successors who accepted and advocated a greater role for state government. Social and welfare legislation of these Republican years have helped make Minnesota one of the ranking states in taxes levied and amounts spent for public assistance programs. In a broader view Stassen's internationalism encouraged thousands of Minnesotans to abandon the isolationism of the 1930s. His view of unprecedented American involvement in world affairs paved the way for a new internationalism in Minnesota politics such as that espoused by Stassen's friend and supporter, Senator Joseph Ball, a former journalist who was one of the most internationally minded senators during World War II. The emergence of Harold Stassen is perhaps symbolic of Minnesota's transition from the isolationist vision of Henrik Shipstead and famed aviator Charles Lindbergh, the son of the former congressman and Farmer-Labor leader, who was one of the country's most vocal opponents of American involvement in European affairs before the United States entry into World War II.

Stassen's 1938 victory was the death knell of the Farmer-Labor Party. Although the party ran state candidates in the next two elections, it was but an echo of what it had been in the days of Floyd Olson. More and more Farmer-Laborites thought of affiliation with the Democrats. The folly of the two small groups independently challenging Minnesota's dominant Republicans and the new liberal image of the Democrats heightened interest in a merger.

The creation of the Democratic-Farmer-Labor Party in 1944 came about under the blessings of President Franklin Roosevelt and partially through the leadership of Hubert Humphrey, who the year before had run unsuccessfully for mayor of Minneapolis. Despite limited success and Roosevelt's victory in Minnesota, the new party was beset with problems. Veteran Farmer-Laborites led by ex-governor Elmer Benson resented the young liberals with their close ties to the academic world and their lack of specific commitment to the old Farmer-Labor ideals. On the other hand, Humphrey and his followers were bothered by the radicalism of the traditional Farmer-Laborites, the strong taint of fiscal mismanagement that continued to haunt the Benson crowd, and the association of Benson and his key supporters with the Communist element.

The differences were exacerbated by sharp clashes over the foreign policy of the Truman administration and came to a head during the Democratic-Farmer-Labor schism of 1948. Most newcomers to the party were internationalists who supported the Marshall Plan and other foreign-assistance programs, while the Benson men saw foreign aid as nothing more than an effort to perpetuate Fascist governments abroad. While most of the party rank and file were ardent Truman backers, the Benson element backed Henry Wallace, the Progressive Party candidate in 1948. Quarreling was bitter at every level within the party, and ultimately Benson and his supporters were rejected and virtually ridden out of the party. In the spectrum of Minnesota politics the Democratic-Farmer-Labor Party, which is invariably nationally noted for its liberalism, actually came under the control of politicians in 1948 who were considerably more moderate than the hard-core Farmer-Laborites. Some of Benson's supporters, after assessing alternatives, came back within the fold; but others including Benson himself had little to do with the party after the schism. Benson to his dedicated followers epitomizes Farmer-Labor ideals and it seemed very appropriate to James M. Shields, Benson's biographer, to call him "Mr. Progressive."

Gaining control of the Democratic-Farmer-Labor Party was only part of the battle for Humphrey and his supporters. They had also to establish their legitimacy with the voters. Elected mayor of Minneapolis in 1945, Humphrey had won a reputation for his advocacy of civil rights during his administration and he led the call for a strong civil rights plank in the Democratic national platform. After winning his party's nomination for the United States Senate, he defeated incumbent Joseph Ball in the November election. At the same time three other Democratic-Farmer-Labor candidates, including Eugene McCarthy, were elected to the U.S. House of Representatives.

The events of 1948 marked an important transition in Minnesota politics: the formation of the Democratic-Farmer-Labor Party and its emergence as a major political force re-established the pattern in Minnesota of two major parties, nationally affiliated, vying for political control. The pattern may have been the same, but the parties were different—different primarily because protesters like Oliver Kelley and Ignatius Donnelly, Arthur Townley and Floyd B. Olson, had insisted over and over that government must be responsive to the needs of its people.

9

Minnesota and the Nation

ISTORY is a tapestry of people great and small; of wilderness and village and cities; of happenings, some notable, some not. Some things have local import only, while others, through a constant repetition, enter the very fabric of society. Sometimes, because of true greatness or just because of time or place, people or events influence the character of a broader area—the state, the nation, or even the world.

So it is that Minnesota has French and Indian names upon its land—Pomme de Terre and Kabetogama; that it has Herman the German and calls the Southern Minnesota bullhead "Iowa trout." The state also has more broadly based traditions: a social conscience, a reputation for responsiveness in government and for political activism. And so, too, has the state made lasting impressions on the character of the United States, as the products of its natural resources and industry contribute to the national economy, and as its people contribute to the national leadership.

It is often observed that Minnesota has produced national leaders far beyond the proportion of its people to the national population. The observation is more easily made than explained, but there is an element of truth in it. Perhaps Minnesota's political activism is a natural byproduct of the long era of agrarian discontent; perhaps Scandinavians, the most politically active ethnic group in the state, are more inclined than others to seek solutions to life's problems through politics and government. Whatever the elusive reasons, there can be little doubt that Minnesota not only had national political impact during the active Populist, Progressive, and Farmer-Labor days, but has earned even more recognition for political contributions during the last three decades.

Hubert Horatio Humphrey has, without doubt, been the central figure in Minnesota's recent political history. Even as a freshman senator Humphrey was not reticent. He expressed himself clearly and frequently on a wide range of national and international affairs and by the mid-1950s he was already recognized as a presidential possibility. In 1960, as his second senatorial term drew to a close, Humphrey made a bid for the Democratic presidential nomination but was outshone by John F. Kennedy in the primaries. During the early part of his third term he was continually in the national and international limelight, because of his role as Senate majority whip and because of his championship of the Civil Rights Act, the Peace Corps and the Food for Peace program. Humphrey was a logical choice for the vice-presidential nomination in 1964 although President Lyndon Johnson flirted with other running mate possibilities—including Minnesota's other senator, Eugene McCarthy.

Humphrey's election to the vice presidency enhanced his presidential prospects but also intertwined more closely than ever his political career with those of Eugene McCarthy and Walter Mondale. Mondale had been appointed by DFL Governor Karl Rolvaag to serve the remainder of Humphrey's senatorial term. At the time of his appointment he was the most respected member of the Democratic-Farmer-Labor Party's younger generation. Friends and critics alike agree that Mondale's political career has been idyllic. At the age of thirty-two in 1960 he was appointed Minnesota attorney general by DFL Governor Orville Freeman, and he was subsequently elected to the post for two more terms. As attorney general Mondale became widely known as a champion of consumer rights. Much of the time during the early 1960s he was more newsworthy than any other state official including the governor. Although Mondale was given his second big break with the senatorial appointment, it soon became evident that he had a solid base of public support. He was elected to a full term in 1966 and was easily re-elected in 1972, even though Richard Nixon defeated Democrat George McGovern in the presidential contest in Minnesota by a wide margin.

Humphrey as vice president initially benefited from the president's domestic accomplishments and nationally was regarded as the natural successor to the popular Johnson. But Humphrey unavoidably became associated with the increasing public distrust of the Johnson administration—a circumstance that put him and his onetime Minnesota ally, Eugene McCarthy, on a collision course toward the bitter Democratic Party split of 1968. The battle lines were drawn when McCarthy on November 30, 1967, announced that he would launch a campaign against American involvement in Vietnam. The declaration had great public appeal because of rapidly growing disillusionment with the country's role in Southeast Asia. Certainly McCarthy's stature as a congressional leader added significance to his crusade. After serving five terms in the House of Representatives he had been elected to the Senate in 1958, defeating Edward J. Thye, the two-term Republican incumbent who had also succeeded Stassen as governor. During his first term McCarthy addressed himself to a variety of domestic and foreign issues and became known as one of the most liberal members of the Senate. He became yet better known nationally in 1964 because of Johnson's consideration of him as a vice presidential possibility, and he was easily re-elected to the Senate.

To those who want things spelled out, McCarthy has always seemed an enigma. Like Humphrey he taught in college for a time, which in some circles helped establish the DFL as the party of the professors. But unlike Humphrey, whose public utterances tended to be both flamboyant and verbose, McCarthy spoke slowly, calmly, and philosophically. In part because of his mannerisms and because he offered questions, not answers, he struck some of his followers as a modern Socrates—a man with profound insight into society's malaise. At a time when the "establishment" defended the Vietnam war McCarthy appealed to many young people, especially college-age students, who took up his anti-establishment cause. During his anti-Vietnam crusade McCarthy was seen by his supporters as a humane philosopher who hoped to save the nation from yet greater tragedy, but many opponents believed that his crusade was nothing more than a vendetta against Johnson for the coquetry of 1964.

McCarthy shocked the nation by easily winning most of New Hampshire's national convention delegates in the first primary of 1968. That success led Senator Robert Kennedy to declare himself for the presidency, and Lyndon Johnson was soon forced to announce that he would not be a candidate in 1968. Johnson's retirement opened the way for Humphrey, and Kennedy's assassination set the stage for a Democratic national convention in Chicago featuring two Minnesotans as the front runners for the presidential nomination.

The bitter rivalry of the Humphrey–McCarthy forces was reflected in the precinct battles in Minnesota. Party regulars who were well acquainted with the long public service of both men tended to support Humphrey, but McCarthy showed great strength among college students and did particularly well in such outstate college communities as Marshall, Winona, Mankato, St. Cloud, and Moorhead. The contest in Minnesota was significant not because Humphrey captured most of the delegates, but because the clashing philosophies over Vietnam created such animosities that even the winner was assured of losing some support. This grassroots struggle in Minnesota, too, was indicative of the schism that was to emerge within the national Democratic Party.

In Chicago Humphrey easily won the presidential nomination on the first ballot, thus becoming the first Minnesotan to run for the presidency as a major party candidate. But Humphrey could not disassociate himself from Johnson's Vietnam policy, and when Chicago police used strong-arm tactics to contain demonstrating anti-Vietnam protesters and Humphrey refused to criticize them, the regular party lost much support. The disaffection of vociferous McCarthy supporters did not seem to be a decisive issue during most of the campaign because the polls regularly showed Humphrey to be far behind Republican candidate Richard Nixon. But Humphrey campaigned tirelessly and enthusiastically like a "Happy Warrior" in the Al Smith tradition, and in the end he lost the election by only 500,000 votes out of 70,000,000 cast. There can be little doubt that the decision would have been different if those who were influenced by the Vietnam dilemma had voted for their party's candidate. McCarthy did not actively campaign, nor did he announce support for Humphrey until just a week and a half before the election, when he gave his onetime friend and fellow builder of Minnesota's Democratic-Farmer-Labor Party an endorsement that at best was perfunctory.

In a sense, both Humphrey and McCarthy lost in 1968. With his defeat Humphrey was temporarily out of public office, but he was easily elected to the United States Senate in 1970, taking the seat left vacant when McCarthy chose not to run. It is very unlikely that McCarthy could have been re-elected even if he had run after having challenged his party in 1968 and, in the minds of many, having ruined the presidential aspirations of his fellow Minnesotan.

In 1972, Humphrey's presidential ambitions were undercut by George McGovern's well-executed campaign, but then during the troubled days of the Watergate investigation Humphrey emerged again as a party favorite. Those who contemplated 1976 presidential possibilities also often mentioned Walter Mondale, and Mondale did launch a short, abortive bid for the nomination in 1974. His withdrawal, prompted by his expressed aversion to the rigors of campaigning, appeared to have seriously damaged his chances for higher office. But the sudden emergence of Jimmy Carter of Georgia as the Democratic Party's favorite presidential candidate, which effectively allayed any serious interest Humphrey may have had in seeking his party's nomination again, also created a situation in which the ticket needed a national balance. By June of 1976 it became apparent that Carter would be nominated and it also became obvious that he needed a running mate from the north, preferably a liberal with close ties to organized labor. After careful screening of potential running mates, and after receiving the nomination at the New York City convention, Carter announced Mondale as his choice for the vice presidential role.

In spite of his earlier aversion to the campaign trail, Mondale worked hard and effectively among party regulars. He also organized labor and blacks in the major industrial states and participated in the historic first debate between candidates for the vice presidency. Polls indicated that he was regarded as an asset to the ticket, and with the Carter–Mondale victory on November 2, 1976, Mondale became the second vice president from Minnesota. There is now speculation that Mondale may well become the Democratic presidential candidate in 1984.

Because of his affliction with cancer, a factor that probably generated some sympathy votes and aided in his easy re-election to the Senate, Humphrey was inactive for most of the campaign season, but Eugene McCarthy as the candidate of the Independent Party threatened to undermine Carter and Mondale. When it became apparent that the election, contrary to initial expectations, would be a close contest, the McCarthy candidacy— which appealed mostly to those inclined to vote for Carter and Mondale—was galling to many Democrats. As in 1968, they were puzzled by McCarthy. To some he seemed to be just the Democratic counterpart to Stassen, to others he appeared an embittered man, and to a small group he offered calm reason in a campaign they thought bereft of thoughtful discussion of the issues by the presidential candidates of the major parties. The closeness of the election, which seemed a dead heat on election eve, magnified McCarthy's importance. His candidacy denied Carter and Mondale the electoral votes for four states and made their victory considerably narrower than it would have been otherwise.

Although Humphrey, McCarthy, and Mondale have been the most conspicuous Democratic-Farmer-Labor politicians, others have served in important national positions as well. Orville L. Freeman, after three terms as governor, was the Secretary of Agriculture in the Kennedy and Johnson administrations; during Johnson's administration Walter Heller of the University of Minnesota served as chairman of the President's Council of Economic Advisers. Eugenie M. Anderson of Red Wing, who was like Humphrey and McCarthy a pioneer in the Democratic-Farmer-Labor Party, was the first woman in the nation's history to hold ambassadorial rank. She was ambassador to Denmark from 1949 to 1953 and later served as minister to Bulgaria and as a representative on the United Nations Trusteeship Council.

The fame of Humphrey, McCarthy, and Mondale leads outsiders to believe that Minnesota is basically a one-party state, but in reality there has been, over the years, an intense and close rivalry between political parties. Stassen Republicans controlled the governorship until 1955, and since then Republicans have held the post two other terms. In spite of losing the governorship so often in recent times, Republicans continued to dominate the state legislature until the election of 1972 and some of the party's members have gained national and international prominence. The persevering Harold Stassen has been newsworthy for nearly four decades, and during the 1950s Congressman Walter Judd of Minneapolis was one of the national leaders of the China lobby—that group which urged strong United States support of Chiang Kai-Shek's Republic of China and the containment of Red China. Judd, a medical doctor who had served as a missionary in China, became an influential figure during the Eisenhower presidency. He reached the pinnacle of his career in 1960 when he delivered the keynote address at the Republican National Convention. But changing voter moods and the appeal of the youthful Donald Fraser unseated Judd in 1962.

Richard Nixon during his first term brought some Minnesotans into prominent government positions. James D. Hodgson, who was born in Dawson, was named Secretary of Labor and Maurice H. Stans of Shakopee was appointed Secretary of Commerce. Stans resigned in 1972 to direct the financial affairs of the Committee to Re-Elect the President. As Nixon's chief fund-raiser Stans was tainted by the Watergate scandal and later in a humiliating end to his public career he pleaded guilty to Watergate-associated misdemeanors. In his efforts to make the Supreme Court more conservative, Nixon appointed to it two Minnesotans who had served on the Circuit Court of Appeals. Warren Burger of St. Paul was named chief justice in 1969 and the next year Harry A. Blackmun of Rochester was also named to the court.

Minnesota has from the beginning had impact on the national

economy because of the extent and nature of its natural resources, and the state's economic character today is but an extension of those frontier bases of agriculture, forestry, and mining. Although each has been drastically changed, each is still
associated with a particular section of the state. Minnesota is
one of the most agricultural of the fifty states, ranking among
the top half-dozen in the production of both crops and livestock.
This dependence on the land unavoidably affects the character
of Minnesotans. There is a preoccupation with weather, particularly during the growing season, because a whole year's work
and investment can depend on the rainfall of but a few days.
During dry years, the week-after-week forecasts of nice weekends that so delight suburbanites can spell disaster for rural residents. And Minnesota is still largely rural. The statistical shift
of the population from rural to urban did not occur until 1950,
and thousands of those who are now classed as urban residents
actually have rural or small town backgrounds. This inherent
ruralness has shaped the perception Minnesotans have of themselves. Sinclair Lewis, Sauk Centre's famous son who won the
Nobel Prize in literature in 1931, first attracted widespread attention with his novel *Main Street,* a classic portrayal of small
town parochialism based on his hometown. Others, however,
have glorified the small towns: for many years, Northfield advertised itself by way of signs at the edge of town as a place of
"Cows, Colleges and Contentment."

Diversification that saved Minnesota farmers from the tyranny
of "King Wheat" has accelerated in recent decades. Although
wheat is still a major crop, it lags far behind corn, since shortly
after World War I the ranking cereal both in acreage and in
bushels. Corn was grown by territorial pioneers in southern
Minnesota, but its successful commercial culture has been a
story of adaptation. At first farmers turned to oats as the main
field crop to replace wheat, partially because of the difficulties
in finding strains of corn suited to Minnesota's climate. From
the 1890s on through World War I, University of Minnesota scientists worked at developing more productive and hardier corn.
They did succeed in drawing the corn belt further north by
pioneering several faster-maturing varieties, but corn yields

even as late as the 1920s were not very much better than those of forty or fifty years earlier.

However, during the last forty years Minnesota corn has experienced its own green revolution. The average yield of 30.4 bushels per acre for the period 1922–1931 increased to 46.6 for the decade 1947–1956. By 1973 it had skyrocketed to 91.4 bushels per acre. This improved production was first of all caused by an almost complete shift to hybrid varieties between 1935 and 1946. But by then yields were also stimulated by better cultivation as horse-drawn equipment was replaced with tractor-powered plows and cultivators. The widespread use of commercial fertilizers, herbicides, and pesticides, especially in the period since World War II, also increased productivity.

Although corn has been a major cash crop it also became a major component of the so-called corn-hog economy when its abundance caused it to be used as the principal fattening cereal. The successful corn culture stimulated the production of both hogs and beef cattle, which, in turn, has made Minnesota one of the major meat-packing states. Such centers as South St. Paul, now the world's largest livestock market, are among the nation's leaders in meat packing. The industry is also significant in such places as Luverne, Worthington, Albert Lea, and Austin, home base of the George Hormel Company, which during its nearly ninety-year history has grown from a small processing plant to one of the country's ranking meat-packing companies with plants in a number of states.

As diversified farmers have shown a remarkable ability to adapt to the land, they have also displayed an acute perception of changing market conditions. Modern farmers, like the pioneer farmers, seek to raise those things that command the greatest market value. Today soybeans in terms of acres are Minnesota's second-ranking crop. Yet as recently as forty years ago soybeans were rarely seen in the state. Some were raised during the drought years of the mid-1930s as a forage crop, but the market for soybean oil led to increased cultivation and the construction of Minnesota's first soybean processing plant at Mankato in 1939. During and after World War II the explosive worldwide demand for soybean oil increased cultivation in Minnesota to the point where the state now ranks fourth in soybean production.

The search for new products and opportunities presented by consumer demands of an increasingly urbanized, industrialized society spurred the production of a great variety of crops nationwide. In Minnesota the major field crops have been supplemented with potatoes, sugar beets, flax, sunflowers, and vegetables. As crops like these increased, that branch of industry related to processing agricultural produce became more complex and varied. Since fresh produce is both bulky and perishable, it is usually processed close to the point of origin or conversely raised close to an existing processing area. As a result, many sugar refineries and other processing plants have developed in Minnesota since the turn of the century.

No other firm better exemplifies the growth of food processing than Green Giant, which has made its giant and the giant's valley world famous. The valley of the "Jolly Green Giant" is the Minnesota River Valley, where the Minnesota Valley Canning Company began modestly at LeSueur in 1903 by canning sweet corn. Gradually the company expanded to other vegetables and during the 1920s began marketing a new variety of peas under the trade name of "Green Giant." In 1928 the company used the name for its other products as well in a national advertising campaign that marked the beginning of an expansive period. The "Green Giant" on the label was a caricature of a rather ugly hunchbacked giant who seems to have been inspired by both Paul Bunyan stories and Grimm's fairy tales. Over the years the giant has mellowed into a very happy, convincing ad man. The success of the label caused the company to change its name officially to Green Giant in 1950. After establishing a number of plants in Minnesota and other states to process an infinite variety of vegetables, the company added an international division in 1961 and is now recognized as one of the world's leaders in vegetable canning and packing.

During its early days the Minnesota Valley Canning Company was only one of many local canning concerns that sprang up in southern Minnesota to process sweet corn and peas. Most of the other small companies were absorbed by such major corporations as Libby's, Del Monte, and General Foods. The plants of these companies when combined with Green Giant make Minnesota one of the foremost states in the production of canned and frozen vegetables.

As modern processing like modern agriculture became more varied, Minnesota's first food processing industry, flour milling, was altered by new circumstances. After Minneapolis became the nation's leading flour producer its annual output continued to rise to a peak of over 18,000,000 barrels in 1916. This growth was dominated by four major corporations, including Pillsbury and Washburn-Crosby, which had absorbed countless smaller companies in an age when consolidation affected all of the country's important industries. Despite consolidation many small town mills persisted, independent of the Minneapolis giants, in places like Winona, Red Wing, and Mankato.

However, the large companies led the way in shifting operations to other parts of the nation. Foreseeing that Minneapolis flour milling would decline, Washburn-Crosby and Company started a mill in Buffalo, New York, in 1903. The anticipated decline came rather abruptly during the 1920s. By the end of that decade the "Mill City" produced only slightly more than half as much flour as it had at its zenith, and it ranked third after Buffalo and Kansas City, Missouri. The decline resulted from a combination of forces that had been building for over two decades. Soil exhaustion and ruinous black stem rust on the northern plains had caused a sharp reduction in production of the varieties of wheat best suited for bread flour. As this was occurring Nebraska, Kansas, Oklahoma, and parts of Texas benefited from the development of a hard winter wheat which was just as desirable as hard spring wheat for flour making. Grain from this southwest region could be more advantageously marketed and milled in Kansas City than in Minneapolis.

Changes in wheat culture were the main reason for the shift to Kansas City, but the rise of Buffalo was more complex. Buffalo, lying between the Great Lakes shipping routes and the large flour market of the Northeast, had traditionally been a flour-milling center, but it could not compete with Minneapolis until it was aided by policies of the federal government.

Through a series of rulings the Interstate Commerce Commission created price differentials in the shipping of bulk wheat and flour from west of the Great Lakes to Buffalo. Because it cost considerably more to transport flour than wheat, millers decided to construct plants at the greatest wheat depot closest to the most consumers: Buffalo, which also became a milling center for Canadian wheat. Under United States tariff regulations there was no import duty on Canadian wheat if the flour was exported. Since Buffalo was ideally situated with respect to both the Canadian shipping routes and the European market, it much more than Minneapolis or any other place benefited from the "milling-in-bond" principle.

The development of Buffalo and Kansas City as milling centers was led by Minneapolis-based companies that readily adapted to the changing conditions. Wasburn-Crosby, the Pillsbury Company, and the International Milling Company, which was started at New Prague in 1892 and today as part of International Multifoods is the world's largest flour miller, all sent men, capital, and technical knowhow to the new centers. But the headquarters of all the companies remained in Minneapolis, which became the nerve center of a national and international complex of terminal elevators, mills, and allied facilities. This outgrowth and extension of milling stimulated cosmopolitanism in Minneapolis as hundreds of businessmen traveled widely in the nation and abroad and returned with new outlooks and perspectives.

As the leading millers were expanding outside Minnesota, they became concerned with diversification. Urbanization and increased demands for convenience foods created opportunities in the breakfast-cereal field. Washburn-Crosby in 1924 began marketing Wheaties, which soon became a household word through the new medium of radio. Several months before Wheaties were introduced, Washburn-Crosby and Company became the major financer of a Twin Cities radio station which they named WCCO after the company's initials. Before the station passed to network ownership the company used it to pioneer a then novel advertising technique—the singing commercial. On Christmas Eve, 1926, WCCO listeners were treated to a quartet singing the Wheaties ad to the melody of "She's a Jazz Baby," a refrain which later became familiar nationwide.

> Have you tried Wheaties?
> They're whole wheat with all of the bran.
> Won't you try Wheaties?
> For wheat is the best food of man.[1]

Through consolidation with some of its own subsidiaries and other milling companies, Washburn-Crosby became General Mills in 1928. The new name was intended to convey the impression that the company was no longer just a Minneapolis flour-milling concern but was in fact general because of its widespread holdings and the diversity of its products. General Mills typifies the modern companies that grew out of the old flour-milling firms. It continued milling and the marketing of Gold Medal flour but also branched out into breakfast foods, cake flours, quick dough mixes, frozen foods, and other products. In the continual quest for new products the companies operate their own laboratories and have developed a great consciousness of consumer interest in the marketing of their wares. In the 1920s General Mills created one of the best known fictional women in American history. "Betty Crocker" was an ad man's dream, inspired by the need to answer consumer inquiries with a human touch. Crocker was the surname of a former Washburn-Crosby official, and Betty was just a good American name. Over her nearly half-century career Betty Crocker has aged while remaining always in keeping with contemporary styles. Her name and her image are so well placed in the public mind that thousands of people assume she is real.

In spite of the exodus to other places during the last half-century, enough milling has continued in Minneapolis and other Minnesota cities to make the state still one of the nation's leading flour producers. Minneapolis flour production in 1960 showed a decline of over seventy per cent from its greatest year, but reputations change slowly; to many farmers and other resi-

---

1. Quoted in James Gray, *Business Without Boundary: The Story of General Mills* (Minneapolis: University of Minnesota Press, 1954), p. 160.

dents throughout the state it was still the "Mill City." The rapid growth of the "brainpower industries"—computer and instrument designing and manufacturing—at last helped the city shed its old image, and the term "Mill City" is only rarely heard today. Minneapolis, in fact, has only two wheat flour mills. The twenty-one other mills in the state still make milling significant and make Minnesota the nation's leading producer of durum wheat products—macaroni, noodles, and other pasta.

Most of Minnesota's reputation as a verdant, scenic state rests on its northern forests. Lush though they may be, those forests have been greatly altered since the lumberman's frontier. As recently as two generations ago lumbermen were felling the last unprotected stands of white and red pine in the final surge of frontier extraction. Today, although a great deal of the state is wooded, the percentage of forested land has been reduced from a pre-frontier seventy per cent to thirty-four per cent. The virtual disappearance of the Big Woods and the farmers' incursion into the western and southern belts of the primary coniferous forest zone account for most of the decrease. Even the remaining forest, which lies mostly in the fourteen northeastern and north central counties, has been drastically changed since frontier days. Once the large conifers such as the white and red pine had been cut, fast-growing aspen, birch, and jack pine replaced them. The change in the type of trees is the main reason for the present nature of forest industries, which emphasize, in addition to cut lumber, posts and Christmas trees, production of wood pulp and chips used in the manufacture of various composition lumber products and paper.

Minnesota's conversion from frontier lumbering to managed forest industries is illustrative of national trends. By the late nineteenth century, as the voracious demands of industry and population growth threatened depletion of natural resources, there was a growing public awareness nationwide that old ways had to be changed. Conservation measures advocated by some Populists and Progressives and other reformers were accepted in principle but implementation was quite another matter, especially in Minnesota where to a large extent the frontier still existed physically and the frontier mentality still ruled.

Nonetheless, even before frontier lumbering had peaked, Minnesota was pushed into the national conservation movement, not because of a great public awareness but rather because of the efforts of a small, far-sighted group which was concerned about the future as well as the present. As early as 1876 there were enough Minnesotans who saw the need for a planned program of forest use to organize the Minnesota State Forestry Association, one of the first groups of its kind in the nation. The association, working through civic groups and fraternal organizations, tried to win public acceptance of the necessary conservation measures. Although the association was effective in marshaling opinion, Minnesota's greatest conservation thrust came from one outstanding individual—Christopher Columbus Andrews.

Andrews, a Massachusetts lawyer, moved to St. Cloud before the Civil War and served as a brigadier general in the Minnesota Volunteers. In 1869, when Andrews was forty years old, President Ulysses S. Grant appointed him United States minister to Sweden and Norway. While serving in this post Andrews, in the course of studying the Swedish economy, was impressed by that country's reforestation projects, in which he saw the future of Minnesota. Although Andrews was absent from the United States for a number of years during the 1870s and 1880s because of his Scandinavian post and his later assignment as consul general in Rio de Janeiro, Brazil, he was more influential than any other single Minnesotan in advocating forest planning.

At first many of Andrews's speeches and writings on the subject had little impact because there was still so much virgin forest standing. However, public awareness of the depletability of its timber resources was jolted by the disastrous Hinckley forest fire of September 1, 1894. The Hinckley disaster, in which over 400 people lost their lives, ranks as one of the greatest forest fires in the nation's history. The very nature of Minnesota with its flat terrain, occasional drought years, and strong sweeping winds is conducive to fires, and in 1894 these conditions were complicated by the carelessness of lumbermen who left stumps and piles of waste in their wake and by the indifference of frontier settlers toward minor fires. After the holocaust,

Minnesotans responded with state aid to survivors, and in 1895 the legislature provided that the state auditor also serve as the state forest commissioner. The auditor was authorized to name a chief fire warden, who could appoint deputy wardens and who was to appraise the state's forest resources and promote reforestation projects. Although he was sixty-six years old, Andrews gladly accepted the position because it provided him at last with a real opportunity to put some of his ideas into practice.

Andrews served as chief fire warden for ten years and as forestry commissioner for six more years before being named secretary of the newly created state forestry board, an agency independent of the auditor's office. It was a difficult time. Conservationists including governors Lind, Van Sant, and Johnson and President Theodore Roosevelt helped popularize the conservation movement, but in Minnesota there was also strong opposition. In spite of this opposition, Andrews was successful in achieving at least a philosophical acceptance of his beliefs that forests should occupy only land unsuited for agriculture, that annual cutting should never exceed annual growth, and that the forests should continually be renewed through reforestation. While Andrews was still chief fire warden the state created a School of Forestry at the University of Minnesota to help professionalize the new directions. The school, created only two years after the first of the nation's forestry schools, was headed for many years by Samuel B. Green, who through his teaching, writing, and speaking helped win acceptance for new forestry practices in Minnesota.

Responding to Andrews's urgings, the legislature authorized a state nursery, made state parks forest reserves, created several new parks with both conservation and recreation in mind, and greatly expanded the forest service through legislation of 1911. Partly because of the influence of Andrews and other Minnesota conservationists, the federal government reserved specified forest tracts under the Morris Act of 1902 and also while Roosevelt was president created two massive national forests in Minnesota—the Superior National Forest, which contained thousands of acres of virgin forest; and the Minnesota National Forest, which became the Chippewa National Forest in

1928. Although both were sizable to begin with, they have subsequently been enlarged and now comprise about one sixth of the state's total forested area. These achievements, although in keeping with the reform spirit of the times, were also prompted by the annual recurrence of forest fires. During every dry year the hundreds of minor fires did not greatly concern the public despite the history of the Hinckley fire. However, the destruction of Chisholm in 1908 and the villages of Baudette and Spooner two years later again aroused public concern and stimulated new forestry legislation. In 1914 Minnesota voters approved a constitutional amendment authorizing the state to set aside as state forests those public lands which were better adapted for forests than for agriculture.

Although conservationists made significant advances during the progressive era, resistance to their movement continued. They had to battle the apathetic who still believed that Minnesota's virgin forests were not really threatened. Further, there was vocal and well-organized opposition from civic boosters, railroads, lumber companies, and land speculators who insisted that the lumbermen were merely opening the way for the farmers. Lumber companies, especially, wanted to sell their cutover land rather than have it remain on the tax rolls, so it was natural for them and others who believed that northern Minnesota could become another agricultural frontier to encourage cutover farming. Strangely enough, the claim that northern Minnesota could become part of the farm belt was strengthened during the period 1880–1920 because there were many opportunities for farmers to sell produce locally to lumbermen or miners. As a result thousands of small farms were started in the least rocky portions of the old forest zone. As late as 1920 the philosophical battle still raged between advocates of reforestation and boosters of cutover farming about the best land use in the wasted forest lands.

Conservationists won the argument as conditions changed in the 1920s. The rapid closing of frontier lumbering and the agricultural depression ruined thousands of farmers, who simply abandoned their land. These small farms in time passed to the state as tax-delinquent lands. By 1930 the situation had reached crisis proportions. About one seventh of the state's entire acreage was on the tax-delinquent rolls and about three fourths of those acres were in the old coniferous forest area. The situation prompted Governor Olson to appoint a land utilization committee, which recommended in 1932 that Minnesota recognize that most of the cutover land was suited only for forests and that the state take steps to create more state forests with the aim of developing economic and recreational opportunities. The tax-delinquent lands helped expand existing forests and became the basis of twenty-six new state forests created during Olson's administration. These changes, which were augmented by New Deal reforestation work done by the Works Project Administration and the Civilian Conservation Corps and by later creations and expansions of state forests, have borne fruit in recent years.

Conservation and management of state and federal forest lands in Minnesota and the recently discovered usefulness of such weed trees as the aspen have stimulated the current forest products industry. The harvest of 1974 exceeded that of 1914—a year when quantities of virgin forest remained—and the industry, with a net worth of $1.3 billion, employed some 40,000 people. Impressive as these statistics are, they in no way reflect the recreational value of the forests to Minnesota's increasingly urban population and to its hundreds of resort operators as well.

In Minnesota as in the nation there is no longer any question about the desirability of preservation or wise use of forest resources, but it would be a mistake to assume that solutions to the problems of one generation will suffice for the next. Currently the controversy is between those who want managed harvesting of virgin forests in the Boundary Waters Canoe Area and those who want to preserve great parts of them in a wilderness condition. The resolution of the conflict over the boundary waters forests will establish precedents affecting the future not only of Minnesota but of the nation.

Although Minnesota is an important agricultural and forest state, its iron resources have had a much greater impact on the nation and the world. Since the opening of the Mesabi Range, Minnesota has produced nearly two thirds of the country's iron ore. Not only was its ore plentiful, but it was rich, easily mined and accessible to water transportation. But like lumbering, iron mining had to undergo a difficult adjustment after the height of its exploitation. As the richest deposits were depleted, Minnesotans converted to mining the more plentiful but poorer taconite, the "mother ore" of the Mesabi Range.

Twentieth-century Minnesota mining has to a large extent been the story of the Mesabi, whose production far surpassed all other American iron regions and completely dwarfed the combined production of Minnesota's three other iron-ore locales— the Vermilion Range, the Cuyuna Range, and ore pits in the southeastern part of the state. The frontier phases of Vermilion and Mesabi mining had run their course by the time the first ore was taken from the Cuyuna Range in 1911. The Cuyuna, a long, narrow range, stretched from near Brainerd in the central part of the state northeastward for about sixty five miles, and it lay across an area that had already been settled by farmers, so the mines were developed right in the midst of established farms, towns, and railroads. The discovery and opening of the Cuyuna Range was principally due to the persistence of Cuyler Adams who first detected signs of magnetic ore in 1895 while surveying land. He worked for another sixteen years, surveying, core testing, and persuading mining companies to invest, before the first ore was taken. Cuyuna sounds like an Indian name, but it was coined by Adams by taking the first syllable of his name and adding to it Una, the name of his dog.

The ore from the Cuyuna, like that of the Vermilion Range, was hard and deep, so most of the early mines developed were underground. The Cuyuna ores were also comparatively rich in manganese, which proved to be very important to the United States during World War I when its importation was limited.

Minnesota's fourth iron-ore area has never been referred to as a range because that ore (in the Spring Valley area in Fillmore County) was found in small pockets of ten to fifty thousand tons under cultivated land. In 1941 contractors took samples, and the next year they removed some 60,000 tons. Because of the value of the land for crop purposes the extraction was carefully done at a time when the ground was not frozen. The valuable topsoil was scraped off and deposited so it could be respread later. Then the iron ore, which usually lay from just below the surface to depths of twenty feet, was scooped into trucks for shipment to a local washing plant and later transshipment by rail. Usually the contractors simply paid the Fillmore County farmers a royalty of about $.25 a ton for ore. Though insignificant when compared to the three iron ranges, this district was quite important during the 1950s. With the end of its mining in 1969 the Fillmore County district had produced slightly over 8,000,000 tons, an amount equal to about one twelfth of the accumulated yield of the Vermilion Range.

Long before the Mesabi reached its full potential, miners discovered that some of the most accessible ore had to be improved before it could be used in blast furnaces. The richest ore, the so-called direct-shipment ore, was simply excavated and shipped to furnaces in Pittsburgh, Erie, and other manufacturing centers; but often adjacent ore was full of impurities such as clay, silica, other rocks, or excessive moisture. The Oliver Mining Company as early as 1907 experimentally removed such substances near the mining sites to produce a concentrated product with a higher ore content. Satisfied that crushing and washing (beneficiating) would improve the quality of the ore, the company commissioned its district manager, John C. Greenway, to construct a concentrating plant at Trout Lake near the company's planned community of Coleraine in 1909. Within a short time other companies built concentrators, and by the mid-1920s about one third of Minnesota's iron ore was improved before being sent east. By the late 1950s there were nearly eighty concentrating facilities spread along the Mesabi Range.

Nineteen fifty-one was, in terms of tonnage, the peak of Minnesota's range production; but in terms of numbers of men employed, the zenith was reached during World War I when approximately 18,000 men worked the mines. By 1932, however, there were less than 6,000 miners, a plunge caused by postwar production cutbacks, increased use of labor-saving machinery, and the onset of the depression.

The World War I era was noteworthy not only because of unprecedented production, but also because of labor unrest fomented in part by the radical Industrial Workers of the World. There was also a renewal of Minnesota resentment against absentee mine owners. Such men as Tower, Oliver, and Carnegie had never been popular with those Minnesotans who saw evil in big business, and they became less so during the time of progressive reforms. Animosity welled up again yet stronger during World War I because of the anti-business stance of the militant Nonpartisan League and the general public belief that war profiteering was rampant.

The League's renewal of the anti-business crusade stimulated a legislative review of iron-ore taxation, which was regarded as the public's most effective check on the excesses of the giant out-of-state steel corporations. Some of the postwar reaction was also caused by a belief that Minnesota had been bilked by the first iron-ore capitalists. Many Minnesotans remembered that Charlemagne Tower had persuaded the state to levy ore duties of only a penny a ton in order to encourage range development. It is true that this original tonnage tax was discontinued in 1897 in favor of an ad valorem property tax based on the assessed valuation of unmined ore; but over the years influential groups and individuals argued that this tax too was insufficient. Proponents of heavier taxation contended that the steel companies were depleting Minnesota's heritage and that within a half-century or so the state would be left with only gaping holes as a stark reminder of its onetime wealth. Reasoning that iron ore (unlike the forests) could not be renewed, legislators concluded that mining should be subjected to what opponents called double taxation. Therefore, the 1921 legislature overwhelmingly passed an act instituting an "occupation tax," an imprecise description of a special tax on the tonnage of extracted ore. Unlike the 1881 tonnage tax, this was a tax not in lieu of property taxes but in addition to them. To forecheck an anticipated challenge of the law's constitutionality it was submitted to the voters of the state, who accepted it as a constitutional amendment in 1922.

Although conservative Governor Jacob Preus did not favor the legislation, he signed it. The act remained controversial for years. Steel companies naturally claimed that it caused higher operating costs, which forced them to reduce the labor force and to charge higher prices for finished steel products. Further, they argued that the burden of double taxation would discourage further exploration and development. But the companies' greatest and probably most justifiable ire was directed at the assessors for the iron-range communities, who used property tax levies to support well-staffed municipal governments and some of the nation's finest public schools. The excesses of the assessors during the early 1920s finally forced the state legislature to place ceilings on property tax assessments in the range communities.

The range economies which were devastated during the depression decade of the 1930s revived sharply during World War II when Minnesota's iron ranges again were assaulted ruthlessly to support the war effort. Heavy wartime production hastened the depletion of direct shipment ore and made thousands of Minnesotans uneasy about the possibility of a future without mines. However, there was enough ore to sustain massive production during most of the 1950s, and in fact the decade's yield exceeded that of the 1940s. But by the late 1950s prospects were bleak. Most of the high-grade ore was gone and the mining economy was suffering in a time of great national affluence. But there was also hope: some mining companies and political leaders were claiming that northern Minnesota could be saved by taconite, a low-grade iron ore.

Although it has become important only recently, taconite has been known for over a century. It was first discovered by a Michigan prospector in the early 1870s and appraised by Newton H. Winchell, Minnesota's state geologist, in the late 1880s and early 1890s. Winchell determined that the hard slate-gray to blackish sedimentary rock underlay the breadth of the Mesabi and contained narrow bands of low-grade magnetite. In his written reports Winchell identified the rock as "taconyte," a word he had borrowed from other geologists. Winchell concluded that the taconite stratum was of a type first identified in the Taconic Mountains of western Massachusetts and Vermont. Winchell used the name to describe a whole era of sedimentary deposits, but his fellow geologists used it only when referring to the Mesabi's mother rock containing the low-grade ores. Since

Winchell's time, however, taconite has been adopted worldwide to describe similar deposits.

The first miners on the Mesabi were obviously aware of taconite, but they were interested only in the soft, rich pockets of ore. Not only was taconite hard, but its mineral bands contained only particles of iron ore and those particles were only about one third as rich as the best Minnesota ores. As the mine owners became aware of the limited quantities of high-grade ore, however, they began to wonder about the commercial potential of taconite. Then in 1913 a Mesabi land owner who was also a University of Minnesota regent sent taconite samples and the problem of utilization to the newly organized Mines Experiment Station at the University. After that time the development of the taconite industry was principally due to the work of Edward W. Davis, an engineer with the Mines Experiment Station. Davis worked on principles and machinery for extracting the ore particles, and within a few years he had developed techniques for crushing and washing the rock and separating out the ore. Utilizing these techniques at experimental plants at Duluth and later at Babbitt, he successfully extracted a moderately rich product from taconite. But unfortunately his experiments also proved that his process was plagued by a host of technical problems and that production was so costly that it was impossible for taconite to compete with direct shipment and concentrated ores. So the experimental plants were soon abandoned and Davis embarked on another phase of his career.

With state research funds he worked for twenty years developing a process that not only would crush the rock, but would ultimately reduce it to a flour-like texture, something that had not been possible in the first plants. There were related problems to solve, too, such as efficiently removing the ore particles by magnetic attraction and discarding the tons of waste, or tailings. By the time of World War II Davis had made enough progress to attract the interest of two new companies, Erie Mining Company and Reserve Mining Company, both of which had been formed by parent steel companies to supply them with iron ore. As more efficient processing steps were devised and refined, both companies became persuaded that commercial taconite production was feasible.

Reserve moved first and in 1946 announced that it would construct a taconite plant at Silver Bay on Lake Superior. The company built not only a large plant which it named in honor of Davis, but a village for its workers as well. At last in 1955 the first pellets were produced, and the next spring they were shipped eastward from the company's harbor alongside the plant. This installation and another taconite facility built by the Erie Mining Company were the culmination of Davis's long years of searching for effective ways of producing quality ore from taconite. The process entailed breaking huge rocks into smaller pieces and then pulverizing the pieces into the flour-like dust from which giant magnets pulled out the usable ore particles. The particles of ore had to be processed into a shippable product, so they were next mixed with a binding clay and pellets about one-fourth inch in diameter were formed. Once the pellets had been hardened by heat of over 2000° they were stockpiled for shipment on ore carriers.

The techniques of producing taconite had been mastered, but the process, especially when compared to earlier mining, was costly. Consequently Reserve and Erie, the steel companies, and many others interested in the economic future of iron mining felt inhibited by the state's mineral tax laws. Rapid depletion of other iron ores and the impending financial doom for Minnesota's ranges gave rise to increasing talk of the need to do something that would encourage the taconite industry. By 1960 there was a general recognition by Minnesotans that something had to be done, but understandably there was long and heated debate over specifics. Many, especially liberal members of the DFL Party, opposed any sort of concession to big business; and the arguments over tax reform began to assume the characteristics of the classic confrontation between the public and the robber barons in an earlier age. Finally in 1963 the state legislature passed a law providing that taxes on taconite and other specified minerals including copper and nickel should not exceed those levied on other industries. Because there was an existing constitutional provision relating to iron-ore taxation, the question had to be submitted to the voters in the form of the "taconite amendment." Both major political parties and the Iron Mining Industry of Minnesota, an association of various mining companies, launched an extensive publicity campaign to inform the electorate about the nature of taconite and the need for the amendment. The mining company association distributed thousands of samples of taconite bits, finely crushed ore, and pellets so voters were made tactilely aware of the issue. Although many voters were not completely convinced that the amendment was desirable, it was accepted; and its passage has had the desired effect of increasing taconite production and stimulating the construction of new plants

Before the amendment Minnesota had just two commercial taconite plants with a combined production of something less than 20,000,000 tons annually. Today there are eight plants with a total production over three times greater than that, and further expansion is yet to come. The amendment has had the effect also of accelerating inevitable change in Minnesota's iron mining. Mining in Fillmore County and in the Vermilion and Cuyuna ranges has ended and the Mesabi remains the state's only ore-producing region. In 1967 taconite shipments for the first time exceeded iron-ore shipments, and presently they comprise over three fourths of Minnesota's iron exports. As the last small deposits of soft ore are scraped from the Mesabi, the balance will swing yet more to taconite, which, based on current production rates, should last for another 150 to 200 years.

Still, taconite is a mixed blessing. It has brought prosperity and renewed hope for the future, but it has also brought controversy. The primary issue is the dumping of taconite tailings into Lake Superior at Reserve Mining's Silver Bay plant. Before Reserve began constructing the plant it requested permission from the federal and state governments to relocate a highway, erect a power plant with a tall smokestack, and construct a harbor. These requests were routinely granted, but state officials were troubled by Reserve's other request: permission to draw water from Lake Superior and, after using it in processing, return it and the suspended waste particles—the tailings—to the lake. The matter was debated for nearly a year before permits were granted, and when they were, there was included the proviso that the tailings should not pollute the lake.

By the late 1960s telltale signs—like the brilliant aquamarine discoloration of the lake water near the plant—were convincing proof to some that the tailings were indeed polluting. Subsequent investigations and vocal public concern caused the federal government, the states of Minnesota, Wisconsin, and Michigan, and the Minnesota-based Environmental Defense Fund to bring a lawsuit against Reserve in federal district court to halt the dumping of tailings in Lake Superior.

The proceedings, which were presided over by Judge Miles Lord, dragged on for nine months and produced so many headline stories that "Reserve Mining" and "taconite tailings" became household words in Minnesota. During the trial the plaintiffs alleged among other things that minute asbestos fibers contained in the tailings were a potential cancer hazard because they had been carried into the water supply of Duluth and other lakeshore communities. Both sides produced witnesses who testified at great length, and charges, countercharges, and defenses sometimes became acrimonious. At last in April 1974 Judge Lord ordered Reserve to immediately halt the dumping of tailings into Lake Superior. However, the company in a series of legal moves appealed the decision to the Eighth Circuit Court of Appeals in St. Louis and even asked that the court remove Lord as trial judge because of his alleged bias in favor of the plaintiffs. In separate actions the court did order Lord's removal, which had the effect of making him a hero to many Minnesotans, and it ordered Reserve to find an on-land disposal site. Despite threats that it might terminate its Minnesota operations, Reserve has seemingly reconciled itself to the use of an on-land site, but the controversy still lingers. The company, pointing out high conversion costs, favors a site closer to the plant than the one that state officials in their concern about detrimental environmental impact have chosen further inland. Whatever the outcome, it is clear that the Reserve case has brought the clash between economic growth and preservation of the environment into sharper focus.

IN A BROAD sense, the Reserve Mining controversy ex-emplifies the dilemma of modern Minnesota, which, like the nation, hangs suspended between the past and the future. Science and technology over the years have extended nature's resources and made them more usable; conservation and preservation have saved some last vestiges of natural and wilderness areas, and yet even the most ardent environmentalists recognize that many of the good and the beautiful things in our present society exist not because resources were conserved, but because they were used—yes, even exploited. The question remaining today, then, is not a simple one of totally preserving what is left, or totally using, but rather arriving at a balance between the two. The problem, though it is national in scope, is particularly significant in Minnesota where urbanization and wilderness are but hours apart, and where the very foundations of the state's heritage are based largely upon nonrenewable resources.

Optimists sometimes think the past can be left behind, but the imprints of past generations can never be erased. From out of the past of exploration and exploitation, out of boom and bust times, out of the experiences of pioneers and immigrants, and out of the heritage of industrialization and the tradition of protest politics has come the Minnesota that is now. The direction has been set; but the road to the future will be determined by those new frontiersmen who, equipped at least with knowledge—if not wisdom—gleaned from the past, must make those decisions that will keep nature and technology and man's needs and desires in balance.

Suggestions For Further Reading

For those interested in a topical introduction to the extensive writings about Minnesota, Michael Brook's *Reference Guide to Minnesota History: A Subject Bibliography of Books, Pamphlets, and Articles in English* (St. Paul: Minnesota Historical Society, 1974) will be invaluable. A well-done, thoroughly illustrated guide to places of historical significance is *Minnesota's Major Historic Sites: A Guide,* 2nd ed. (St. Paul: Minnesota Historical Society, 1972), by June Drenning Holmquist and Jean A. Brookins. Minnesota place naming is comprehensively detailed in Warren Upham's *Minnesota Geographic Names: their Origin and Historic Significance* (1920; reprint ed., St. Paul: Minnesota Historical Society, 1969).

The best of the multivolume general histories is William Watts Folwell's exhaustive, well-documented four-volume *A History of Minnesota,* rev. ed. (St. Paul: Minnesota Historical Society, 1956–1969). Theodore Christianson's five-volume work, *Minnesota, the Land of Sky-Tinted Waters: A History of the State and Its People* (Chicago: American Historical Society, 1935), contains a good chronicle of political developments. The standard one-volume general history is Theodore C. Blegen's *Minnesota: A History of the State,* with a new concluding chapter by Russell W. Fridley, rev. ed. (Minneapolis: University of Minnesota Press, 1975). Many photographs and other illustrations of Minnesota's history are featured in *The Thirty-Second State: A Pictorial History of Minnesota,* 2nd ed. (St. Paul: Minnesota Historical Society, 1966), by Bertha L. Heilbron.

Among the best works on French and British activities are Louise Phelps Kellogg's *The French Régime in Wisconsin and the Northwest* (Madison: State Historical Society of Wisconsin, 1925) and *The British Régime in Wisconsin and the Northwest* (Madison: State Historical Society of Wisconsin, 1935); *The North West Company,* by Gordon Charles Davidson (1918; reprint ed., New York: Russell and Russell, 1967); *The Northwest Fur Trade, 1763–1800,* by Wayne Edson Stevens (Urbana: University of Illinois, 1928); and Grace Lee Nute's *The*

216

Voyageur (1931; reprint ed., St. Paul: Minnesota Historical Society, 1955).

There are many useful works on Minnesota's Indians. Prehistoric Indians as well as the customs and history of both the Chippewa and the Sioux are extensively covered in the somewhat dated *The Aborigines of Minnesota,* by N[ewton] H. Winchell (St. Paul: Minnesota Historical Society, 1911). The history of the Minnesota Sioux is comprehensively treated in Roy Meyer's excellent *History of the Santee Sioux: United States Indian Policy on Trial* (Lincoln: University of Nebraska Press, 1967). The best introduction to the voluminous literature about the Sioux War is Kenneth Carley's *The Sioux Uprising of 1862,* 2nd ed. (St. Paul: Minnesota Historical Society, 1976), which contains a brief, objective narrative, dozens of photographs and other illustrations, and a most complete bibliography about the war.

Frontier expansion, a popular theme in Minnesota history writings, is well described in *Old Fort Snelling, 1819–1858,* by Marcus L. Hansen (1918; reprint ed., Minneapolis: Ross & Haines, 1958); Evan Jones's *Citadel in the Wilderness: The Story of Fort Snelling and the Old Northwest Frontier* (New York: Coward-McCann, 1966); and *Minnesota and the Manifest Destiny of the Canadian Northwest: A Study in Canadian-American Relations,* by Alvin M. Glueck, Jr. (Toronto: University of Toronto Press, 1965).

Existing histories of agriculture, lumbering, and iron mining generally emphasize the frontier period. The most comprehensive work about pioneer farming and the beginnings of diversified agriculture is *The Earth Brought Forth: A History of Minnesota Agriculture to 1885,* by Merrill E. Jarchow (St. Paul: Minnesota Historical Society, 1949). An excellent description of a fascinating aspect of Red River Valley history will be found in Hiram M. Drache's *The Day of the Bonanza: A History of Bonanza Farming in the Red River Valley of the North* (Fargo: North Dakota Institute for Regional Studies, 1964). A solid economic history of frontier and postfrontier agriculture in the valley was done by Stanley Norman Murray in *The Valley Comes of Age: A History of Agriculture in the Valley of the Red River of the North, 1812–1920* (Fargo: North Dakota Institute for Regional Studies, 1967).

The most detailed history of the lumberman's frontier was written by Agnes M. Larson in *History of the White Pine Industry in Minnesota* (Minneapolis: University of Minnesota Press, 1949). Min-

nesota's frontier lumbering is also extensively recounted in William G.
Rector's *Log Transportation in the Lake States Lumber Industry,
1840–1918* (Glendale, Calif.: Arthur H. Clark, 1953). The most general histories of the Lake Superior iron ranges of Michigan, Wisconsin, and Minnesota are Harlan Hatcher's *A Century of Iron and Men*
(Indianapolis: Bobbs-Merrill Co., 1950) and *Iron Brew: A Century of
American Ore and Steel*, by Stewart H. Holbrook (New York: Macmillan, 1939). The intriguing story of the Merritts was told by Paul De
Kruif in *Seven Iron Men* (New York: Harcourt, Brace and Co., 1929),
a popularly written, readable account that suffers somewhat because of
inaccuracies and lack of documentation. The most complete history of
taconite's development from early experimentation through the construction of the Silver Bay plant was written by E. W. Davis, who
vividly recalled his experiences in *Pioneering with Taconite* (St. Paul:
Minnesota Historical Society, 1964).

The significance of Minneapolis and St. Paul in Minnesota's history
is dealt with in numerous writings. Among the most important are *The
Waterfall That Built a City: The Falls of St. Anthony in Minneapolis*,
by Lucile M. Kane (St. Paul: Minnesota Historical Society, 1966);
Charles Byron Kuhlmann's *The Development of the Flour-Milling Industry in the United States with Special Reference to the Industry in
Minneapolis* (Boston: Houghton Mifflin, 1929); and *The Twin Cities*,
an interesting portrait of the modern cities in their historic setting, by
Carol R. Brink (New York: Macmillan, 1961).

An excellent survey of political issues from territorial years to the
early 1970s was done by Rhoda R. Gilman in *Minnesota: Political
Maverick*, a small work written as part of *Minnesota Politics and Government: A History Resource Unit* (St. Paul: Minnesota Historical Society, 1975). *Politics in Minnesota*, 2nd rev. ed. (Minneapolis: University of Minnesota Press, 1970), by G. Theodore Mitau, is a concise,
well-written résumé of Minnesota's political character, institutions,
and history. The story of the Nonpartisan League's beginnings is best
described in Robert L. Morlan's vivid *Political Prairie Fire: The Nonpartisan League, 1915–1922* (Minneapolis: University of Minnesota
Press, 1955), and the nature and impact of progressive age politics is
analytically portrayed in *The Progressive Era in Minnesota,
1899–1918*, by Carl H. Chrislock (St. Paul: Minnesota Historical Society, 1971).

Index

219